The Question
of Parole

Retention, Reform,
or Abolition?

The Question of Parole

Retention, Reform, or Abolition?

Andrew von Hirsch
Kathleen J. Hanrahan
Rutgers University

Introduction by Sheldon L. Messinger

Ballinger Publishing Company ● **Cambridge, Massachusetts**
A Subsidiary of Harper & Row, Publishers, Inc.

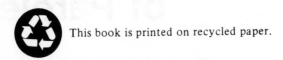

This book is printed on recycled paper.

Prepared under Grant Number 76−NI−99−0038 from the National Institute of Law Enforcement and Criminal Justice, Law Enforcement Assistance Administration, U.S. Department of Justice. Points of view or opinions stated in this document are those of the authors and do not necessarily represent the official position or policies of the Institute, the Law Enforcement Assistance Administration, or the Department of Justice.

International Standard Book Number: 0−88410−796−5

Library of Congress Catalog Card Number: 78−21131

Printed in the United States of America

Library of Congress Cataloging in Publication Data

Von Hirsch, Andrew.
  The question of parole.

  An enlarged version of the authors' Abolish parole? which was published in 1978.
  Includes bibliographical references.
  1. Parole—United States. I. Hanrahan, Kathleen J., joint author.
II. Title.
KF9750.V66   364.6'2'0973   78−21131
ISBN 0−88410−796−5

Contents

Preface

A summary of this study was published in September 1978 as a monograph by the National Institute of Law Enforcement and Criminal Justice (NILECJ) under the title *Abolish Parole?* This book represents a full statement of our views—as we have more space here to elaborate, and have had more time to review and rethink the argument.

The book, as well as the monograph, grew out of the Project on Parole Alternatives, which was funded by NILECJ, a division of the Law Enforcement Administration of the U.S. Department of Justice. The Project was administered by the Center for Policy Research, Inc., New York City. The Center's director, Dr. Amitai Etzioni, was most helpful in developing the initial ideas for the project, and the Center's staff was cooperative throughout.

We are greatly indebted to the project's Board of Consultants, and our analysis relies heavily on the Board's guidance and advice. However, it was contemplated from the outset of the project that the final work would be that of the two authors, rather than a committee report. Thus the conclusions are our own.

The members of the Board of Consultants were: Paul Chernoff, Judge of the District Court of Newton, Massachusetts, and former Chairman of the Massachusetts Parole Board; Walter W. Cohen, Master of the Court of Common Pleas of Philadelphia, and former Chief Assistant District Attorney of Philadelphia; Alan M. Dershowitz, Professor of Law at Harvard Law School; Don M. Gottfredson, Dean of the Graduate School of Criminal Justice, Rutgers University, Newark; Morris E. Lasker, Judge of the U.S. District Court for the Southern District of New York; Sheldon L. Messinger, Professor of Law at the Law School of the University of California at Berkeley, and former Dean of the School of Criminology at that University; Vincent O'Leary, President of the State University of New York at Albany, and former Dean of the School of Criminal Justice at that University; Arthur Rosett, Professor of Law at the University of California at Los Angeles; David J. Rothman, Professor of History at Columbia University, and Senior Research Associate at the Center for Policy Research, Inc. in New York City; and Linda R. Singer, a partner in the law firm of Goldfarb, Singer and Austern, Washington, D.C. In addition, Elliot Studt, Professor of Social Welfare (emeritus) at the University of California at Los Angeles, participated in the Board's sessions on parole supervision.

We are indebted to our Project Monitor, Dr. Phyllis Jo Baunach of NILECJ, who was supportive and helpful throughout our entire effort; and also to George Bohlinger and Marlene Beckman, formerly of that agency, who guided the first steps of our undertaking.

Anne W. Murphy and Antonia Goldsmith served successively as the project's administrative assistant, and we thank them for their patience, cooperation, and care in doing the administrative and secretarial work for the project. We also thank Deborah Koster, the project's research assistant, for her work in locating sources, as well as for her thoughtful comments on the drafts.

Conversations with several of our colleagues during the project provided us with valuable ideas: Peter B. Hoffman, Ira Blalock, Richard F. Sparks, Susan Steward, John J. Gibbs, and Vicki Jackson.

Several other colleagues and friends went through the drafts of the report and furnished us with lengthy and helpful comments: Richard G. Singer, Marvin Wolfgang, Leslie T. Wilkins, Diane Steelman, Richard A. Tropp, Michael Tonry, Robert Carter, William Wilbanks, John Conrad, John Kleinig, Hyman Gross and Katrina de Hirsch. Further valuable comments on the drafts were provided by John Monahan, Martin R. Gardner, David T. Stanley, Lawrence Travis, and Louis B. Schwartz.

Finally, we are indebted to the members of the Advisory Commission on Prison Terms and Parole Standards of the State of Oregon, from whose work we learned much.

Introduction

Sheldon L. Messinger
School of Law
University of California, Berkeley

In this volume, Andrew von Hirsch and Kathleen J. Hanrahan take a close, critical look at the implications of parole for doing justice. They find it wanting as currently conceived and practiced, and they propose some changes.

I

Parole has a double referent. On the one hand, it refers to the procedures used to fix the actual periods of confinement served by most persons committed to state or federal prisons. On the other hand, it refers to ways of regulating the conditions of such persons' post-prison lives until final discharge from sentence. The authors refer to the first as "parole release"; the second as "parole supervision." It is a useful distinction that is too seldom clearly made.

Under parole release, a prisoner's actual term of confinement is fixed by a centralized board; this period is to be within a maximum possible term of confinement as imposed by a criminal court. Typically this maximum term authorizes confinement for a period much longer than the prisoner or anyone else expects will actually be served in prison. In some jurisdictions, the court may impose a minimum term as well, fixing a period that must be served in confinement before the centralized board can release the prisoner. With or without such a minimum term, the board ordinarily can fix widely varying actual terms of confinement for prisoners with similar (or different) court-imposed maxima or minima. The result is a kind of chaos. Some boards do tend to fix standard terms for the kinds of prisoners they see repetitively. But even if this informal strategy develops in a jurisdiction, the board need not impose a standard term on any specific individual. Nor need it justify "exceptions"—which are difficult to identify anyway, given the absence of a "rule." Various parole boards, further, have different, if usually equally obscure, ideas about "standard terms."

Prisoners cannot, moreover, be certain when their actual terms will be fixed because most boards have discretion in this matter as well. And most choose to delay term-fixing actions until considerable time in confinement has passed and the prisoner, as board members say, is "ready for release." This means, of course, when the board is ready.

Parole release ends neither the sentence imposed by the court nor the authority of the parole board over the sentenced person. Until the court-imposed maximum term lapses, or until otherwise discharged from sentence, the prisoner remains under "parole supervision." During the parole supervision period, the parolee is required to abide by rules imposed by the board. Such rules are typically broad and vague, and amount to a generalized jeopardy to reimprisonment at the discretion of the board for the remainder of the court-imposed term. Most parolees are required to report regularly to state-employed parole officers, who will work out a program of surveillance and service for them. Surveillance regularly includes unannounced visits at home and sometimes at work, as well as report-gathering from "collaterals," such as relatives. Sometimes parolees are required to accept psychiatric "help" as a condition of staying on parole, or to take and "pass" narcotics tests. Services, when there are any, may include assistance in finding employment, or aid in getting needed documents, such as a driver's license.

As noted, parolees are subject to reimprisonment. Parole officers can recommend "revocation" of parole—that is, reimprisonment—on a variety of grounds, including failure to report or to follow an imposed program. Such a recommendation leads to a hearing before board members or representatives at which the parolee is "tried," in effect, for violating the conditions of parole. The standards of evidence and proof required and employed are lower than those constitutionally provided for others facing imprisonment. Further, since it has at its disposal the unserved portion of the court-imposed maximum possible term (and, in some places, time on parole does not count as service of that term), the penalties available to the board often exceed those that could be imposed through the judicial process for a similar "offense."

Both parole release and parole supervision are under attack from several directions as part of a broader challenge to the wide, unstructured, and unchecked discretion of officials over criminal sentences generally. One view is that the way parole officials exercise discretion has resulted in insufficient protection for the community: parole boards release too many too soon; and parole officers permit too many to remain too long in the community. Another view finds parole boards holding too many too long in terms of the risks involved; and that parole officers interfere with the adjustment of many ex-prisoners in the community—all of which causes needless suffering and taxes the public purse unnecessarily.

Still another attack is more fundamental, going to the purposes of sentencing and parole rather than failure of officials to accomplish the purposes imputed to them. In this view, although crime control in its various guises is among the general purposes of punishment, it is not to be pursued in a manner inconsistent with fairness and justice; fairness and justice should be the first priority in sentencing, and other goals may be pursued only so far as they do not reverse this order of priorities. Existing laws authorizing parole permit, and parole officials produce, punishments that are unjust and unfair. Terms are unrelated, or arbitrarily related, to the seriousness of offenders' past criminal conduct. They are meted out in ways that do not provide a reasonable opportunity for challenge. Parolees do not receive the benefit of basic constitutional protections. This is the view put forward by the authors and, in light of it, they propose certain changes to enhance fairness and justice in sentencing.

II

Von Hirsch and Hanrahan isolate for discussion the central legal and procedural arrangements that are generally held to be essential for an effective parole system. Statutes providing parole boards with wide options over prisoners' terms of confinement and over the conditions of parolees' lives are the core legal underpinning of parole. Such statutes typically do not constrain choices among these options; nor have the courts, until very recently, undertaken to check on how this wide, unguided discretion has been exercised.

Many parole boards can release prisoners on the day they arrive at the prison gates; and most have authority to keep prisoners confined for long periods. Parole "dates" can be fixed when the parole board feels moved to fix them; and they can be "pulled" and refixed at any time the board feels this is justified. Parole periods can be brief or, in the case of those imprisoned for "life," terminate only at death. The board may impose virtually any rules on parolees it wishes. Until the Supreme Court's *Morrissey* decision of 1972, it was unclear that parole revocation required a hearing, although it has been quite clear that hearings, when held, were often the most perfunctory charades. Parole officials have been free to impose "intensive" supervision, and parole officers free to be intrusive in ways that would be little countenanced with respect to any but "ex-cons." Statutes have permitted all these things, most still do, and case law has done little to change the situation (except in the area of parole revocation procedures). The authors believe that the justifications for such unusually unfettered discretion should be explored in depth.

Parole as a whole, and each of its features, has come to be justified principally by its purported contribution to crime control, and its effectiveness has conventionally been assessed in terms of this purpose. Wide options over periods of confinement are supposed, on the one hand, to motivate prisoners to cooperate in the process of "rehabilitation" while in prison in the hope of release considerably before the maximum legally possible period of confinement. On the other hand, these options are supposed to permit the board—composed of "experts"—carefully to fit the actual term to the rehabilitative progress of individual prisoners; in particular, they are supposed to facilitate the continued confinement of the insufficiently reformed. Wide latitude is needed, it is claimed, because of the great variations in time needed to assure sufficient rehabilitation among prisoners with vastly different backgrounds and commitments to criminal ways, notwithstanding their similar criminal histories. Ideally, in some views, this latitude would extend to possible life terms for all, or at least to possible very long terms for very many. Many jurisdictions have achieved the latter.

Delaying the term-fixing decision is supposed to give the board time to collect needed information and to observe and evaluate the rehabilitative progress of prisoners. Fixing a term early would be the merest guesswork in the opinion of many; delay permits a more rational and discriminating decision. Further, say some, the anxieties induced by such delays are "therapeutic"; they keep prisoners' attention focused on improving themselves.

The various conditions of parole are also supposed to serve to control crime by encouraging parolee avoidance of crime and crime-producing situations, and by furthering rehabilitation. The threat of return to prison for violating these conditions is said to help assure parolee adherence to them. Supervision by parole officers, and parole services, will enhance these effects during the post-prison period, as well as permit prompt detection and reimprisonment of parolees gone astray.

In summary, through their effects on prisoners and parolees, parole release and parole supervision are supposed to encourage rehabilitation and deter parolees from crime. If these effects are not forth-coming, parole is supposed to permit parole boards to be able to know and keep likely repeaters in prison or, with the help of parole officers, quickly return them to confinement. In other words, in the absence of deterrent effectiveness, parole is supposed to facilitate effective incapacitation of likely or proven repeaters. Since individual prisoners and parolees differ so much in rehabilitative potential and risk—each, in the end, being "unique"—there is no good way to establish criteria for appropriate lengths or conditions of prison or parole terms. That, as noted, had best be left to "experts."

III

When the practices of parole officials have been assessed in terms of the purposes presented in section II, they have usually been found seriously deficient. In response, critical thought has typically turned to trying to find ways to assist boards and officers to improve their capacity to achieve these objectives. The literature on parole is awash with arguments for enlarging the options of officials to permit them to respond more "flexibly" to the prisoners and parolees before them; with recommendations for removing parole boards from "poli-tics" and "upgrading" parole personnel so that more "scientific" judgments might be made; with predictive instruments and advice about how best to use them; and with proposals for modifying pa-role supervision patterns so that recidivism among parolees might be reduced.

Prison and parole officials have urged legislatures to change laws and supply resources to permit the introduction of hopefully im-proved practices. By and large, legislators have done so—although, as one might expect, resources have been more slowly appropriated than discretion. It is my impression that over the course of this cen-tury, legislatures have greatly increased the maximum possible terms that courts could impose, thereby giving the boards "more time to play with," as is sometimes said. Boards have also received increased discretion to release prisoners "early." At the same time—partly be-cause it is seen as a way of saving money by avoiding prison-build-ing—parole supervisory resources have expanded considerably. In some states, the numbers of persons on parole at any given time has approached the numbers in prison.

But the results of almost 100 years of tinkering with parole release and parole supervision do not appear to have made them particularly effective in controlling crime—crime committed by prisoners and ex-prisoners, much less that committed by others. Participation in prison programs of rehabilitation, where such programs exist, seems loosely if at all related to recidivism. Delaying the release decision—in order to observe the offender's "progress" in prison—does not seem to enhance one's ability to predict crime, particularly violent criminal activities. Even when parole conditions seem rationally related to the reduction of recidivism—and they often do not seem so-related—inquiry fails clearly to confirm their effectiveness. And varying forms of parole supervision and service seem neither to decrease the frequency of recidivism nor to increase very much the chance that parole officers will detect recidivists.

With these kinds of findings in mind, the authors review the cases for a delayed term-fix and for parole supervision. Their conclusion is that, given current knowledge, the support for either is, at best, weak. Further, they speculate about the differences that improved knowledge might make, and suggest ways to improve knowledge. Among the most interesting consequences of their discussion are the questions it raises about needed knowledge. For example, if time served in prison and on parole is properly limited by the seriousness of the offender's past criminal conduct, and if rehabilitative efforts are to continue, knowledge about the time "successful" efforts may be expected to take is needed. There appears to be little, if any, research on this question.

IV

Whether or not parole contributes to crime control is not the main issue the authors choose to raise. Unlike almost all but the most recent critics of parole—and not all of these—von Hirsch and Hanrahan refuse to take for granted what it should mean to say that a parole system is operating "effectively." A judgment about a system's effectiveness, they properly insist, depends on how one orders the several purposes it is claimed to serve. Since they order these purposes quite differently from the way many other commentators do—putting justice foremost—they are led to assess the legal and procedural arrangements constituting and sustaining parole in the light of standards that have too seldom been applied. They ask whether parole contributes to or interferes with justice and fairness in the distribution of punishment for crime. To gauge the effectiveness of parole in this respect is decidedly unusual.

Parole release, as they note, is the decision process that nowadays determines the quantum of punishment meted out to most prisoners. Longer periods of confinement are, other things equal, more severe punishments, while shorter periods are less severe punishments. For reasons von Hirsch and Hanrahan set forth at length, punishments should be commensurate with the seriousness of the offenses that justify them. Further, they should be issued fairly, and be open to timely challenge. Seen in this light, the questions to be asked are whether the practice of parole release is a fair method of issuing punishments, and whether it results in a just distribution of them. It may also be asked whether parole release as we know it is humane. The authors develop compelling reasons to believe it is ineffective on all these counts.

Similar questions are raised about parole supervision, particularly with respect to the grounds and procedures used to reimprison parolees who violate their conditions of release. The parole period is part of the punishment expected and experienced by most persons sentenced to prison today; it, too, should be assessed in light of the standards appropriate for punishment for crime. By these standards, parole supervision is often "ineffective," as well.

Von Hirsch and Hanrahan are not satisfied to pronounce judgment on the effectiveness of parole practices. One conceivable answer to objections about parole's effectiveness is that the situation will improve when expertise increases: when more is known, and when parole personnel are "upgraded." The thrust of the authors' position, however, is that a punishment system mainly steered by crime control purposes is misguided; more knowledge will not change that. As for upgrading personnel—the most familiar reform proposal in all fields, perhaps—this might be taken to imply a theory of governance that I infer is not shared by von Hirsch and Hanrahan. Such a theory places much emphasis on the intelligence and goodwill of officials, and little emphasis on constraining officials. Correspondingly, it places too little emphasis on the ways the purposes of official actions come to be defined, how these purposes come to be or fail to be reflected in the laws and rules which authorize and limit those actions, and on the logic of the situations in which officials find themselves as the result, in part, of the purposes they are supposed to serve and the laws and rules provided to facilitate and guide them.

The authors place great emphasis on these matters, not, I think, from any underevaluation of the importance of intelligence or goodwill, but from a conviction—shared by those who wrote the Constitution—that intelligence and goodwill, while clearly needed to produce right actions, are simply not enough. Not only is it wise to be on guard against *wrong* actions, but one must also clarify what is *right*. One must mark it off as clearly as possible from what is wrong, and one must support the selection of right actions both by providing continuing incentives to choose them and disincentives to do otherwise. Interestingly enough, officials find this logic compelling when they consider how to treat the governed—particularly con-victed felons—even though they are somewhat less likely to apply it to the governance of their own actions.

Von Hirsch and Hanrahan are less disposed to make a distinction in this regard. This leads them to pay particular attention to what parole laws authorize officials to do, as well as to what such laws fail to constrain officials from doing. And it leads them to propose changes designed both to limit the options easily available to officials and to guide their choices among those available. They also examine how such options might be designed and institutionalized.

V

Given what the practice of parole has become, one might rightly wonder how it ever came to be accepted so widely—and, indeed, with such enthusiasm. As yet no satisfactory history of parole exists, so I can only speculate. My speculations are based on what I know mainly from secondary sources, and from some considerable explora-tion of primary sources in California.

All sources suggest dissatisfaction with the way prison terms were fixed in the late nineteenth and early twentieth centuries in the United States. Generally, the way was as follows. Statutes gave the courts much discretionary control over the length of prison terms: a sentence varying between one and fifteen years was possible in Cali-fornia, for example, for offenders convicted of a single charge of bur-glary. The courts fixed a "definite" sentence within such ranges for each offender committed to state prison. Sentences could be reduced by prison authorities in most places through the award of "good-time credits." In California, good time reduced sentences—and, thus, periods of confinement in prison—by about one-fifth for those with shorter sentences, up to about half for those with longer ones; stat-utes in other states were similar. Most prisoners received such credits. Further, gubernatorial clemency actions were much more frequent than has since become the custom. Commutations and pardons seem to have been sought by most prisoners, and many received them. Over the several decades preceding the adoption of parole in Califor-nia (in 1893), over 10 percent of prisoners had their terms shortened through clemency actions; again, other states acted similarly.

Complaints about the prison terms issuing from this process were frequent, and most were of long standing. Rising crime rates were blamed on the leniency of the courts in fixing too-short terms, espe-cially for "confirmed criminals." Good-time credit grants and guber-natorial clemency actions were held to exacerbate the situation, the latter coming in for particular criticism. The following excerpt from an editorial is a fair sample of such criticism:

> Governor Stoneman is piling up a fine record of pardons in the closing days of his administration. Murderers, burglars, thieves, confidence men, defaulters, all of these have been allowed to go free.

There also were those who felt that sentences were often much longer than needed for many of those convicted, especially young, first-time offenders, many of whom could be released sooner with no great risk to public safety and with some saving for the public purse. Besides considerations of future-oriented effectiveness and cost, many objected to the visible sentence variations, then as now, on grounds of justice and fairness. Prisoners and their supporters were foremost among those making this kind of complaint, but they were not alone. Some way should be found to assure that prison terms were distributed more even-handedly, it was said; and some way should be found to see that all of those deserving executive clemency could be heard.

Such complaints, as noted, seem to have been of long standing. A new theme was added in the latter decades of the nineteenth century, however, by prison officials and those for whom they worked. The early enthusiasm for prisons, well described by David Rothman in *The Discovery of the Asylum* (Boston: Little, Brown, 1971), had faded among prison officials, as well as others. Some officials decided that a major problem was insufficient discretion over the terms prisoners would serve. For all their variation, sentences continued to be roughly tied to, and principally rationalized in terms of, the severity of the past criminal offenses of prisoners. But this often seemed to bear little relation to the time it might take to produce a rehabilitated prisoner. Some had to be released before rehabilitation was apparent; others had to be kept, even though they seemed safe bets for release. True, prison officials could recommend clemency, but the governor could not extend terms, and often would not shorten them. Sometimes, too, the governor would shorten the terms of those who were undeserving in the eyes of the prison officials. And overall, when prisoners compared the terms they had received, prisons were becoming more and more difficult to manage—or so, at least, officials claimed.

A greater measure of "indeterminacy" was the solution proposed by such officials. In its extreme form, the proposal was for all prisoners to be confined until prison officials decided they were ready for release. The California State Penological Commission, exploring possible reforms, noted in its 1887 *Report* (Sacramento, California: State Printing Office) that "at the present time our people are not prepared to accept this code, that draws no distinction between crimes." It suggested a parole law similar to that adopted by Ohio in 1884. As proposed and later adopted, parole would authorize the prison directors to release all first-time offenders, except those convicted of murder, after one year, whatever the length of sentence imposed by the courts. Released prisoners would remain on parole, subject to reimprisonment by the board, until their court-fixed sentences lapsed. Good-time credits would continue to be given, reducing the overall sentence.

What would this accomplish? First and foremost, the California commission said, it would provide a means for "discrimination between those who are criminals by nature and those who, not bad at heart, have committed crime." While it is not at all clear what the board could have hoped to accomplish relative to "criminals by nature," since they could not extend confinement beyond the sentence imposed by the court, it is apparent that they hoped to be able radically to reduce the terms of some first-termers.

It is also apparent that the commission hoped to shift the rationale for imprisonment away from what von Hirsch and Hanrahan term a "just deserts" rationale toward one giving more emphasis to crime control because secondly, parole would permit:

> Abandoning the idea that a prison is nothing more than a place for the detention and punishment of offenders, and accepting the more reasonable as well as humane view that the great majority of prisoners . . . may at their release, by proper management and discipline, be sent into the world useful and law-abiding citizens. . . .

Put differently, parole release moved toward a system of sentencing that was more consistent, in this view, with a reformative prison: one that used sentences to encourage—or coerce—reformation, and assure incapacitation if that did not work.

It would also help quell complaints about the inequalities of sentences, partly, it seems, by permitting parole authorities to rectify gross disparities, at least for first-termers, and partly, though this wasn't expressly said, by changing the basis for assessing "inequality." California commission members were quite explicit about the need to deal with sentencing disparities; the commission, in 1887, said:

> It will be admitted that for the same offense as defined by statute, different persons, under different circumstances aggravating or mitigating their

crime, should receive different sentences. But it is not right that the same
person, for the same offense, should receive a punishment out of all proportion to what he would receive, depending upon the accident of appear-
ing before one or another Judge of the same Court, or from a temporary
excitement of the public mind, either with reference to that offense or
that particular offender or offenders generally.

This would ease problems of prison management since: "there is
nothing that produces so much discontent and disaffection among
prisoners as this inequality of sentences." Further, equalizing sentences would serve, perhaps, to reduce recidivism:

> If one man has received a sentence of ten or twelve years for an offense for
> which another has received a sentence of but one year, the former feels
> that he has suffered a grievous wrong, and when he leaves the prison does
> it with feelings of resentment and an ardent desire "to get even." How
> much better to have him feel that he should have no grudge against society.

Again, how such equalization could be produced with recidivism-risk
being the standard for term-fixing is not immediately apparent. But
it was intended that a parole board, and not the governor, would
shoulder the main burden of producing such equalization as was possible. Those recommending parole in California and elsewhere at that
time were aware of this fact, and indeed parole was intended to
reduce the occasions when the governor would be called upon to
grant clemency.

Looking back, it seems that from the start parole was intended
to serve crime-control purposes; it would permit a closer match of
term to risk (although judicial maximum sentences would limit this
"matching" somewhat); and it would permit manipulation of the
sentence in the interest of prison management personnel, who prom-
ised disciplinary regimes calculated to produce reformation. Further,
by permitting the quick release of the rehabilitated, it might produce
some fiscal savings. At the same time, however contradictory it now
seems, parole would serve the end of justice by facilitating the equalization of terms. And, not least, it would relieve the governor of the
"unpleasant and arduous duties" connected with considering hun-
dreds of applications for pardons. Relieving the governor of such
duties would also enhance fairness, and the appearance thereof, because *all* prisoners would have access to the board.

Little was said about parole supervision, and in most places, including California, no provision was made for such supervision except insofar as local police might furnish it. Prisoners on parole
would be required to have jobs and to avoid evil companions, among

other prohibitions, and to report by mail regularly to the board. They could be reimprisoned at any time the board felt they were headed toward a life of crime. This was not emphasized at first, for focus was on releasing "deserving" prisoners "early."

It is worth noting that, as originally adopted in California and elsewhere, parole involved a transfer of already existing discretion, with prison authorities being the main beneficiaries of that transferred discretion. They could use terms, within judicially imposed limits, to induce conformance to prison regimes; they could also take population pressures into account, should they want to do so. Prisoners were about where they were before—almost totally dependent on official choices—but some could hope to serve shorter terms than might otherwise have been the case. It seemed a laudable reform for all concerned.

Parole was first seriously urged in California in 1887; it was not adopted until 1893. The sources of resistance are not fully clear, but newspaper comments pressing the governor not to approve the legislation suggest that law-enforcement officials opposed any move that would authorize shorter terms. Other newspaper comments emphasized the need for care and caution on the part of officials in issuing paroles. Parole was seen, patently, as a device certain to result in increased leniency toward prisoners. How one felt about it seemed to depend mainly on one's assessment of the need for, and likely results of, such leniency.

The California board appears to have been careful and cautious. In the first decade during which parole was possible, fewer than 160 of 6,100 releases from prison—less than 3 percent—were by parole. The proportion of releases involving executive clemency was even smaller. Among the reasons for such scanty use of parole was quite clearly concern by the prison directors, doubtless shared by the governor, that they would be held responsible for having released prisoners who went on to commit violent crimes, when it was in their power to retain these persons in confinement. Several such incidents occurred. There was a move to repeal the parole law.

Resistance to shortening prison terms appears to have been a major source weakening the resolve of the directors to use parole either to release many low-risk prisoners or to shorten many terms in the interest of justice. The parole law did nothing to *make* the board issue a parole, and set forth no standards for deciding when it was appropriate to do so. The board's exposed position made it attentive to the resistance to releasing prisoners "early,"—that is, before they were required to do so by law. The board quickly emphasized its sensitivity to such pressures by adopting a rule that no prisoner would be considered for parole until he had served half his court-fixed sentence, which suggests how easily equity can be abandoned when there are no clear standards to interpose between strong local feelings and centralized decisionmaking.

The problems of managing the state prisons, however, gave incentives to use parole somewhat differently than first envisioned. The prison population kept increasing. In the first few years of the century, the legislature (following the urging of the prison directors) appropriated funds to expand the prisons. But before the expansion was completed, it was quite clear that it would not solve the problem of crowding. Rather than appropriate more funds, the legislature suggested that parole be used more freely, a suggestion the governor supported. Confronted with crowded, difficult-to-manage institutions, and with a continuing inflow of new prisoners—an inflow the prison directors could not affect, as they saw it—the directors complied. In 1906, 8 percent of those released from prison were paroled; by 1910) the figure was 31 percent. In 1903, murderers became eligible for parole after seven years; in 1909, the law was changed to permit the board to parole second-termers. In 1908, the first state parole officer had been appointed, to keep better track of parolees.

Along with these changes came a shift in the way parole was justified. As noted, at its inception (in California, at least) emphasis fell almost exclusively on the benefits of parole release, not parole supervision; and the main supposed benefits were that the possibility of such release would motivate reformation, while its actuality would result in shorter terms for those first-time offenders who apparently posed no threat to society. At the same time, the board would be able to equalize prison terms. Although the latter was a somewhat contradictory aim, it was only so if one believed that past criminal conduct alone should be taken into account in rendering a "just" sentence. When the board began to parole a larger proportion of prisoners, including murderers and those who had served prior terms, it began to emphasize the benefits of parole supervision. At first, when parole officers were scarce, it talked about the financial savings of parole. It would carefully select those who didn't "need" to be in prison, and they would have the chance to rehabilitate themselves still further in the community at less expense to the state. Also, the state would be saved the expense of building more prisons. As the number of parolees continued to increase and, from time to time, to make crime news, and as further prison expansion was funded, another rationale was heard: since almost all prisoners would be released sometime, it was better to release them under supervision, for the community would be better protected. By the early 1920s, a large majority of prisoners were being released on parole. By then, the contemporary rationale for parole had developed; it emphasized the benefits of releasing prisoners when they were "ready"—but releasing them *prior* to the expiration of sentence, so that supervision could be exercised.

Sentencing law did nothing to prevent this development. Indeed, both substantive and procedural sentencing laws were changed to facilitate it. Formal standards had never guided judicial discretion over sentences within the wide statutory ranges available; the introduction of parole did nothing to encourage the development of standards. There was increasing emphasis on the protection of the community through decisions meant to apportion prison terms on the basis of risk, and to continue protection through supervision and revocation after imprisonment. That emphasis, in turn, generated a steady resistance to the articulation of standards by decisionmakers. What was needed, in the view of parole officials and their supporters, was "flexibility" to take all relevant matters into account. But who knew what might prove relevant?

The introduction of still further "indeterminacy" in California served to confirm and reinforce this development. About the time it started paroling a larger proportion of prisoners, the board began to press actively for authority to fix the maximum possible term (still imposed by the courts) in addition to the actual prison duration within this limit. The justification offered publicly was that this would free the board to parole similarly situated prisoners after a similar period of confinement, an action hampered by different judicially imposed sentences.

Although this sounds like a "just deserts" argument—and the board emphasized the "justice" of being able to act in this fashion—in fact it was much more ambiguous both in intent, and, certainly, in effect. Under existing law, the board already *could* parole almost all prisoners after equal terms of confinement, notwithstanding court-imposed sentences. They did not do so, however, choosing instead to take court-imposed maxima into account, generally keeping those with longer sentences longer than those with shorter sentences, whatever the underlying facts. Doubtless they wanted to be free from this constraint, but not necessarily because justice would be served; more immediate objectives could also be better served, like rewarding "worthy" prisoners, or accommodating continuing population pressures. Further, court-imposed maxima forced "early" release on some occasions, and both discipline and seeming public protection could be better served if this were not the case. Finally, but not least important, as parole supervision became more important, so, too, did the board find it needed more "time to play with" in order to impose conformance on parolees. Control over the maximum possible term would expand the board's powers of parole supervision, as well.

Whatever the prison directors' intention in pressing for authority to fix the maximum term, when this change was legislated in 1917, additional pressure was placed on the board to define its powers as aimed at providing crime control. Complaints about releasing prisoners too soon from prison, or discharging them too quickly from parole—never in short supply—were now more than ever properly directed at the board: it had the power, within increasingly broad statutory limits, to do almost anything. Most of all, it had the power to keep prisoners locked up for very long periods. So long as any doubt remained, so to speak, about their readiness to stop criminal activities, they could be incarcerated. Further, should they violate parole conditions, offenders could be reimprisoned for very long periods.

It should finally be added that the development of an extensive staff of parole officers seems closely related to these changes and pressures. The staff may be seen both as a consequence of, and as a contributor to, them. Paroling prisoners when they were presumed safe is now and was seen then as an inherently risky enterprise. The risk could be reduced, it was reasoned, by increasing surveillance over ex-prisoners. Parole officers, given their task, wanted as much discretion as possible to reduce risks. One way of doing so would be to increase the threat that action would be taken against parole violators, and to increase the certainty that the threat would be carried out when threat alone proved insufficient.

The California parole board from the start adopted rules for parolees permitting reimprisonment under a wide variety of circumstances, and it never seems to have felt required to extend full due process protections to parolees. But revocation of parole, particularly in the absence of conviction for a new serious crime, appears to have been much less frequent before the parole officer staff burgeoned. It is difficult to believe that parolees were better behaved, although the selectivity of the early years may have had some such effect. It is easier to believe that minor violations came to official attention less frequently, and that without parole officers worried about *their* records, the board may have had less impulse to reimprison "technical" parole violators when they did. Whatever the reasons, the heyday of parole violation in California came long after parole was introduced, and was justified as a means for preventing serious crimes by reimprisoning ex-prisoners headed for recidivism. Whether the community has benefitted is arguable; that parolees have been given less than the full protection of the law is patent.

One last matter. It is generally believed that parole, initially adopted in many places as a way of selectively shortening prison terms, has resulted in the end in lengthening them. Although California developments, as portrayed above, suggest both how and why this may have happened, the fact is that there is no compelling evidence one way or the other. The few studies that exist, mainly done earlier in this century, do not consistently or compellingly show that prisoners, on the average, served shorter or longer terms after parole was adopted; most do not even consider the parole supervision period as part of the "prison" term, that is, the punishment. Not only are comparisons with the pre-parole situation in the same states badly made, there are no comparisons of states with and without parole during comparable periods. Information exists that will permit an answer, even now, and there is some possibility that it will be mined in the future. In the meantime, one should suspend judgment on the matter. One should suspend judgment, too, on whether parole boards have served to equalize terms, since again, so far as I know, no really satisfactory studies exist.

VI

Saying that one should suspend judgment on the above matters is not the same as advocating that one should suspend judgment on parole boards as they have traditionally operated, however, or that one should not make recommendations for change. As von Hirsch and Hanrahan ably demonstrate, there is scant reason to believe that parole boards have had any special success in achieving their supposed crime-control purposes; and there is considerable reason to believe that in the process of trying to do so—if that, in fact, is what parole boards have been attempting to do—they and their supervisory arms have been instruments of injustice.

There is no doubt that the situation of parole boards—a situation that members have actively sought, in many instances—has contributed to their propensity to act as they have. They have been and continue to be under pressure not to release prisoners until it is "certain" that the prisoners will not commit further crimes; clearly this is an impossible certainty to achieve. The demand for this kind of certainty has surely been one of the pressures important in moving boards to delay specification of the prisoner's parole "date" and thereby his term of imprisonment—a characteristic procedure the authors severely criticize. The delayed "term-fix" is justified as necessary for a rational decision, but so far as "rational" means ability to predict recidivism, there is little reason to suppose the delay helps. And clearly, as the authors point out, it is not needed to fix a just penalty.

Seen this way, delaying the decision is hardly necessary, and it is arguably both inhumane and unfair. Seen in the light of the pressures on boards to produce certain decisions with respect to "a hoard of vicious robbers, rapists, and killers"—a common phrasing—it is understandable. Delay, or more exactly, freedom to decide when the board is "ready," permits parole boards not only to keep up a front of rational caution, but also permits them to do what needs to be done when the doing is best, politically speaking, even if neither crime control nor justice is served.

What the authors' excellent analysis reveals most sharply, I think, is that sentencing laws and the ways they have been rationalized leaves the process of punishment-determination largely uncontrolled. Perhaps better said, they leave it open to tacking to the prevailing political winds, and subject to the influences that criminal justice officials themselves create in the interests of the organizations they are charged to manage. Having observed parole boards in action many times, I have found them usually quite concerned to see that prisoners receive the full measure of punishment that board members believe is their due. Unfortunately, in the absence of standards for assessing the quantity of a full measure, or criteria for applying such standards, such judgments tend to be quite varied among parole board members, or even for the same member at different times. To add to the difficulty, as a result of "public" pressures, a full measure (however defined) was typically only the minimum time of confinement. Having served that, the next consideration was whether it was "safe" to release the prisoner. Since it is almost always safer to keep a prisoner, I found myself sometimes amazed at the bravery or recklessness of boards in deciding the time for release had arrived.

The lesson I draw is the one that I believe the authors wish drawn. Given the "public's" steady, understandable concern with crime control, if it is wanted to distribute punishment justly and humanely, ways must be found to limit the options available to those who mete out punishment. Their situations must be structured in ways that encourage them to select appropriate options and discourage them from selecting inappropriate options. This is not the same thing as urging that official discretion be "eliminated," a goal as chimerical as some of the others the criminal justice system has entertained. It is a suggestion that we give careful scrutiny to the design of our institutions: to the laws and rules that constitute and hopefully guide them, to the purposes embodied in those laws and rules, and to the organizational vehicles we construct to implement these laws, rules, and purposes.

The same kind of analysis is pertinent for the legal and organizational supports for parole supervision. Given a mandate to rehabilitate parolees and, above all, to see that they stay out of serious trouble while on parole, parole officers have continually sought to increase the options available for moving parolees to conform. Simultaneously, they have felt moved to "intervene" earlier and earlier in those sets of events that they regard as indicative of more serious trouble. Like parole board members, parole officers are sensitive to the expressed demands of the "public," particularly those of the law enforcement and judicial communities whose cooperation they often need in order to keep their own records good. All of this and more has made them satisfied with the loose administrative procedures for reimprisoning parolees, and with the heavy back-up sanctions available to them. Indeed, "satisfied" is not the point; parole officers have been among those urging boards to adopt and retain such procedures and sanctions.

Again, I find this not too difficult to understand. One usually seeks to widen one's own discretion, and is relatively certain that it will be exercised judiciously. Our ideas about judicious action, however, are heavily influenced by what we are expected to do, and by the actions we might have taken, but did not take. Parole officers usually might have reimprisoned most parolees for something before they robbed another store or pistol-whipped a helpless aged widow. They are subject to blame in the views of many for not having done so, given current laws and arrangements. With the authors, I believe we should change our laws and arrangements so that such blame, and the expectation of blame, is not forthcoming. I think we have little to lose but our bad faith, but much to gain.

VII

One general way of characterizing the authors' recommendations is to say that they propose relieving those who fix the actual terms served by persons committed to prison of the burdens of large unstructured discretion to be exercised in the name of crime control. More specifically, they propose that when decisions are made about the duration of prison terms, those decisions be governed by standards based primarily on "desert"—that is, the seriousness of the past criminal conduct of the person being punished. Further, those decisions should be made early rather than delayed, and subject to little later modification.

Finally, they recommend that parole supervision, if it is retained at all, should be sharply curtailed in its potential effects on those subject to it. If parolees are suspected of new crimes, they should be prosecuted. If parolees are to be sanctioned for technical parole violations, the severity of those should be carefully restricted. If services to parolees are to continue to be offered, they should be offered because parolees need them, not because it is expected that recidivism will be reduced; and services should be refusable. All of this and more is put forward with force and, at the same time, modesty.

The authors exhibit full awareness of the many problems that their analysis and recommendations leave unsolved—or, indeed, help create. What should the *specific* content of the standards be? (Von Hirsch has elsewhere begun to address this question, but he readily concedes that much work remains to be done.) To what extent will the standards, when applied to the complex realities of an existing criminal justice system, succeed in reducing disparity? (This will require empirical inquiry into the experience of states that have tried to adopt standards, but it would be wise not to be too hopeful.) And there may be other difficulties, also. If "good-time" laws are established to help prison authorities manage their mega-prisons in the face of an early term-fix, they could easily build much disparity back into the terms of prisoners. And whether parole supervision organizations could be moved to adopt a social welfare role in a period of emphasis on "just deserts" is also questionable. Von Hirsch and Hanrahan are aware of these and other problems; they are aware, that is, of both the theoretical and *practical* problems raised by their analysis.

I would like, finally, to make particular mention in this introduction of the topic of choosing the decisionmakers. This is among the most novel parts of the authors' treatment of parole. First, the authors consider what the best means for developing sentencing standards might be. They argue convincingly that the legislature is probably *not* the best forum for development, and they discuss alternatives. Second, they consider whether centralized term-fixing boards should be abolished if such standards are developed and adopted; for example, should the courts alone apply such standards? This leads to a long-needed discussion of "real time" (that is, where sentences represent time actually to be served) vs. the current practice of "dual time" (that is, where the court fixes a sentencing limit and a centralized board the actual, lower period of confinement).

They present reasons for retaining "dual time," at least during a period of transition. It will surprise many to learn that, in view of that conclusion (and the reasons for it), they also suggest that a "parole board"—but not a traditional one—may be a useful medium, during that transition, for applying (as well as helping develop) sentencing standards.

VIII

Will the reforms presented by the authors, if instituted, cure the difficulties presented by sentencing? I doubt it, and so do they, if "cure" is taken to mean either that inequality of sentences—even of prison terms—will be over; or that the thrust to bend the system to provide ever more crime control, even at the expense of justice, will cease. The latter will, I think, always be with us, and will move us continually to compromises. Cure of sentencing inequalities calls for consideration of much more than what happens to that small fraction of those caught up in the criminal justice process who end up in state or federal prisons. But one must start somewhere. And it seems reasonable and just to start by trying to ameliorate the lives of those penalized most severely.

※ *Chapter 1*

Posing the Question

Parole is now a central feature of America's penal system.[1]
When a convicted offender is sentenced to prison, it is largely the parole board's responsibility to decide how long he will stay, and what will happen to him after release.

When developed in the early 1900s, parole was hailed as a reform. Until the 1970s, it continued to command a broad consensus of support. Now, parole is under attack. Abolition has been urged by persons representing a wide spectrum of political and philosophical viewpoints, ranging from Jessica Mitford to Ernest van den Haag.[2] Parole has been abolished in Maine,[3] and curtailed in California, Indiana, and Illinois.[4] Several other jurisdictions are considering similar actions.[5]

This book will analyze whether parole should be retained, reformed, or eliminated. We focus on parole of adult felons. While the issues we raise are also relevant to other forms of parole (such as parole for misdemeanants and for juvenile offenders), we do not deal specifically with the latter.

There is considerable variation in how parole systems work. Many states parole a large percentage of imprisoned offenders, but some do not.[6] The grounds for granting or denying release also differ among states,[7] as do parole supervision and revocation practices,[8] and the organization and staffing of paroling authorities.[9] We shall, however, direct our attention to the common features of parole systems, rather than to the differences. Here, then, is a thumbnail sketch of how parole works.

Parole Release.   When an offender is sentenced to prison, it is normally the parole board that determines how long he or she will in fact remain confined. Ordinarily, the judge's sentence sets the maximum permitted duration of confinement: a six-year prison sentence means the offender may be confined for no more than six years. The parole board is empowered to release an offender on parole well prior to sentence expiration. In some states, the parole board has discretion to release a prisoner at *any* time before the sentence expires. In others, the offender must serve one-third of his sentence, or a similar fraction, before he may be considered for release. In still others, the judge has the power to set a minimum term of confinement of up to, say, a third of the maximum sentence.[10] *

It has been customary for the parole board to wait until the inmate has served a substantial period in confinement before considering him for parole. In jurisdictions where the offender becomes legally eligible for parole only after serving a prescribed fraction of his sentence, a board will delay considering the prisoner's case until shortly before the eligibility date. Even in jurisdictions where the board has power to parole at any time, it is common practice to impose a similar waiting period before hearing the case. If parole is considered and denied, the decision is delayed still further. Parole release thus is typically a deferred decision: the inmate will not know when he can expect to be released until well into his prison sentence.[11]

The decision to grant or deny release takes place at a parole hearing.[12] The hearing usually consists of a brief interview conducted by a hearing officer or parole board member.[13]

The basis for the release decision varies considerably among different boards. The theory traditionally has been one emphasizing rehabilitation and prediction: parole officials typically assert that the offender will be released when it appears that he is "progressing" toward a law-abiding existence. Studies of parole decisionmaking have indicated, however, that other factors are given weight.[14] Analyses of the past practice of the U.S. Parole Commission[15] suggest that it relied heavily upon the seriousness of the offense, as well as the estimated likelihood of recidivism. Some boards have been found to rely on such other factors as the inmate's disciplinary record and his local community's attitude about his release.[16]

---

*In most jurisdictions, the board's power to release is constrained by the operation of "good time" laws. Traditional good time is time deducted from sentence for good behavior in the institution; usually, good time reduces the maximum term by some fraction (e.g. one-third) and in some cases it also reduces the minimum term. The operation of this system thus determines to some extent the time frame within which the parole board operates.

Until recently, parole boards operated without any explicit guidelines for release decisions. Decisions were supposedly made on a case-by-case basis, considering any factors the board deemed "relevant." In the early 1970s' however, the U.S. Parole Commission began instituting guidelines for release, derived from studies of its own past decisionmaking practices.[17] Since then, the parole boards of several states (including Oregon, Minnesota, and New York) have followed suit.[18]

Parole Supervision. When the inmate is granted parole, he is released to the community under supervision. As a prerequisite to release, the inmate must sign an agreement listing the parole conditions he must obey. The parolee is required to comply with the law; he is directed to engage in certain activities believed conducive to a law-abiding existence (such as seeking a job); and he must avoid other activities thought criminogenic (such as associating with known criminals).[19]

At release, the parolee is assigned to the caseload of a parole agent. The agent is responsible for monitoring the parolee's activities and for providing him with assistance in readjusting to life in the community. Parolees must report periodically (e.g., monthly) to the parole officer, and can expect unscheduled visits. The parole officer may also contact individuals connected with the parolee, such as family, friends, or employers, to secure information on the parolee's activities.[20]

The period of supervision must terminate at the expiration of the sentence. Most jurisdictions, however, authorize discharge of the parolee from supervision prior to sentence expiration.[21]

If the parolee violates any of the conditions of his release, parole may be revoked by the board—in which event he returns to prison. Revocation proceedings do not have the full safeguards of a new trial, although certain elementary procedural protections (such as notice of the charges and opportunity to present rebuttal evidence) are now required.[22] If parole is revoked, the board determines how long the parolee will be reconfined, since it has the power to decide whether and when he may be paroled again. However, the period of reconfinement may not exceed the unexpired portion of his original sentence (reduced in some jurisdictions by "street time," which is the time the parolee has already served in the community).[23] With few exceptions, parole boards have not issued guidelines on their revocation policies.[24]

THE CURRENT CRITICISM

The attack on parole began by calling attention to the arbitrariness of its practice—the absence of substantive standards and procedural safeguards for parole decisions. M. Kay Harris, writing in 1975, summarized the complaint as follows:

> The overall picture of parole release in the United States . . . [has been] one of systems unguided by rules, policy statements, or explicit decision-making criteria, unbounded by requirements for statements of findings and reasons, . . . devoid of procedural safeguards [and] unchecked by administrative review. . . .[25]

The U.S. Parole Commission and some state boards responded by developing explicit guidelines for their release decisions, and by adding some due-process safeguards to their procedures.[26] Meanwhile, however, the critics have found what they assert to be more fundamental defects.

Parole, it is said, tries to perform impossible tasks. One claimed purpose has been to promote rehabilitation by permitting the offender to be released when he is "responding" to treatment. But rehabilitation programs, when tested for effectiveness, have generally shown disappointing results.[27] How can parole promote rehabilitation, critics ask, if the treatment programs do not work?[28]

Another claimed purpose has been predictive: parole authorities are supposed to observe the imprisoned offender's behavior and determine when he becomes a good risk for release. Yet, critics point out, behavior inside the prison appears to be an indifferent predictor of subsequent behavior in the community.[29]

Parole was also supposed to facilitate law-abiding behavior after the offender's release from prison, by requiring him to maintain regular contact with a parole agent who has special surveillance and counselling responsibilities. But, critics assert, the parole agent's dual functions of policing the parolee and "helping" him tend to conflict with each other.[30] And both the surveillance and the "help" seem to be of questionable effectiveness.[31]

A different kind of criticism addresses the moral appropriateness of the goals of parole. *Should* decisions about confinement be based on someone's estimate of the offender's responsiveness to treatment or likelihood of recidivism, even if those estimates could be made accurately? It has been argued that it is unjust to make the severity of the offender's punishment depend on what he supposedly will do in the future, rather than on the basis of the blameworthiness of his past actions.[32]

These criticisms, however, leave a number of important questions unanswered.

When parole is challenged on grounds of ineffectiveness, this leaves the question: What if knowledge about treatment and prediction were to increase? Suppose, for example, that some prison-based treatment methods were developed that *did* work. Or suppose further research discovered that some behavior in prison (or on furlough or parole supervision) *were* useful in predicting recidivism. Would such discoveries strengthen the case for keeping parole?

When the rehabilitative-predictive ideology is criticized as unjust, one must then ask: Might not parole be supported on a different penal philosophy? One needs to analyze how parole would fare, for example, on a philosophy of punishment that put more emphasis on the blameworthiness of the offender's past behavior, and less on prediction and rehabilitation.

One must also inquire whether some features of parole might be more worthwhile than others. Parole has a number of distinguishable functions, including: (1) having an administrative board decide how long the offender will stay in prison; (2) having this decision occur late, rather than immediately upon commitment; and (3) requiring the offender to undergo supervision in the community after release from prison. Might it be advisable, for example, to keep the board while eliminating the second and third features?

Finally, one must consider what the alternatives are. If any of parole's major functions were eliminated, what compensating measures would be necessary? How could one ensure that altering or abolishing parole does not produce undesirable consequences elsewhere?

The present study addresses such issues. We shall try to describe which problems of parole are currently remediable; which would require new empirical knowledge to solve; and which, if any, raise fundamental ethical objections. We shall identify which features of parole we would like to see retained, and which eliminated; and where we suggest the latter, we shall explore what the alternatives are, and what problems those alternative present.

A study such as this necessarily involves value judgments, since the issues raised by critics concern not only what works but what is fair. Rather than avoiding such issues, we shall try to deal with them as explicitly as we can. This, in turn, requires us to state what moral principles we believe should be fundamental to a penal system. Those principles are the topic of the next two chapters.

Part I

Premises

※ *Chapter 2*

General Assumptions

Our analysis of parole will be based on certain general premises, which we will state explicitly. Let us begin with moral assumptions. The liberty and freedom of choice of each individual are to be preserved to the full extent consistent with the freedom of others. The convicted offender should retain all the rights of a free individual, save those rights whose deprivation can affirmatively be justified by the state.[1] It should be up to the state to establish the case for any proposed intrusion into the offender's life, not up to the offender to show the inappropriateness of the intrusion.

The basic notions of procedural fairness should apply to convicted persons. If, for example, an offender is to be penalized for supposed new misconduct occurring after plea or verdict of guilt, there should be fair procedures for determining whether the individual did, in fact, commit that misconduct.

Wards of the state, including convicted criminals, must be treated with common decency. Cruel punishments, intolerable living conditions, and the like are impermissible because the state ought never to inflict such deprivations for *any* purpose. This obligation should take precedence over whatever penal goals the state is purportedly pursuing. Inhumane conditions of imprisonment should be ruled out even if they were, for example, to serve deterrent or other penal purposes, for those latter purposes must be subordinate to the idea that prisoners be treated in a manner befitting a civilized society.

Our next assumptions concern the control of discretion. Specific, carefully drawn standards should govern the disposition of convicted offenders.

The widest discretion has characterized sentencing and parole. In a typical felony case, the sentencing judge has been free to impose from as little as a suspended sentence to as much as a ten, fifteen, or twenty year sentence of imprisonment. If the judge chooses a prison sentence, the parole board then has been free within broad limits to decide what portion of the term will actually be served in prison, what the conditions of release will be, and what circumstances warrant reconfinement.[2] Until recently, no explicit standards, guidelines, or precedents have applied to these decisions.

The dangers of disparity are obvious. Officials whose decisions are unchecked by general standards decide similar cases differently.[3] And the idea of rule of law is offended: such unstructured discretion, as former U.S. District Court Judge Marvin Frankel has aptly written, "is *prima facie* at war with such concepts . . . as equality, objectivity, and consistency in the law."[4]

It was long assumed that broad, standardless discretion was necessary to allow the sentencing judge and parole board to tailor the disposition to the particular offender's needs for treatment.[5] But this claim does not bear analysis. *Any* theory of punishment, even a rehabilitatively oriented one, requires standards to assure that individual decisionmakers will pursue that specified purpose (not ulterior ones of their own choosing), and to assure that they will do so in a reasonably consistent fashion. The choice of penal philosophy—that is, whether rehabilitation, incapacitation, deterrence, or desert should have priority—concerns a different question. It is not whether there should be standards (yes, there should!), but what the standards' content should be: what characteristics of the offender or the offense should determine the disposition.

The standards should set forth the type and severity of penalties with reasonable definiteness. In the next chapter, we shall be more specific about the standards' aim and content, and about the problems involved in formulating them. But general maxims are clearly insufficient: exhortations such as those found in the Model Penal Code—which call upon the decisionmaker to consider such factors as whether the penalty would "depreciate the seriousness of the defendant's crime"[6] —fail to provide the necessary guidance.

Our third set of assumptions concern the nature of imprisonment. The miseries of life in today's prisons, the Atticas and Statevilles, have been too well documented to need restating. Imprisonment would still be a great deprivation, however, even if conditions could be improved, were there smaller size, better location, superior facilities and less regimentation than is customary in American prisons today. As Erving Goffman and other observers have pointed out,[7] it is intrinsically painful to lose one's liberty; to be cut off from the pursuits important in one's life; to be denied the company of family and associates; to have one's daily existence controlled by prison authorities; to reside in enforced intimacy with (uncongenial and possibly menacing) strangers; and to live in a place that embodies the public stigma of criminality.

The severe character of imprisonment is crucial to bear in mind. It calls for strict economy in the use of the prison sanction. Lengthy confinements bear an especially heavy onus of justification.[8] An obstacle to careful thinking about parole has been the notion that the offender is fortunate to be considered for release and supervision, since he otherwise would have remained in prison. Because parole was thus seen as a "privilege" or "act of grace," its fairness was not thought to need inquiry.[9] Our assumption about the harsh nature of imprisonment undercuts this notion. If imprisonment is as onerous as we believe it is, lengthy, judicially imposed sentences are not necessarily warranted—in which case earlier release is not merely a "privilege." The justice of this process, by which some remain imprisoned longer than others, and by which some are reimprisoned while others are not, urgently requires scrutiny.

Chapter 3

The Purposes of Punishing—
The Desert and Modified
Desert Models

Since parole is part of the penal process, we should specify what aims are to be achieved in choosing punishments.

At least four different notions have been said to underlie the punishment of offenders. Three of these concern reduction of crime in the future: rehabilitation, incapacitation, and general deterrence.[1]* The fourth concerns the blameworthiness of the offender's past criminal conduct: desert. Which of these should be given primacy when selecting penalties has long been a matter of debate. During most of this century, rehabilitation and incapacitation[2] (and to a lesser degree, deterrence)[3] were penologists' favored notions. Now there is renewed interest in desert[4] —although how much emphasis it should receive is still far from settled.

---

*We define "rehabilitation" as changing a convicted offender's character, habits, or behavior patterns so as to diminish his criminal propensities. Its success is measured by the treatment's impact on recidivism rates. It includes not only traditional correctional treatments (such as psychiatric therapy, counselling, and vocational training), but also more novel techniques such as behavior modification.

"Incapacitation," as we use the term, is restraining the convicted offender so he is unable to commit further crimes against persons in the community even if he were inclined to do so. Like rehabilitation, its success is measured by recidivism rates. Unlike the latter, however, it does not involve efforts to change the offender, but only to limit his access to potential victims.

"General deterrence" is the effect that a threat to punish has, in inducing potential offenders to desist from prohibited conduct. It seeks to alter the behavior not only of convicted criminals but also of unconvicted members of the public who otherwise might have been disposed to commit crimes. It thus is concerned with the effects of penalties (or their threat) on overall crime rates, not just on recidivism rates.

Given the continuing dispute over aims, why is it necessary to make a choice? Why not, instead, pursue all four purposes at once? Unfortunately for such a strategy, the aims are in potential conflict. The best treatment may be a poor deterrent; the best deterrent may be undeservedly severe. One must choose which of the aims should have priority.[5] We therefore shall devote this chapter to stating our own assumptions about the aims the state should pursue when deciding how much to punish. This will provide the necessary conceptual framework for our inquiry into parole.

DESERT AS A REQUIREMENT OF JUSTICE: THE PRINCIPLE OF COMMENSURATE DESERTS

It is the fundamental requirement of justice in punishing the convicted, we assume, that *the severity of the punishment be commensurate with the seriousness of the offender's criminal conduct.* This is called the principle of "commensurate deserts."[6] Of the variety of philosophical arguments that have been suggested in support of this principle,[7]* the most persuasive in our view is that addressed to the condemnatory implications of punishment. It may be summarized as follows.[8]

Punishment involves blame; it is a defining characteristic of punishment that it is not merely unpleasant (for so are taxes and conscription), but treats the person punished as a wrongdoer who is being censured for his criminal act. The severity of the penalty connotes the amount of blame: the sterner the punishment, the greater the implicit censure. A period of years of imprisonment implies that the actor is more to be condemned than does a brief stint in jail or a suspended sentence.

The amount of punishment, therefore, should comport with the seriousness of the offender's criminal conduct. When this requirement of commensurateness is not observed, the degree of blame becomes inappropriate. Giving severe punishment to a lesser offense overstates the blame. Giving a mild punishment to one convicted of serious criminal conduct understates the censure due.

Undeservedly severe or lenient penalties are impermissible, even when imposed for the sake of crime prevention. Suppose, for example, that a certain type of lesser criminal conduct could be deterred efficiently by invoking a severe penalty against a very few offenders.

---

*The rationale of the principle is developed more fully in *Doing Justice*, and in the philosopher John Kleinig's valuable book, *Punishment and Desert*.

On a utilitarian theory of punishment, such a sanction could be supported if its aggregate social benefits (prevention of even small loss to numerous potential victims) exceeded its aggregate costs (severe penalties imposed on only a few offenders). Nevertheless, it would be unfair to impose so much censure, if the conduct cannot be shown to be highly reprehensible.

This principle calls for more than the mere setting of broad outer limits on the amount of penalties for various crimes. It permits variations in punishment among offenders only to the extent that these reflect variations in the blameworthiness of their conduct. Concededly, it is easier to discern gross excess in lenience or severity than to decide on specific proportions between crimes and punishments. But the commensurateness principle is infringed whenever divergent penalties are imposed on equally deserving offenders—even if such disparities are kept within specified latitudes. If A and B have committed crimes of equal injuriousness under circumstances suggesting similar culpability, they deserve the same amount of punishment. Imposing unequal penalties on them unfairly treats one offender as though he were more to blame than the other.

The principle of commensurate deserts, it should be noted, addresses the question of *allocation* of punishments: that is, how much to punish various convicted offenders. The allocation question is distinct from the issue of the *general justification* of punishment, namely, why the criminal sanction should exist at all. In arguing for the commensurate-deserts principle on the basis of punishment's condemnatory overtones, one need not adopt the view that reprobation for wrongdoing is necessarily the only reason for the criminal law's existence. The institution of legal punishment may serve other ends as well (in *Doing Justice*, it was suggested that it exists to deter crime as well as to condemn.[9]) But punishment—once established, for whatever reason—necessarily implies blame. Therefore, it ought in fairness to be distributed among convicted offenders in a manner that is consistent with those overtones of blame.

We would like to emphasize that the principle of commensurate deserts is concerned only with severity; it thus allows the pursuit of crime-control goals to the extent these do not affect severity in ways the principle prohibits. It is permissible, for example, to try to rehabilitate the offender, provided this is done without significantly changing the amount of his penalty from that which he deserves.[10]

The Desert Model

To analyze parole, we shall posit two alternative conceptual models, and then trace the implications of each. The first is the "Desert

Model": it is the conception of punishment that emerges when the principle of commensurate deserts is rigorously observed.

The Desert Model constitutes a radical departure from the penological theory that has traditionally sustained parole. That theory stressed forward-looking considerations: the likelihood of the offender's returning to crime and his expected responsiveness to treatment. The Desert Model, by contrast, gives primacy to retrospective considerations; severity is to be determined by the seriousness of the offender's *past* criminal behavior. Does this mean the model necessarily rules out parole? Sometimes it is said that parole must be abandoned once the rehabilitatively oriented theory that sustained it is no longer accepted.[11] But it is not so simple. Even if parole were historically supported by predictive-rehabilitative ideas, it is still necessary to examine whether any of its features might be re-justified under a desert-oriented conception.

If the Desert Model is so different from the traditional assumptions of parole, why begin with it? We do so because we think it is the most equitable conception of punishing. It is the model that best complies with the principle of proportionality between offense and punishment that we believe justice requires.

What would a penalty system using a Desert Model look like? Attempts to sketch such a scheme are found in *Doing Justice* and in John Kleinig's *Punishment and Desert*.[12] Basically, what is involved is grading criminal conduct according to its seriousness and then constructing a scale of penalties that corresponds to those gradations of seriousness. In this grading and scaling task, the following major issues still need to be resolved.

Criteria for Seriousness. Analytically, the seriousness of criminal conduct has two components: *harm* and *culpability*. Harm refers to the amount of injury done or risked by the act. Culpability refers to the factors of intent, motive, and circumstance that bear on the degree of the actor's blameworthiness—whether, for example, the act was done with knowledge of its consequences or only in negligent disregard of them; whether, and to what extent the act was precipitated by the victim's own misconduct, and so forth.[13] To date, efforts to develop criteria for seriousness have been hampered by the absence of theory on how harm and culpability are to be assessed.[14]

Marvin Wolfgang has proposed that criteria for seriousness be developed using empirical studies of popular perceptions of the gravity of offenses. Beginning with his and Thorsten Sellin's work in 1964, several surveys have measured perceptions of seriousness and found considerable agreement.[15] When asked to rate the gravity of common acts of fraud, theft, and violence, people from different walks of life tend to give similar ratings. Such popular ratings might provide a useful starting point in constructing the criteria,[16] especially after more data are developed.[17] It is doubtful, however, that such ratings could be relied upon exclusively. Consider the question of mitigating factors that might bear on an offender's culpability. One study found that such matters as whether there was provocation by the victim had little apparent effect on popular ratings of seriousness. It is arguable, nevertheless, that the criteria for seriousness should take such mitigating factors into account, because—irrespective of the survey results—they *do* in fairness affect how reprehensible the act was.[18]

Relevance of Prior Offenses. In assessing an offender's deserts, is it appropriate to consider whether or not he has a record of prior convictions? In *Doing Justice*, it was argued that (for reasons which we shall refer to later)[19] the presence or absence of a prior criminal record bears on the offender's culpability and thus is an appropriate factor to consider. The report proposed a two-dimensional penalty scale in which the severity of the punishment would depend upon: (1) the seriousness of the current offense; and (2) the number and seriousness of crimes for which the offender was previously convicted. The matter has prompted dispute, however. Some commentators have argued that, in a desert theory, only the current offense (not the priors) should be considered.[20]

Magnitude of the Penalty Scale. So far we have spoken of the desert requirements that govern the *internal* structure of the penalty scale—that is, the ordering of penalties relative to each other. Punishments are to be arranged so that their relative painfulness corresponds to the comparative seriousness of offenses; infractions of equal seriousness are to be punished equally. More problematic, however, is the question of the absolute dimensions of the scale. How severe should the highest penalty on the scale be, and how lenient the lowest?

In deciding the scale's overall magnitude, the commensurate-deserts principle would require that, at all points on the scale, there be a reasonable proportion between the quantum of punishment and the gravity of the conduct. The scale should not be inflated so much that less-than-serious conduct is severely punished—not even if worse crimes were punishable more harshly still. Conversely, the scale should not be so much deflated that even grave offenses are punished leniently. But "reasonable proportion" is an imprecise notion: a more specific account is called for. It needs to be decided, for example, whether the commensurate deserts principle would leave any room for other considerations—for example, crime-control aims such as deterrence, or notions of parsimony—in deciding among alternative proposed magnitudes-of-scale. *Doing Justice* suggests that there could be room for such considerations within certain limits; Kleinig's *Punishment and Desert* argues that there should not.[21] To what degree, moreover, is it proper to look to a jurisdiction's past practice as a starting point for decisions about magnitude? Is there an inescapable element of arbitrariness in choosing the anchoring points and overall dimensions of the scale, and might there be a better and worse way of making such "arbitrary" choices? All these issues urgently need more thought.

The Desert Model does, nevertheless, impose this critical limitation. Once criteria for seriousness are assumed, and once the absolute dimensions of the scale have been chosen, the model narrowly restricts the extent to which the internal structure of the penalty scale can be varied for purposes unrelated to offenders' deserts. Of particular relevance to parole, it prohibits raising or lowering a particular offender's punishment because of his predicted likelihood of recidivism or his supposed need for treatment.

The Modified Desert Model

The Desert Model, as we have seen, requires strict adherence to the commensurate-deserts principle. No deviation from deserved severity is permitted. We shall, however, also consider a second conceptual model that gives somewhat greater scope for future-oriented considerations in deciding how much to punish. We shall call it the "Modified Desert Model": it permits limited deviations from the constraints of commensurateness.

The commensurate-deserts principle, we noted, requires equal punishment of those whose criminal conduct was equally blameworthy. The Modified Desert Model permits some relaxation of this requirement. Limited variations in punishment of equally deserving offenders would be permitted for the purpose of enhancing the incapacitative, rehabilitative, or deterrent usefulness of the sanction. On this model, therefore, desert would determine the range of penalties applicable to conduct of a given degree of seriousness; but, within the range, other factors could be considered in fixing the specific penalty.[22]

The deviations permitted in the Modified Desert Model would, however, have to be modest. Large departures from the requirements of commensurate-deserts would continue to be barred as unjust. The model thus represents a compromise: the basic structure of the penalty system would still be shaped by the desert principle, but other considerations would be allowed some scope in choosing the penalty.

The model has its drawbacks. There are problems of equity: how could there justly be even "modest" differences in punishment among those whose conduct is assumed equally blameworthy?[23] The notion of "modest" deviations is worrisomely plastic: how can moderate reliance on nondesert factors in sentencing decisions be distinguished from reliance that is too extensive to satisfy minimal requirements of justice? It will not be easy to draw a principled demarcation.

Nevertheless, we think the Modified Desert Model is useful as a heuristic device. It furnishes a conceptual framework in which both desert and the traditional crime-control aims would have a role in deciding an offender's disposition. This allows a fuller analysis of parole than would have been possible using the Desert Model, with the preeminence the latter gives to the single idea of desert in deciding the individual sentence. Besides considering whether desert requirements are met, the Modified Desert Model requires us to inquire whether and to what extent parole does actually serve the rehabilitative and other forward-looking aims that traditionally were thought to constitute its reason for existence. However, the model still would require, as we think justice minimally demands, that the degree of blameworthiness of the offense be the primary (although no longer the exclusive) determinant of the punishment.

STANDARDS—WHAT FORM?

Earlier we discussed the need for dispositional standards. Under either the Desert or Modified Desert models it is essential that there be rules governing how serious various categories of crimes are and how much punishment they deserve. Otherwise, dispositions will not be consistent: one sentencer could treat an offense as serious and punish accordingly, while another sentencer, having a different set of values, could treat the same infraction as minor.

The Desert Model calls for a definite disposition for each gradation of gravity in order to satisfy the principle of punishing equally serious conduct equally. A proposed method of accomplishing this is through a system of "presumptive sentences."[24] Each seriousness gradation would be assigned a specific penalty, and that would be the disposition applicable in the usual case. However, departures from the presumptive disposition would be permitted in unusual cases where mitigating or aggravating circumstances were present. The standards would define what kind of circumstances qualified as mitigating or aggravating—and, under the Desert Model, only those circumstances which affected the harm or the culpability of the criminal conduct would qualify. The standards would also define how much deviation from the presumptive disposition was permissible in such instances. Uniform treatment would thus be ensured for the unexceptional cases that make up the bulk of the sentencers' caseloads, while still allowing variation for the out-of-the-ordinary cases.

The drafting of a system of presumptive penalties will involve some difficult choices. The system could be more or less detailed, and allow for more or less discretion in dealing with mitigated or aggravated cases. One could try to devise an intricate code of penalties, as the Twentieth Century Fund's report, *Fair and Certain Punishment*, recommends.[25] Each major offense category would be broken down into several subcategories of distinct gravity, with a presumptive amount of punishment assigned to each subcategory. Aggravating and mitigating circumstances would be defined in detail, and narrow limits imposed on the permitted amounts of variation from the presumptive disposition. Alternatively, one could—as *Doing Justice* suggests[26]—devise a simpler and more flexible system. The penalty scale would consist of a limited number of gradations of gravity, each possibly embracing several offense categories, with a presumptive penalty assigned to each gradation. Wider variations from the presumptive penalty would be permitted on account of aggravating or mitigating circumstances; and the rules specifying what constitutes aggravation and mitigation would be less detailed, leaving more to the sentencer's discretion.

The latter scheme would be easier to draft and implement, but with its greater leeway, it involves greater risks of disparity. The detailed code would reduce that risk, but puts on those drafting the standards a heavier burden of anticipating a large number of contingencies that may affect seriousness. Perhaps one solution would be to start with more general standards, and then refine them over time on the basis of experience.

In any event, a "feedback" process would be needed. The standard-setter should regularly monitor decisions made in individual cases, in order to identify areas where the standards need alteration or more specificity.[27]

A Modified Desert Model may call for somewhat differently drafted standards, since it would make some use of information about offenders that does not concern their deserts. Suppose, for example, that the standards use a numerical scoring system for selecting the applicable presumptive penalty. Under the Desert Model, all the points on the score would have to relate to the offender's criminal conduct. On a Modified Desert Model, however, a limited number of points (but *not* the bulk of them) might be assigned to other, "non-desert" items, if these were useful, say, in helping the sentencer assess the likelihood of recidivism.[28]

Let us emphasize that in recommending standards, we are not presupposing that the legislature should be the agency to set them. The question of which agency—the legislature, the courts, the parole board, or a special rule-making authority—should bear the standard-setting responsibility will merit a chapter in itself (Chapter 9). We shall be arguing, in fact, that a body other than the legislature is preferable for the task.

IMPRISONMENT: WHETHER
AND FOR HOW LONG

A parole system assumes the existence of imprisonment. It determines when the imprisoned offender will be released, how he is to be supervised after release, and whether he may be returned to confinement. When, if ever, *should* imprisonment be used?

The principle of commensurate-deserts is concerned with severity, and does not direct that penalties take any specific form. The principle's relevance is that it restricts severe punishments to criminal conduct that is serious. Imprisonment, as pointed out in Chapter 2, is a severe punishment. It is thus unsuitable as a penalty for nonserious offenses. But what of criminal conduct that is grave enough to deserve severe punishment? This must either be punished by imprisonment, or else an alternative form of severe sanction would have to be devised.

Given that choice, we think there are reasons for retaining imprisonment. First, there are no known satisfactory alternatives. Other possible severe punishments (such as corporal punishment, exile, or house arrest) seem either barbaric or impractical. Second, imprisonment has collateral usefulness as an incapacitant: those confined cannot commit crimes, during their confinement, against persons on the outside. This use of incapacitation would not violate commensurate-desert constraints, since we are speaking of the choice between imprisonment and another hypothetical sanction that would be equally severe.[29]

However, the duration of imprisonment should be stringently rationed. Given the deprivations of confinement, time crawls for the incarcerated individual. Lengthy terms of confinement are very harsh sanctions, deserved for none but the most heinous offenses. *Doing Justice* thus recommended that most terms of imprisonment be kept below three years' actual confinement, and that imprisonments in excess of five years be used extremely sparingly.[30] One might debate these specific figures, but the principle of strict durational limits on imprisonment remains crucial.

In measuring the severity of imprisonment by its duration, we are assuming that restrictions imposed on inmates within the prison should be limited to those necessary to ensure their safe presence.[31] Otherwise, even a few months' confinement could be made very harsh by stepping up the rigors of institutional life. We endorse neither the imposition of intentionally Spartan prison regimes, nor, of course, the miserable conditions that prevail in many U.S. prisons today.

THE PROBLEM OF
PROSECUTORIAL DISCRETION

There is a problem in developing standards and limiting the use of imprisonment that we shall not address: prosecutorial discretion. We make this omission not because we think the topic is unimportant, but quite the reverse—because it is so important that it requires a full separate study.

Critics of recent proposals to create sentencing standards, such as Albert Alschuler,[32] have suggested a "hydraulic" view: that such standards are likely not to reduce discretion effectively, but merely to make the discretion flow to prosecutors. As the formal sentencing agencies (judges and parole boards) are allowed less leeway, dispositions will increasingly become controlled by the prosecutor through plea-bargaining decisions. Others, such as James Q. Wilson, question whether this hydraulic effect will occur.[33] Sentencing standards are capable of influencing dispositions, Wilson argues, provided that the prescribed penalties are perceived as reasonable by the participants in the process.

Since standards regulating the severity of punishments are a recent development, there is little empirical evidence to support or refute either position. Considerable disparity will doubtless persist as long as there are no guidelines governing prosecutors' charging and bargaining decisions. But the dimensions of the problem will become known only as sentencing standards are tried and evaluated.[34]

The extent of the problem may vary with the manner in which the standards are drafted—particularly with the severity of the penalties. Arthur Rosett has pointed out that the harsher the stated sanctions, the greater the incentive of prosecution and defense to bypass them through plea-bargaining.[35] (This is a practical consideration which supports our earlier recommendation that penalties be kept modest.)

Even if standards for the later, formal stages of the process are not a sufficient solution, we think they are a necessary first step. It would be extremely difficult to address the complex and elusive issues of prosecutorial discretion without first attempting to bring some order into the sentencing and parole system. Should there, as some have suggested,[36] be guidelines for prosecutors' charging and bargaining decisions? It would be difficult to describe what form such guidelines could possibly take, until one had first developed norms for how much an offender should be penalized *if* convicted on one or another charge, and until experience provides an indication of how prosecutors respond to such norms.

OTHER MODELS

The foregoing assumptions about the aims of punishing are admittedly controversial ones. Some will prefer conceptual models that put less stress on desert and give crime-control aims more prominence in deciding how much to punish.

Some of these models may overlap with ours; that is, they may derive similar results from a different theory. Compare, for example, the model used by the U.S. Parole Commission, in its guidelines, with the Desert Model. Theoretically there are important differences: the Parole Commission's model was derived from historical practice, and relies upon predictions of recidivism as well as upon judgments about offense seriousness; whereas the Desert Model is based on theoretical arguments, looks to the gravity of the offender's criminal conduct, and does not rely on predictions. Yet it has been pointed out—by Gottfredson, Wilkins, and Hoffman in their recent book, *Guidelines for Parole and Sentencing*—that there may be considerable congruence in practice between the two models.[37] This is, they assert, because the best (known) predictor of recidivism is the offender's prior criminal history; and the latter is, at least according to some versions of desert theory, also a factor in assessing the degree of the offender's blameworthiness.[38] (How much congruence there is will be difficult to estimate, however, until there is further analysis of how criminal history should bear on blameworthiness.)

Other conceptual models, however, could be so different from ours that little congruence would exist. There, the conclusions about parole could well differ from those we shall develop here. We will, at various points, suggest how the analysis might change if the assumed aims of punishment differed from ours. But these will only be tentative suggestions: one cannot develop any single analysis of parole that will hold ineluctably for all penal philosophies.

Having described our assumptions, we may proceed with the analysis. In the next Part (Chapters 4 and 5), we will examine parole's process for releasing offenders from prison. In Part III (Chapters 6-8), we will discuss the supervision of parolees in the community. In the final Part, we shall consider which decisionmakers could best set the standards for punishment and apply those standards—and there, we shall address whether or not parole boards should continue to play any major role in the sentencing system.

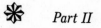 *Part II*

Release of Prisoners

Chapter 4

The Case for an Early Time-Fix

Parole typically involves deferral of the decision on how long a prisoner will remain confined. At the time an offender is sent to prison, he ordinarily does not know what portion of the judicially imposed sentence he will have to serve: that is decided at a much later date by the parole board. This deferral of the duration-of-confinement decision is sometimes known as "indeterminacy" of sentence. But as that expression has been used with a variety of other connotations,[1] we prefer to coin our own term: "deferred time-fix."

In prevailing parole practice, the inmate's case is first heard by the parole board after he has served a specified portion (in many jurisdictions, about one-third) of the judicial sentence. If the board decides favorably, a release date is set and the inmate is notified of it. If the decision is unfavorable, the case is put off until the next hearing. Most jurisdictions have a schedule of rehearing dates, with annual rehearings being common.[2] On rehearing, the procedure is the same: a release date is set if the decision is favorable; otherwise, the case is postponed again. The release decision thus is not only delayed but "floats": there is no fixed time at which the inmate must be told when release will occur. Until the board decides, the inmate cannot be certain about how long he will remain in prison.[3]

Recently, deferral has become a much criticized feature of parole. It is said to rest on outdated assumptions, and to subject prisoners to the needless cruelty of waiting for a decision. A number of penologists and study commissions—Norval Morris,[4] Richard McGee,[5] David Fogel,[6] David Stanley,[7] and the Citizens' Inquiry on Parole[8] —

have advocated an early decision on the duration of imprisonment. And several jurisdictions—Maine,[9] California,[10] Indiana,[11] Illinois,[12] Oregon,[13] and Florida,[14] as well as the Federal system[15]—have shifted to an early time-fix.

Sometimes this change has been linked with abolition of the parole board's power over duration of confinement. Under the new California statute, for example, the judge's sentence determines the actual duration of confinement (subject to prescribed reductions for satisfactory behavior in prison).[16] The Indiana and Illinois statutes likewise eliminate parole release.

Sometimes, however, the change is made while retaining the parole agency's authority. Under the new Oregon statute, release from prison continues to be decided by the parole board, but the board must adopt standards for duration of confinement and notify the offender of his expected release date shortly after he enters prison. The new Florida statute requires a similar procedure. The U.S. Parole Commission has recently amended its rules to call for an early decision on the prisoner's release date.

MODE OF ANALYSIS

To resolve whether the time-fix should be early or late, we should examine what, if anything, is learned by waiting. Which items of information are relevant to deciding the duration of confinement? Are any such items of information knowable only late—that is, well after sentence is imposed? If so, this would be a reason for delaying the time-fix. If all such items can be known at or about the time of sentence, however, that would support an early fix.

What information is relevant depends, of course, on the assumed goals of punishment. We shall therefore consider the Desert and the Modified Desert Models and, with respect to each, ask what kinds of information would be germane to deciding the duration of prisoners' confinement, and when that information is available.

Our conclusion will be that the decision should occur early under either of these models. We shall advocate that each prisoner be notified of his release date at or soon after sentencing. Then, in Chapter 5, we will consider whether this conclusion needs to be altered in order to deal with the practical problems of prison discipline and prison overcrowding.

WHY DEFER?—ON A DESERT MODEL

We begin with the Desert Model, for it is the one we prefer. Not surprisingly, it creates the strongest case for an early time-fix.

This model, as we saw in Chapter 3, requires that the duration of the individual offender's confinement be based only on an assessment of the gravity of his criminal conduct.[17] In making that assessment, is any "late" information necessary? Generally not. Judgments about the seriousness of criminal behavior are judgments about *past* events. An offender's desert is normally just as well ascertainable at or about the time of sentence—when the nature of his crimes can already be known—as at a later date. By waiting longer to fix the time-in-prison, one learns nothing new.[18]

One limited class of exceptions comes to mind, however. This is where the seriousness-rating assigned to a given type of crime alters over time because of changes in beliefs about how reprehensible the conduct is. Suppose, for example, that—some time after the initial adoption of the standards on length of confinement—cocaine possession ceases to be classified as a serious crime because of growing skepticism about the harmfulness of the drug or about the moral appropriateness of severely penalizing conduct that seems hurtful primarily to the perpetrator.[19] In this case, there would be good cause for reducing the prison terms of previously convicted cocaine offenders who are still undergoing punishment. For what is in question is the appropriateness of *ever* having treated such behavior as serious, and hence of having treated such offenders as deserving severe punishment.*

To accommodate such cases, however, there would be no need to keep all prisoners in suspense about when they will be released. Each prisoner should promptly be notified of the date of his expected release from prison. That release date could subsequently be altered only in cases where there was a change in the standards for the seriousness of the offense, which would warrant a reduction in the punishment of those previously convicted. Since few crimes are apt to be reclassified during any given time period, such changes in release dates would be the exception not the rule. Rather than being kept waiting, prisoners would know when they would be likely to leave prison.

This re-fixing of the release date should be limited, moreover, to cases where the altered standards treat the offense as *less* serious. The

*The conclusion might be different, however, in cases where the seriousness-rating of an offense has been reduced solely because a change in external circumstances has altered the conduct's *actual* consequences. (For example: creating a certain species of public-health hazard becomes classified as less serious, after the technology for counteracting it has improved.) Here, the later events would not have affected the degree of injuriousness of such acts at the time they were originally committed, so that the deserts of the original actors arguably remain unchanged. Such situations are apt to be rare, however, as the cited example suggests.

converse should not obtain: even if a crime comes to be classified as more serious than it once was, those formerly convicted and still undergoing punishment ought not have their prison terms extended. The reason is, of course, fair notice: at the time the individual committed the crime, he could not foresee that it would later be seen as more blameworthy and hence as punishable more harshly. To increase the length of "deserved" confinement retroactively would be objectionable as a form of *ex post facto* punishment.[20]

WHY DEFER?—ON A MODIFIED DESERT MODEL

The analysis becomes more complicated if one adopts the Modified Desert Model, for that model permits more factors to influence the penalty, and hence more items of information to affect the time-fixing decision. We must attempt to determine whether any of these added items of information could be known only later.

Incapacitation.   A common method of incapacitating criminals is to rely on predictions in deciding the amount of an individual offender's confinement. If the offender is deemed to be in a high risk category, he would be kept out of circulation longer; if he is in a lower risk category, he would be restrained for less time (or else not confined at all).[21] The Modified Desert Model could allow some room for this, since it permits incapacitative considerations to influence the disposition to a limited extent.[22] *

Assuming this much scope for incapacitation, does it require deferral of the time-fix? The conventional answer was "yes." To predict whether an offender would or would not be law-abiding, it was thought, one had to wait for post-sentence information about, for example, the prisoner's performance in prison, plans for employment, or the nature of the social milieu to which he would be returning. But is this really the case? To answer that question, we must go to the prediction literature and ask how well forecasting techniques succeed, and what information they require.

*There is, however, another method of incapacitation—discussed by James Q. Wilson and Reuel and Shlomo Shinnar—that would not call for any effort to predict an individual offender's likelihood of recidivism. It is to impose a given period of confinement on *all* offenders convicted of a given type of crime. So long as some (even if by no means all) of the imprisoned offenders would have committed new crimes had they been allowed at large, this sanction will have an incapacitative effect. This technique of "collective incapacitation" would not require a deferred time-fix, because the duration of confinement is *ex hypothesi* determined at the outset.

Actuarial prediction methods have had some success in identifying subgroups of offenders having the higher statistical likelihood of returning to crime.[23] They achieve this success, however, at the expense of overpredicting: a substantial number of those identified as potential recidivists will be "false positives"—persons who are mistakenly identified as recidivists, and who would not have offended again. Some writers—Norval Morris[24] and one of the present authors[25] among them—have argued that, even aside from desert considerations, it is unfair to rely on predictions in deciding how much to punish, because of the risk of mistakenly penalizing the persons who are false positives. But an advocate of the Modified Desert Model might reach a different conclusion. Such a person, being willing to accept modest differences in punishment among those equally deserving, might also be prepared to tolerate errors of overprediction so long as their consequences were not severe. And the consequences would not be severe under the Modified Desert Model because of the limits it imposes on the extent to which incapacitative considerations could increase punishments.

Assuming predictions are permitted, what information do they require? The available forecasting techniques rely on information that is available at the time of sentence.[26] The best-known prediction index, the California Base Expectancy Score, makes exclusive use of "early" information. Base Expectancy scores are derived from the following data, in descending order of predictive weight:

> ... arrest-free period of five years or more, no history of opiate use, few jail commitments (two or less), present commitment based on offense other than checks or burglary, no family crime record, no alcohol involvement, first arrest for offense other than auto theft, one job held at least six months, no alias, present sentence on original commitment, favorable living arrangement (not transient), and two or fewer prior arrests.[27]

Other prediction indices use similar information.[28]* Current methods of predicting violent recidivism also rely principally on facts about

---

*This raises the question whether matters of status such as employment history, residential stability, or age—which may be partly or wholly beyond the offender's control—should be considered in sentencing decisions. On a Desert Model they could not, because they do not relate to the gravity of the criminal conduct. On a Modified Desert Model, they might be considered if they had predictive usefulness, although some advocates of the latter model may prefer to rule out such matters of status for other reasons, e.g., reasons of social equity. Our point here is that even if such factors *were* taken into account (and we would not wish them to be), they are knowable early, and hence do not require a delayed time-fix.

the offender knowable at the time of sentence, such as prior record of violence, psychiatric history, age, and sex.[29]

Personality tests, such as the California Personality Inventory or the MMPI, have been tried as predictors of recidivism, but so far with only mixed results.[30] And while little attention has been paid to the issue, it appears that these work no better when administered late than when administered when the offender first enters prison.[31]

Some studies have measured how prisoners' behavior during confinement correlates with recidivism.[32] These studies generally find little correlation. This is not surprising, given that living conditions in the institution are so different from those outside.

With increasing use of furloughs, work release, and halfway houses, it has been suggested that offenders' behavior while on partial release should be useful in assessing risk of recidivism, since temporary liberty better approximates the milieu to which the offender will be returning.[33] But what behavior? It is still not known, for example, to what extent noncriminal conduct on furlough or work-release helps predict recidivism. In fact, this whole question has received scant study.[34]

What of clinical, instead of statistical, prediction? Clinicians have attempted to predict recidivism, with varying success—usually, less confirmed success than statistical techniques have had.[35] In some instances, the forecasts are made before sentence; in others, at a diagnostic center when the offender first enters prison; in still others, they are made later. Even to the limited extent that successes have been achieved,[36] however, we know of no evidence that delaying the clinical evaluation significantly enhances clinicians' ability to predict. The question has, to our knowledge, never been systematically addressed.

Rehabilitation. It was also conventionally assumed that rehabilitation would require deferral of time-fix. Since, supposedly, the sentencing judge cannot know in advance how quickly the offender will respond to treatment, the date of release (to the extent determined by rehabilitative considerations) must be set later, after observing the inmate's progress in the program.

To delay the time-fix for reasons of treatment presupposes that there are programs known to be effective in reducing recidivism. This brings us to the question of what treatments work, if any. A number of surveys of treatment programs—by Bailey,[37] Robison and Smith,[38] Lipton, Martinson and Wilks,[39] and Greenberg[40]—have reached pessimistic conclusions. Supporters of treatment have challenged the findings of these surveys, asserting that their authors have drawn more negative inferences than the cited evidence warranted; and have also claimed success with particular programs.[41]

Do any successful treatments exist, then? Surveys of more recent programs are now underway.[42] Until the results are analyzed and reported, it is premature to reach a definitive verdict. Nevertheless, we think a case has *not* been made for deferring the time-fix on rehabilitative grounds. This is so for several reasons.

First, even if certain categories of offenders are thought amenable to treatment, the entire population of prisoners is unlikely to be. There are large segments of the criminal population—those who engage in criminal enterprises for profit, for example—who could be expected to remain intractable to treatment even on optimistic assumptions about rehabilitation.[43] Why, then, routinely defer the time-fix for all prisoners?

Second, the time-fixer can consider only those treatments that can be administered before the release decision occurs—namely, those designed for a prison setting or for furlough or work release. Prison-based programs have, thus far, been a particular disappointment;[44] and comparatively little rigorous research has been done on furlough or work-release-based programs.[45]

Third, were a treatment for a certain type of prisoner to work, it would not necessarily affect the duration of his imprisonment. If the offender is deemed to deserve, say, eighteen months of imprisonment, it might be possible to give him the treatment without accelerating or postponing release. The time-fix is not at issue at all, unless the rehabilitative program calls for a different term of confinement. This brings us to the largely ignored question: How long will the treatment take? Existing studies have made little effort either to assess the extent to which longer or shorter durations might affect successful outcome, or to develop methods of estimating the needed duration of treatment for different types of offenders.

Finally, treatment would not necessarily require a deferred time-fix, even if it were to call for some change in the duration of imprisonment. One still would have to ask the same question as we did about incapacitation: What kind of information relevant to the duration-of-treatment is gained by waiting? It may be that information needed to place the offender in a suitable treatment program and to estimate the treatment's duration is largely known at the time of sentence.[46] Again, there has been no empirical research on this question of the usefulness of "late" information for treatment decisions. Until such research has been undertaken, there would be no reason for deferring the time-fix.

General Deterrence. The Modified Desert Model would theoretically permit limited adjustments in duration of confinement to enhance a penalty's deterrent impact. But the technology does not exist today to calculate deterrent returns with any precision,[47] and crime rates are not likely to be very sensitive to moderate variations in severity.[48] In any event, there is no reason to expect that one will gain new information about a penalty's deterrent utility by delaying the time-fix. Certainly, "late" information about what has befallen the prisoner himself would hardly be useful, since general deterrence depends on how much others are intimidated.[49]*

Deferral of the time-fix thus would be unnecessary, even when one considers the complicating factors that a Modified Desert Model introduces. The addition of these factors has made our conclusions depend partially on the state of empirical knowledge; but, based on the current state of the art, we can say that the relevant information is available early, at or shortly after sentence.

CHANGES IN EMPIRICAL KNOWLEDGE

What if empirical knowledge were to change, however? Consider prediction. While existing prediction methods rely on information available at sentence, that may be due, in part, to its being more readily at hand. Usually, better records are kept of an offender's prior history than of his post-sentence behavior in prison or on furlough.[50] Were "late" information more carefully recorded than it is today, and were there a systematic effort made to explore its predictive usefulness, might not instances be found where it did enhance prediction?

Perhaps so, but the difficulties of finding such information should not be underestimated. Even if an item of late information were found to be correlated with recidivism, it would not necessarily tell the predictor anything new—for it may predict essentially similar outcomes as information that was available earlier.[51] (Among various data that are correlated with recidivism, there is a considerable de-

---

*It has sometimes been suggested that deferral enhances deterrence by permitting the system to *seem* to punish more severely than it in fact does. Judges can intimidate potential offenders by imposing long purported prison sentences; later, the parole board can quietly scale down the time actually served. The deterrent usefulness of this strategy depends, however, on which segment of the public would be fooled. Those prone to accept the illusion may be the more law-abiding citizens, who would be least tempted to commit crimes in any case, and most readily deterrable with modest sanctions. Those having the greatest potential for offending may be more familiar with the actual workings of the system. (See also Chapter 9.)

gree of substitutability: one item can replace another in a prediction instrument without appreciable loss of forecasting power.[52]) Any proposed item of late information thus would have to meet a more stringent test: whether the inclusion of the item would substantially enhance predictive efficacy in ways that could not be achieved by substituting an item or items of information available at time of sentence.

Suppose, nevertheless, that instances were found where late information could meet this test. To what extent would we then have to alter our conclusion favoring an early time-fix? On a Desert Model, there would be no difference—for there, prediction is not a factor in the time-fix at all. It is only on a Modified Desert Model (or other assumptions stressing prediction still more) that the question arises.

Even then, prisoners would not have routinely to be kept ignorant of when they will be released. Were new research to find instances where items of late information enhanced prediction, such cases could be accommodated through a limited modification in what we have recommended: namely, an early presumptive time-fix. Each prisoner would be informed immediately of his anticipated release date, which would be based on the seriousness of his offense and (to the extent one's assumptions permitted) the estimated risk of his recidivism. That date could be altered on the basis of subsequently-available information *only* when there was strong evidence that the information did, in fact, alter the estimated probability of the offender's returning to crime.* And, under a Modified Desert Model, the alteration could not be great, because of the Model's limits on how much incapacitative considerations may affect the disposition. This suggested modification, moreover, would be called for only at some future date, if ever, when the predictive technology had changed substantially.

THE BURDEN OF JUSTIFICATION

Thus far we have been asking, Why have a deferred time-fix? In other words, we have been assuming that the burden of justification lies

---

*While further experimentation would be needed to find out when late information was useful, the experimentation would not itself require a delayed time-fix. Suppose one were exploring the predictive usefulness of a particular item of late information—say, the presence or absence of an adequate release plan by the prospective parolee. That can only be determined by fixing the time early, and then finding out whether releasees with good work plans perform better than those with bad ones. If the time-fixer were allowed to delay release for offenders whose plan is deemed inadequate, this would make it impossible to determine whether adequacy or inadequacy of the plan is linked to recidivism.

with the proponents of deferral. Why should the burden lie there? Why shouldn't we be asking, instead: Why not defer?

Were the latter question asked, the penal aims of which we have been speaking would not compel an early fix. Consider desert; and suppose one were asking whether desert *precluded* deferral. It would not: even though the seriousness of the crime can be determined at the time of conviction, it also could be assessed later. The same holds for crime-control aims, to the extent one's assumptions permit their use. While predictive information, for example, is available at the time of sentence, this information could simply be preserved for later use.[53]*

Why, then, put the burden of justification where we have put it— on the proponents of deferral? There are two reasons. One is the painfulness of waiting. A deferred release decision, Marvin Frankel notes, "is experienced as a steadily galling affliction."[54] There are numerous accounts of the anxiety prisoners feel because of uncertainty about release.[55] And the one systematic study, conducted by Maurice Farber in 1944, found that uncertainty about duration of confinement was correlated with heightened suffering among prisoners.[56]

Some of the suffering, admittedly, may stem not from the deferred time-fix *per se*, but from the absence of discernible standards concerning release. A prisoner could better estimate his length of stay if durational standards were adopted. But even with standards, uncertainty will remain when the time-fix is delayed, as long as the time-fixer retains any significant degree of discretion (for example, to increase or decrease the term on account of aggravating or mitigating circumstances). The question thus remains: Ought the prisoner be subjected to *any* uncertainty about his release in the absence of affirmative justifying grounds for deferring the fix?

Our answer is that he should not. Whenever the state undertakes any substantial interference with an individual's life, that individual should *prima facie* be entitled to know as promptly as possible the proposed nature and extent of the interference. This holds also for the imprisoned offender. He has a legitimate interest in being swiftly informed of how long he is to be deprived of his liberty, so that he

---

*The former practice of the U.S. Parole Commission is a case in point. The Commission's guidelines on duration of confinement have been based on: (1) the seriousness of the offense; and (2) a predictive index known as the salient factor score. The items used in this index are all knowable at time of sentence— prior convictions, prior parole revocations, history of drug use, and the like. The Commission, prior to 1977, nevertheless used a deferred time-fix. It decided the release date after about one-third the sentence had expired, and obtained such information from the available records.

can try to inure himself to the pains of confinement, and so that he can plan his life.

A second, more pragmatic, concern is the ability to appeal. An appellate procedure of some sort, either judicial or administrative,[57] is needed to ensure that the durational standards are being properly applied. An early fix is needed to give sufficient time for the appeal. Suppose the durational standards provide that, for crime X, the presumptive duration of confinement is eighteen months, but that four months' increase is permitted for specified aggravating circumstances. Suppose that the state claims such circumstances were present in a particular offender's case; that the time-fixer has accepted this claim; and that the offender wishes to appeal on grounds that the standards were erroneously applied. If the time-fix occurs when the defendant is sentenced or first enters prison, there will be time for the appeal. But if the time-fix is delayed—if, for example, it occurs only shortly before the time of normal release—the appeal may be too late.

CAVEATS

In thus recommending an early time-fix, we should mention these caveats. First, we have done the analysis on two conceptual models, both (albeit to a different extent) emphasizing desert. That leaves the question whether our conclusion favoring an early fix would hold on more thoroughly crime-control-oriented penal philosophies. At first impression, the answer would seem to be "yes." Suppose, for example, that one assumed that duration of confinement should be based *primarily* on the offender's predicted likelihood of offending again. If one asks what information is useful in making such forecasts, the answer remains (at least, on the existing state of the art): information knowable at time of sentence. Because we doubt the justice of so future-oriented a scheme, however, we have not explored its ramifications systematically. That being the case, we cannot categorically state whether our conclusions extend to it.

Second, the shift from a late to an early time-fix still leaves open, as a *separate* issue, the question of which agency should act as time-fixer. An early fix does not necessarily require that the parole board be abolished and that the time-fixing decision be transferred to judges; instead, the board could decide offenders' release dates shortly after their entry into prison, as is now the practice in Oregon and the Federal parole system. The choice of time-fixer, which is discussed at length in Chapter 9, involves difficult questions about, for example, which agency is best capable of applying a complex set of durational standards.

Finally, an early time-fix is a useful reform only when durational standards are also adopted. To accelerate the time-fix without limiting the time-fixer's discretion will perpetuate the disparities and confusion that characterize so much of today's parole release decision-making. The recent Maine statute is a case in point. By law that took effect in 1976, Maine moved to an early fix—by eliminating the parole board and requiring judges to specify the duration of confinement. Yet the statute sets virtually no standards to guide judges' decisions.[58] Maine's new system is now under study and its results have yet to be reported.[59] But the hazard is evident: without explicit norms to guide their decisions, judicial time-fixers can assess the seriousness of similar offenses differently; give different weights to the competing aims of desert, deterrence, incapacitation, and rehabilitation; and have different policies of leniency or severity.

Chapter 5

The Early Time-Fix and Problems of the Prison

We have yet to speak of more practical concerns. How can a system with an early time-fix cope with problems of prison overcrowding and prison discipline? We are interested in such problems of management only from a limited perspective—their relevance to our recommendation for an early time-fix. For that purpose, we need not deal comprehensively with space and order in prisons, complex topics that are developing a substantial literature of their own.

PRISON POPULATIONS

Overcrowding is, perhaps, the most serious problem facing prisons today.[1] Crowding may continue to be a problem even if one were to adopt dispositional standards of the kind we recommended in Chapter 3. True, those standards would restrict imprisonment to serious crimes and put particularly stringent limits on the use of long confinements. But those convicted of serious criminal conduct would have to go to prison. Hence, if the number of convictions for such crimes were large enough, or if it should increase, the prison population would rise also.

If prison populations grow, crowding will become worse—unless prison capacity expands concurrently. Many jurisdictions will have difficulty affording extra space, given the high cost of building and operating new facilities.[2] It has been questioned, also, whether it is desirable to expand prison capacity, as that may generate pressures to keep the new facilities filled (irrespective of need) once they are built.[3]

Severe overcrowding renders imprisonment intolerable.[4] When two, three or four prisoners are forced to live in a cell designed for one person, the daily discomforts of prison life become much worse; frictions among inmates that can lead to violence are exacerbated; and the institution's ability to ensure prisoners' safety diminishes.

When there is no additional space, crowding can be alleviated by shortening prisoners' terms. Traditional parole was capable of being used in this fashion; the parole board, with its wide discretion, could simply release offenders sooner.[5] The extent to which parole boards exercised this power has varied from jurisdiction to jurisdiction. A recent study suggests, for example, that the Massachusetts and Iowa boards have been sensitive to population pressures in their release decisions, while the Illinois board has been much less so.[6]

One must ask, first, whether it is desirable to deal with overcrowding by shortening stays in prison. Why should an offender receive any less confinement than he deserves, through the happenstance that the prisons are too full? We think this is proper, because there exists an overriding obligation to refrain from cruelty. Our suggested conceptual models assume that desert should have priority among the aims of punishing. Yet certain constraints of a civilized society, as we suggested in Chapter 2, should take precedence over *any* penal purposes, even desert.[7] One is the obligation to avoid barbaric treatment of persons in the state's custody.

Suppose, for example, that the standards prescribe that offenders convicted of crimes of a given degree of gravity normally deserve X number of months of imprisonment, but that, because of insufficient prison capacity, they can be held for that period only by so overcrowding the prisons as to make life inside intolerable. The obligation to punish as deserved should then give way to a still more fundamental obligation of the state to treat its wards in a manner befitting a civilized society. The argument is that no penal aim, not even desert, justifies confining people in severely overcrowded prisons, because such privations should never be inflicted for *any* reason.[8]

Assuming it is proper to shorten stays in prison to alleviate overcrowding, the making of such adjustments should be governed by explicit guidelines. The guidelines should define what constitutes overpopulation for various types of facilities. In formulating the definition, it would be useful to consult the recommendations on adequate prison living space that have now been made by several study commissions.[9] The guidelines should also suggest the methods of calculating term-reductions, when situations of overcrowding are found to occur. To the extent possible, the benefits of such reductions should be distributed evenhandedly among those confined at the time.

How can such crowding-adjustments be reconciled with an early time-fix? The technology of projecting prison populations is still quite rudimentary. A recent LEAA-sponsored report to Congress concludes that population-projection technologies have not progressed beyond the making of rough approximations on the basis of alternative scenarios.[10] When an offender enters prison, therefore, one may not be able to foretell whether crowding can be expected to develop or become worse during his term of confinement.

Adjustments in prison terms to alleviate overcrowding may thus require short lead times. This, in turn, would call for a limited modification in the early time-fix. If unanticipated situations of overcrowding develop after the offender's release date has initially been set, it may become necessary to set a new, earlier date pursuant to the guidelines on overcrowding.

PRISON DISCIPLINE

Where the state punishes by imprisoning, there need to be sanctions to preserve order in the prison. Traditional parole often served as such a sanction, through the threat of denying release to prisoners who misbehaved.[11] A study by Peter Hoffman of the U.S. Parole Board's release decisions found that, at second hearings, the offender's "institutional adjustment" was an important factor in decisions to grant or deny release;[12] studies conducted in some states have reached similar conclusions.[13]

When, if ever, should the authorities be allowed to extend the prison stays of refractory prisoners through an administrative procedure? There are three kinds of misconduct in prison that should be distinguished.

First, there are serious crimes committed inside the institution: murder, rape, aggravated assaults, and the like. These *deserve* added incarceration for substantial periods. The violator should, however, be prosecuted.[14] Granted, there may be special problems in prosecuting such crimes: fear of reprisals may make witnesses harder to obtain, for example. But where the accused stands in jeopardy of so severe a sanction, any procedure that lacks the high burden of proof and other protections of a criminal trial, in our view, entails an unacceptable risk of penalizing the innocent.[15]

Second, there are the minor disciplinary infractions: routine acts of disobeying staff orders, petty thefts, and the like. These, generally, are not serious enough to warrant any added confinement. For such violations, lesser penalties would be appropriate, such as loss of specified privileges within the institution.[16]

Third are violations in the middle range: significant disruptions of prison discipline that do not involve major felonies. These may warrant brief extensions of time in prison. How much time, and for which violations, may vary somewhat, depending on whether the Desert or Modified Desert model is adopted. (The Desert Model would be the more difficult to satisfy, as one would have to establish that the proposed penalty was strictly commensurate with the gravity of the prisoner's infraction).[17]

If administratively imposed time extensions are justified at all, it could only be for this third category of middle-range infractions. Where some extra time (but not much) is called for, prison administrators' arguments about the impracticability of seeking new prosecutions have some plausibility. And the extent of the prisoner's jeopardy is less, because the amount of the potential punishment has been restricted. The stringency of the procedures would thus depend on the amount of the penalty. A limited stint of extra prison time could be imposed in an administrative proceeding; but the severe sanction of lengthy extra imprisonment would necessitate a criminal prosecution with its greater procedural safeguards.[18]

How could such a solution be incorporated into a system having an early time-fix? The simplest method, perhaps, would be as follows. The prisoner would be notified of his expected release date at or shortly after sentence. He would be informed, however, that his release could be postponed beyond that expected date by specified amounts if, after a hearing by a designated administrative body, he is found to have committed specified rule infractions in prison. Any such extensions should, however, be hedged by the following safeguards:

1. There should, as stated already, be prescribed limits on the amount of such postponements. Large extensions of confinement should require a new prosecution.

2. There should be a specification by rule of which kinds of infractions lead to how much added time. The amount of time-extensions should bear a reasonable relationship to the gravity of the conduct. The kinds of misconduct subject to such penalties should be described with enough specificity so the offender knows what to avoid if he wishes to be released on his scheduled date.[19]

3. The hearing body should be independent of the prison authorities, or else there should be an independent reviewing body. Institutional disciplinary committees cannot be expected to be sufficiently disinterested to act as final arbiter, given their understandable concerns about the smooth running of the institution and about staff morale.[20]

The new Oregon statute partially adopts this kind of procedure.[21] The offender is notified of his expected release date shortly after he enters prison, but is told the date may be extended for disciplinary violations. The law attempts to incorporate the second and third of the safeguards just suggested. Release may be postponed only if the violation involves "serious misconduct"—and a rulemaking agency (in Oregon's case, the parole board*) must define what constitutes "serious misconduct" and adopt rules "specifying periods of postponement for such misconduct."[22] The penalty may be imposed in an individual case only if an agency independent of the prison authorities (again, the parole board) finds that the misconduct has, in fact, occurred. However, the first safeguard is missing: the statute specifies no maximum limit on the amount of postponements.[23]

The foregoing may be described as "bad time": the offender's initially set term is *extended* by specified amounts if he commits infractions. An alternative technique would be "good time": the term of confinement, fixed early, would be *reduced* by so many days per month if the prisoner refrains from specified rule infractions.[24]** If the term initially fixed is appropriately adjusted, the latter system could lead to similar results in practice as a "bad-time" system. And the needed safeguards are the same. There should be maximum limits on the amount of good-time that may be lost for any infraction[25]† so that an alleged violator cannot be punished se-

---

*In Oregon, the parole board is also the body that writes the rules governing duration of actual confinement for various kinds of criminal conduct. For discussion of why the parole board was chosen for the standard-setting and time-fixing tasks, see Chapter 9.

**This system differs from the so-called good time statutes that have traditionally existed in most states, in that it would govern the actual date of release. In the latter, good time was merely deducted from the judge's minimum or maximum sentence, and did not necessarily affect the time when the parole board granted release.

†The new California law limits the amount of good time that can be lost through any single infraction, by "vesting" the good time accumulated by the violator before his infraction, and by not permitting the authorities to deprive the violator of the right to earn good time in the future. Thus, while the amount of good time is comparatively large on the face of the statute (it amounts to a one-third deduction), the offender's jeopardy for any given violation is considerably smaller.

verely through an administrative proceeding. There should be rules stating with reasonable specificity how much good time can be lost for what kinds of infractions. And the final arbiter of lost good time in individual cases should be a hearing or review body that is independent of institutional authorities.

While the problems of devising fair and workable methods of coping with prison infractions are difficult ones, they are not unique to the early time-fix. They would also have to be confronted were the time-fix delayed, so long as the release decision were made according to explicit standards. Irrespective of whether the decision occurs early or late, the standard-setter would have to decide the extent to which refractory prisoners should serve more time, and determine the procedures that are appropriate for deciding such cases. The reason traditional parole never confronted such questions was that it operated without any set standards at all.

We would like to add a word of warning: good time or bad time, if adopted without foregoing safeguards, can duplicate many of the ills of unreformed parole. If one replaces the old evil of standardless parole with the new evil of standardless control over release by prison disciplinary bodies, neither the fairness nor the predictability of punishments will be enhanced.[26] An illustration of what to avoid is found in the new Indiana sentencing code. According to this statute, each convict sentenced to prison is to receive a "definite sentence" of a specified number of years, but is entitled to receive a deduction from that sentence of up to *50 percent* if he maintains a clean disciplinary record.[27] Any disciplinary violation may, in the discretion of a designated corrections department disciplinary committee, result in loss of accumulated good time and in denial of the right to receive future good time.[28] The department's rules on what constitutes disciplinary violations contain much that is trivial or vaguely defined.[29] The upshot is that a disciplinary committee is given huge, uncharted leeway to decide how long an offender will in fact remain confined.

The dangers of such a system are evident. The hope of having fair and commensurate punishments will be lost if duration of confinement depends so much upon a prisoner's disciplinary record, rather than upon the degree of blameworthiness of his criminal conduct. A true early time-fix will also be lost: if any infraction inside the prison, even a minor one, can result in nearly a doubling of the time the prisoner serves, he will remain uncertain of the duration of his stay.[30]

NET EFFECT OF THESE
RECOMMENDATIONS

Even with the modifications discussed in this chapter, the procedure we recommend differs markedly from traditional parole release practice. Instead of a largely discretionary release decision, the time-fix would be guided by explicit standards. Instead of the decision being delayed, as it still is in many jurisdictions, the decision would occur early: all prisoners would swiftly be informed of their expected release dates. The prisoner would know that his date could be altered only in two contingencies:* he could serve less time than expected if severe overcrowding developed; and he would serve more time (within specified limits) if he is found to have committed certain violations in the prison.

---

*There is, however, the possibility of a third—namely, where a long term of confinement has been imposed because the crime was found to be especially heinous. Should there in such cases, be a special "cooling off" procedure, involving a second look at the term subsequent to the initial time-fix? The pros and cons of this issue are discussed in Appendix I.

 *Part III*

Supervision of Ex-Prisoners

 *Chapter 6*

Parole as a Separate Adjudicative System for New Crimes

It is nearly always a condition of parole that the parolee refrain from new crimes.[1] Any violation of the law can result in revocation of parole and reimprisonment. The revocation process differs from a new trial in that the hearing is conducted by an administrative agency (the parole board instead of a court); the standard of proof is lower, and the procedural protections are slighter; and the system of dispositions is different. Should this separate system for adjudicating new crimes be preserved?

CURRENT PRACTICE

New criminal conduct by parolees is probably the most common reason for revoking parole.[2] When a parolee is suspected of new criminal activity, his parole may be revoked in lieu of prosecution.[3] From the state's point of view, revocation in lieu of prosecution has advantages of convenience. The parole board retains control over the case, and can decide the parole violator's fate in a brief, uncomplicated procedure. Prosecutors and judges are saved time and resources, for revocation keeps such cases off their calendars.[4] For the parolee, revocation has the disadvantage of a lower standard of proof, which makes a defense more difficult to conduct. (He may, however, derive a few benefits: In some states, the revoked parolee is eligible for re-release sooner than he would be were he given a new sentence.)[5]

When a parolee is arrested, what determines whether he will be prosecuted or have his parole revoked in lieu of prosecution? One major factor seems to be the permitted period of reconfinement. Upon revocation, the parolee can be incarcerated only until expiration of his original sentence.[6] If sentence expiration would cut the desired amount of reconfinement short, a new prosecution may be sought; if substantial unexpired time on the original sentence remains, revocation in lieu of prosecution may be chosen. Authorities may also opt for revocation, it has been alleged, where evidence of criminal activity would be inadmissible at trial.[7]

The parolee accused of a new crime may, however, be prosecuted *and* have his parole revoked.[8] Depending on the policy of the parole board, he may have to serve both time on his new prison sentence and time for the revocation.[9]

It sometimes occurs that a parolee suspected of a new crime will be charged in the revocation proceeding with violating one of the "technical" conditions of parole, rather than with violating the condition that he remain law-abiding.[10] This may occur, for example, when the agent feels that he lacks sufficient evidence to substantiate his suspicions, or has gained information from an informant. Evidence of such violations is easily obtained, because some technical parole conditions are very restrictive while others are quite vague.[11] Since the real reason for revocation is not officially recorded in these cases, it is difficult to determine the extent to which the revocations for technical violations are actually based on suspected criminal conduct.[12]

The parole revocation procedures currently in effect were shaped by two Supreme Court decisions: *Morrissey* v. *Brewer*[13] and *Gagnon* v. *Scarpelli*.[14] *Morrissey* established the minimum procedural requirements for revocation, while *Gagnon* addressed the issue of the right to counsel.

Morrissey requires a two-stage revocation process. The first stage consists of a preliminary hearing, held "as promptly as convenient"[15] after arrest of the parolee, at or near the site of the alleged violation. The hearing is conducted by an individual other than the parolee's parole officer. Its purpose is to determine whether there is "probable cause" that a violation of parole has occurred.

The parolee must receive written notice of the hearing, its purpose, and of the alleged violations. At the hearing, the parolee may present letters or documents, and may call witnesses. Upon request, individuals who have supplied information adverse to the parolee's case are to be made available for questioning in his presence unless the hearing officer "determines that the informant would be subjected to risk of harm if his identity were disclosed."[16] A summary of the proceedings is prepared. If probable cause is found, the parolee may, at the board's discretion, be returned to an institution to await a final revocation hearing.

The second hearing—which is the final revocation hearing—is held to evaluate any contested facts and to determine if the facts warrant revocation. The hearing must be conducted by the parole board or a "neutral and detached"[17] hearing body. The procedures for notice, evidence, and confrontation are substantially the same as those of the preliminary hearing. In addition, the evidence against the parolee must be disclosed to him and the hearing body must prepare a written statement of the evidence relied upon and the reasons for the revocation decision. *Morrissey* did not specifically deal with the question of right to counsel, but that question was addressed in *Gagnon*— which left the hearing body considerable discretion in deciding whether to permit or exclude counsel.[18]

If the offender's parole is revoked, he returns to prison. Depending on the nature of the charge and the parole board's policy, the period of reconfinement may be lengthy. The rules of the U.S. Parole Commission provide, for example, that a person whose parole is revoked for new criminal conduct should be held (subject to expiration of his original sentence) as long as would a new prisoner whose crime had a similar seriousness-rating, and who has scored poorly on the Commission's prediction index.[19]

In existing parole practice, this special adjudicative system for new crimes is interwoven with supervision of the parolee in the community. However, it would not have to be: one could imagine a system where the adjudicative function existed separately and alone. Offenders would be released from prison on the *sole* condition that they abide by the law. As long as they remained law-abiding, releasees would not be subject to any control by parole authorities. The latter would enter the picture only if a releasee were charged by the police with a new crime. Then the parole authorities would be empowered to detain the individual, hold a hearing, and decide whether to revoke and reimprison in the same manner as they now do when they charge a parolee with new criminal behavior. Eliminating the supervision would probably entail little or no loss in the capacity to detect new crimes by parolees or apprehend them for such crimes. Detection and apprehension are usually done by the police, and the parole agent first learns of the event when he is notified that one of his parolees is in police custody.[20]

The special adjudicative system for parolees has been abolished in only one state, Maine, which has done so by eliminating parole supervision altogether.[21] However, no data are available on the effects of this change.

THE STANDARD OF PROOF IN REVOCATION PROCEEDINGS: THE RISK OF MISTAKENLY IMPUTING GUILT

A parolee suspected of committing a new crime can have his parole revoked and be reimprisoned on less evidence than it takes to convict. The standard of proof in revocation proceedings is not that of "beyond a reasonable doubt," constitutionally mandated in criminal trials,[22] but a lower standard. The *Morrissey* decision did not address the standard-of-proof question.[23] A 1975 survey of statutory and case law found that:

> [T]he vast majority of state statutes, as well as the federal parole and probation statutes, contain no direction as to the necessary burden of proof. In most of the statutes, the matter of revocation is totally within the discretion of the supervisory authority and the establishment of the violation is either referred to without qualification or the appropriate authority is directed to proceed by its own rules and regulations.
>
> Standards for proof in such proceedings did emerge, however, through judicial review of revocation decisions. All courts required as a minimum that there be no abuse of discretion by the revoking authority, in that the revoking authority may not act arbitrarily or capriciously or without any basis for its actions. Where the court is willing to review the sufficiency of the evidence within the discretionary standard, the level of adequate evidence may range from "slight" to "substantial." Alternatively, the court may look to see if the "evidence and facts be such as to reasonably satisfy the judge that the conduct of the probationer has not been as good as required by the conditions of probation." A number of recent decisions have found the "reasonably satisfy" test to be adequate even under the due process mandate of *Morrissey*.
>
> A small minority of courts had required a preponderance of the evidence as a basis for revocation of probation or parole even prior to *Morrissey*. Subsequent to *Morrissey*, a number of state courts also held that such a standard of proof is required to satisfy due process. No court has held, and a number of courts have expressly rejected, the contention that a violation need be proved beyond a reasonable doubt.[24]

The procedures for parole revocation also lead to less rigor in requirements of proof. Instead of the unanimous (or near-unanimous)[25] jury required in criminal trials, only the members of the hearing body (frequently, one or two board members or hearing officers) need be persuaded;[26] and they, as David Stanley asserts, "have a natural inclination to back up the parole officer [who makes the charges] as their colleague in the correctional establishment."[27] Rights of counsel[28] and cross-examination[29] are more restricted than in a criminal trial, and evidentiary standards are more lax.[30]

In a criminal prosecution, it is true, the defendant will have the benefit of these procedural safeguards only if the case goes to trial; and he may face strong inducements to forego his right of trial and accept a plea-bargain instead.[31] But ultimately it will be *his* choice whether to demand a trial or plead guilty. A parolee cannot insist on a trial if the board prefers to pursue the revocation route. Nor can he, in cases where there is a trial, prevent the board from conducting a revocation hearing with its lower standards, and reaching its own decision as to his guilt or innocence.[32]

These lax procedures were founded on such notions as the "custody" theory of parole. While the offender was on parole, that theory asserted, he was still legally serving part of his prison sentence. Therefore, a return to prison was merely the substitution of one form of custody for another, which called for no rigorous safeguards.[33] But that is mere fiction; being returned to prison is, in fact, a painful sanction. When that sanction is visited upon a parolee because of new criminal conduct he supposedly committed, he is really being punished for a new crime. That necessitates a fair procedure for determining his guilt.

The purpose of a high standard of proof is to keep to a minimum the risk of punishing the innocent. That is a fundamental requirement of fairness, as the Supreme Court stated in *In re Winship*[34] when it decided that a "proof beyond a reasonable doubt" standard was constitutionally mandated in criminal trials. In the Court's words:

> The accused during a criminal prosecution has interests of immense importance, both because of the possibility that he may lose his liberty upon conviction and because of the certainty that he would be stigmatized by the conviction. Accordingly a society that values the good name and freedom of every individual should not condemn a man for commission of a crime when there is reasonable doubt about his guilt.[35]

Reducing the standard of proof, while making it easier to punish the possibly guilty, would entail the unacceptable moral cost of increasing the exposure of innocent persons to punishment. As Justice Harlan stated in his concurring opinion in *Winship*:

> ... I view the requirement of proof beyond a reasonable doubt in a criminal case as bottomed on a fundamental value determination of our society

that it is far worse to convict an innocent man than to let a guilty man go free.[36]

This principle has as much applicability to persons previously convicted and imprisoned as it does to persons accused for the first time. It is no less unfair to punish a parolee for an alleged new offense he may not have committed than to punish an alleged first offender who may be innocent. This holds even if one were to assume that parolees are, as a group, more likely to commit crimes than members of the general population. For whatever that group's statistical probability of recidivism may be, the *individual* parolee still could be innocent of the new crime of which he is suspected. It is that danger —of injustice to the individual wrongly accused—that the high standard of proof in criminal trials aims to prevent.

The potential severity of the sanction makes these risks particularly worrisome. We are not speaking here, as we did in the preceding chapter, of limited modifications in the terms of those already in prison on account of alleged disciplinary violations. What is involved here is, rather, removing an ex-prisoner from the community, sending him *back* to prison, and possibly keeping him there for a long time.[37] We are speaking, in other words, of potentially harsh punishments based on truncated procedures.

DISPOSITIONS IN REVOCATION PROCEEDINGS

There also exists a separate system of dispositions for parolees found to have violated their paroles by committing new crimes. Revocation and reimprisonment is authorized for *any* criminal behavior, irrespective of its seriousness. The maximum duration of reimprisonment depends not on the character of the new offense, but on the amount of the parolee's unexpired sentence.

Ought the standards of disposition for ex-offenders who commit new offenses differ from those applicable to first offenders? On our assumptions, the answer would be yes, but only to a limited extent.

Under a Desert Model, an argument can be made for penalizing first offenders somewhat less severely than those previously convicted. In *Doing Justice*, it was contended that (given criminal conduct of equal harmfulness) a first offense suggests a lower degree of culpability than a second or third. The first offender, that study argued, is at the time of his offense only one of a large audience to whom the law had impersonally addressed its prohibitions; the repeater, by contrast, has committed the conduct *after* having been personally visited with moral disapproval for such actions through his prior conviction and punishment.[38] This position has been disputed by some,[39] but it is at least arguable under desert theory.

The differentiation between first and repeat offenders could be somewhat greater on a Modified Desert Model. That model permits limited deviations from deserved severity on the basis of incapacitative considerations. According to most prediction studies, the existence of prior criminal history is a factor pointing toward greater likelihood of recidivism.[40]

Yet the power to revoke permits a much larger differential between parolees and first offenders than either model would allow, since even parolees apprehended for minor crimes could be reimprisoned, for example. This may occur, for example, when the board believes that the offense, while unimportant in itself, augurs for more serious criminal behavior in the future.

ABOLITION OF THE SEPARATE SYSTEM

Standard of Proof

What if this separate adjudicative system for parolees suspected of new crimes were eliminated? In that event, the suspect would have to be prosecuted. In principle, this should make the process fairer. If the accused wishes to contest the charge, the prosecution would have to meet the normal standards of proof, and the defense would have available the normal protections of a criminal trial. The substitution of these higher standards should help reduce the risk of punishing the possibly innocent.

Practice, concededly, will often prove less satisfactory. For what would be guaranteed is not a *trial* but merely being put through the criminal process; in many jurisdictions, this usually means plea-bargaining. As Albert Alschuler and other critics have pointed out,[41] a defendant who feels he has a valid defense may still feel compelled to plead guilty. This may occur because he has reason to fear that if he refuses to bargain and insists on his right of trial, he will be punished with greater severity in the event he is found guilty. Or it may be that his defense would require him to take the stand, and then his credibility could be impeached by proof of prior convictions. Or it may be that he lacks the resources to hire competent counsel.

We do not wish to underestimate the difficulty of remedying such ills. But there is beginning to be interest in reforming guilty-plea practice to alleviate some of the abuses.[42] * And the traditions of the

---

*Albert Alschuler has recommended a ban on plea-bargaining, and the state of Alaska has recently been experimenting with such a ban. Other, more modest proposals include guidelines for prosecutors to follow in their bargaining decisions, and fuller judicial review of proposed plea bargains.

criminal trial, with its emphasis on the rights of the accused, at least makes it easier to define the abuses as such. One can readily explain why it is unfair to force a defendant to surrender a plausible defense by threatening him with exemplary penalties if he insists on a trial and loses. It is harder to explain the evil of truncating opportunities for defense in revocation proceedings, since they have been perceived as informal processes concerned not with guilt or innocence but with ensuring parolees' compliance with parole rules.

Even with the criminal process as it is today, moreover, there will be cases where requiring a new prosecution will serve the interests of justice. Some ex-offenders charged with new crimes will be convinced they have valid defenses; will have competent counsel; and will be willing to risk a trial rather than plead guilty. Here, the higher standards could allow them to defend themselves effectively, where they could not have prevailed in a revocation proceeding.

Could the revocation process be reformed to provide higher standards of proof? One could, conceivably, require the parole board, before revoking parole, to make a determination that the parolee was guilty of the new offense "beyond a reasonable doubt"; or else the board could adopt this standard on its own initiative. But the high requirements of proof in criminal trials stem not only from this formal standard, but a host of ancillary protections, such as strict evidentiary standards and the requirement that a jury of the defendant's peers be convinced of guilt. To approximate these protections, parole revocation would have to be recast so as to closely approximate the criminal process; and if so, why not be done with it and require a criminal proceeding?

Moreover, the criminal process would be less vulnerable. In criminal trials, the main procedural safeguards are *constitutionally* mandated. Efforts to lower the requirement of proof beyond reasonable doubt could be resisted under the Due Process Clause, or efforts to eliminate the jury as fact-finder challenged under the Seventh Amendment. Were equivalent procedural standards adopted in revocation proceedings, they could later be diluted, because parole revocation has not been similarly hedged with constitutional protections.

Eliminating the separate adjudicative system could increase court caseloads. Charges against parolees can now be kept off court calendars and handled separately through revocation. With abolition of this separate system, those charges would have to flow through the courts. Depending on how large the additional caseload is, this might add to pressures to bargain charges down.[43] The dimensions of this problem, however, will become known only as studies are done of caseload experience in jurisdictions that eliminate or restrict parole revocation.

Standards of Disposition

Abolition of the separate adjudicative system could also alter the penalties for ex-prisoners who commit new crimes. The extent of the change, and its desirability, would depend on whether the jurisdiction had adopted dispositional standards for convicted persons, and what these standards were.

Suppose a jurisdiction had adopted explicit dispositional standards of the kind we recommended in Chapter 3. Here, the ex-prisoner convicted of a new crime would simply receive the punishment provided in those standards. And while his penalty could (for reasons previously mentioned)[44] be somewhat higher than that of a first offender, the amount of such increase would be governed by the norms.

This method of disposition should be an improvement over the parole revocation process as it exists today. Because desert constraints would be built into the dispositional standards, an ex-prisoner found guilty of a minor new offense could not be reimprisoned, as can occur through revocation. On the other hand, an ex-prisoner convicted of a serious new offense would face a period of imprisonment long enough to reflect the gravity of his crime.

Would it be possible to reform the revocation process to achieve equivalent results? A parole board could try to move in that direction by adopting dispositional rules for its revocation proceedings. Those could, at least, bar reimprisonment for minor new offenses. But the board could not ensure that serious offenses were penalized proportionately to their gravity, since parole reconfinements are limited to the unexpired portion of the offender's original sentence.

Were the system of criminal dispositions not reformed, however, the results could be much less desirable. There will be no gain in the predictability of the penalties, if the jurisdiction has not adopted standards or guidelines on whether and how much to punish convicted criminals. Penalty levels are another problem: absent explicit standards, it will be difficult to foretell how the quantum of punishment might change when the criminal process replaces revocation. There could, conceivably, be unjustifiable increases in severity.[45] *

Bail

Parolees who are arrested for new crimes do not have the same right to prehearing release as other defendants. A criminal defendant is ordinarily entitled to bail. A parolee has no similar right in a revocation proceeding; when a parolee is apprehended, he may be detained pending the final decision at the board's discretion.[46]

---

*This problem could also arise if the state has adopted explicit standards, but ones that violated desert constraints. An example is Indiana's 30-year minimum sentence for persons convicted of any third felony.

Were the separate adjudicative system abolished, the parolee charged with a new crime would have to be prosecuted, which means he would be entitled to bail as other defendants are. How much difference would this make in practice? It is difficult to say, since the discretion that parole boards explicitly have to deny prehearing release is matched, to some extent, by a less visible discretion that magistrates have to deny pretrial release. While "excessive bail" is forbidden by the U.S. Constitution, this provision has not been read as precluding the setting of bail beyond the defendant's means. Thus the magistrate has, in fact, considerable leeway to deny a defendant release by fixing bail above what he can afford.[47] Many parolees who would have been subject to prehearing detention under the parole system might still find themselves denied release when prosecuted, through the decision fixing the amount of bail.

Because the bail system has given the magistrate such unfettered discretion, and because it favors the affluent over the indigent, it has often been advocated that bail be replaced by a nonmonetary scheme of pretrial release.[48] Defendants would be presumed entitled to release unless they fell within designated categories, such as those having characteristics associated with absconding. Were there no parole revocation, ex-prisoners suspected of new crimes would be subject to these release rules.

This seems to us a proper result. We cannot here enter into the hotly contested question of what the content of the reformed pretrial release rules should be. And in deciding which categories of defendants should be presumptively releasable and which not, it might be relevant under some schemes to look to their prior criminal histories—to see, for instance, whether they had previously absconded. But any different treatment of ex-prisoners ought to be justified in terms of the specific purpose of the rules on pretrial release. There is no reason for a blanket denial to ex-prisoners of such pretrial release rights as other accused criminal defendants have. Where, for example, an ex-prisoner has in no fashion abused the right of pretrial release in the past, why should a different standard apply to him than to other defendants?

Eliminating the separate adjudication system for parolees suspected of new crimes would, in summary, permit a fairer procedure for deciding guilt: the higher standards of proof and other safeguards of the criminal process absent in parole revocation proceedings, would become available to the suspect. Whether eliminating the separate system would improve dispositions in such cases would depend on how far the jurisdiction has gone in reforming its manner of punishing the convicted.

Chapter 7

Parole Supervision

Besides facing a different system of adjudication if suspected of a new crime, the parolee is supervised in the community. Parole conditions regulate conduct on his part that is not criminal in itself but is thought linked with possible future criminality. To ensure compliance with these conditions, a parole agent is assigned to and maintains regular contact with the parolee. Violation of any of the conditions—even in the absence of a new criminal offense—is grounds for revocation of parole and reimprisonment. Is this system of supervision worth preserving?

CURRENT SUPERVISION PRACTICE[1]

Parole supervision is supposed to consist of both surveillance of the parolee and provision of services to him. Of the two functions, control tends to predominate[2] —but even the control is sporadic.

The parolee is assigned to the caseload of a parole officer, who is responsible for him. Caseloads vary in size, with the average ranging between 50 and 70 parolees per agent.[3] Usually the assignment of a parolee to one or another officer is made on the basis of the parolee's area of residence or the number of cases the officer is carrying already.[4]

The resources given to parole agents to supervise their cases are meagre. Ordinarily the parole officer is given little more than a manual, a car, a gun (in some jurisdictions), and the power to grant or deny permission for certain activities. Training is also limited: often it consists of a brief orientation period, followed by a period of working with an experienced agent.[5]

Parole conditions are typically comprehensive in scope: they allow official scrutiny of much of the parolee's life. They also tend to be written in a manner that gives the parole officer broad discretion as to what does and does not constitute a violation.[6] One result of this broad discretion is considerable variation in style and extent of enforcement from one parole agent to another. As Elliot Studt notes, "[P]arolees who are supervised by different agents tend to experience quite different control systems."[7]

The principal technique of supervision is periodic agent-parolee visits. The parole officer, traditionally, has been expected to visit the parolee's home and place of employment, and to make "collateral contacts" (that is, contacts with the parolee's family, work supervisors, and associates) to verify and collect information. Parolees must, in turn, report periodically to the agent—usually by visiting his office—to keep him informed of their residence and employment. David Stanley reports that office visits are becoming the principal means of contact, and describes these meetings as "typically amiable, superficial, and brief." (In some cases, even office visits are not required; parolees call the agent periodically or mail a monthly report.)[8]

Typically, little time is spent on the individual parolee. A study of Federal parole reported that each offender could expect "7.7 hours of supervision per year—or 38 minutes a month or 9 minutes a week." The same study reported that face-to-face contacts averaged 3 minutes a week.[9]

The parole officer is also supposed to provide treatment services to parolees; but usually he has few programs at his disposal and must rely on his individual efforts to help or counsel the parolee. Absent guidance from the agency, individual agents tend to develop their own service techniques. Thus, Studt notes, "[E]ach parolee experiences a different service agency than that available to other parolees on other caseloads, regardless of his needs or of the range of services actually provided somewhere within the district office."[10]

REVOCATION PRACTICE

Revocation is the parole officer's strongest weapon. While revocation is the responsibility of the parole board, agents' recommendations appear to be influential; a California study found that the board followed agents' advice 80 to 90 percent of the time.[11]

Theoretically, any violation of the conditions of parole can result in revocation. Actually, the philosophy of the individual agent largely determines which violations will be acted upon and which overlooked, and some agents are more prone to recommend revocation than others.[12] The attitude of the agent's supervisor, in turn, may influence the agent's decisions, as may the expressed bureaucratic concerns of senior agency officials.[13]

How many parolees have their paroles revoked? The Uniform Parole Reports' three-year follow-up of male parolees released in 1972 indicates that, nationally, 15 percent were revoked for technical violations (excluding absconding); of those, 8 percent (or about half this group) were "pure" technical revocations, involving neither new convictions nor revocation in lieu of prosecution.[14] Information on individual jurisdictions is more difficult to obtain, and revocation rates appear to vary greatly from jurisdiction to jurisdiction.[15]

The duration of reconfinement for revoked parolees is a still more elusive figure. The Federal Parole Commission has issued guidelines on duration of reimprisonment for technical parole violations. These recommend 0–8 months for revoked parolees who do not have a history of previous violations—and a longer period of 8–16 months for persistent violators, those whose violation has occurred less than eight months after release on parole, and those found to have "a negative employment/school record during supervision."[16] Oregon, whose system is more desert-oriented, has guidelines recommending shorter periods of reconfinement.[17] The majority of states have no guidelines, and little information is available on their average durations of reconfinement.

Whatever the averages are, the *potential* duration is long. A revoked parolee faces reimprisonment, at the board's discretion, for up to his full unexpired sentence—and that may be several years hence. In New York, for example, over 25 percent of parolees revoked in 1975 had, at the time of revocation, unexpired parole periods in excess of two years.[18]

DOES SUPERVISION WORK?–
THE EFFECTIVENESS CRITERION

The ostensible purpose of parole supervision is to prevent crimes by the supervised. Were supervision incapable of achieving this purpose, there would be no need for its existence. Offenders convicted of serious criminal conduct could be punished as they deserved simply by being imprisoned for prescribed periods, and then released unconditionally.* Before one can make even a *prima facie* case for supervision, therefore, the threshold criterion of effectiveness must be

*See Appendix II for fuller discussion.

satisfied: there must be empirical evidence that parole supervision is capable of reducing recidivism rates among parolees. Thus far, the effectiveness of parole supervision has not been established.

A number of studies have compared recidivism rates by parolees with those of offenders released at expiration of sentence. Some studies, reporting that parolees do better, are inconclusive because they do not control for possible differences in the selection of the two groups.[19] The parolees may have recidivated less often not because of any virtues of supervision *per se*, but because the parole board has selected the better risks for release on parole.

A few studies do attempt to control for such differences in selection. Two of them report favorable results. One study, described by Don Gottfredson,[20] found that parolees in the Federal system perform better than persons discharged without supervision at expiration of sentence. Another investigation found that misdemeanants released on parole did better than those discharged.[21]

Two other studies, however, report less favorable, albeit mixed, results. In a Canadian study, conducted by Irwin Waller,[22] the arrest rates of parolees and dischargees were compared at six, twelve, and twenty-four months. Some difference was found at six months, but none at twelve and twenty-four. The author concludes:

> The effectiveness of parole in terms of reducing recidivism within twelve and twenty-four months, or in the long run generally, is an illusion. First, those selected for parole are no less likely to be re-arrested than predicted . . . though parole is, however, granted in the first place to those with lower probabilities. . . . It does appear that parole delays the arrest of a parolee from the first six months to a later period within twenty-four months. . . .[23]

Preliminary findings of a study of juvenile offenders conducted by the California Youth Authority found there were no differences in arrest rates between parolees and those discharged early from parole.[24] The groups did, however, differ in types of offenses for both the first and most serious arrest; dischargees were more likely to be arrested for crimes against the person and drug and alcohol offenses, while parolees were more likely to be arrested for property offenses.[25] *

*Several studies have examined the effects of supervision with small caseloads where, supposedly, individual parolees can receive more attention from their parole agents. The results have generally been disappointing: parolees in small caseloads generally recidivate no less than parolees in normal-sized caseloads. However, one cannot infer much about the effectiveness of parole from these studies, since they examine only one feature of supervision (caseload size), and

This research is too scanty and its results are too equivocal to warrant the inference that supervision succeeds—at least, if the burden of proving success rests on the proponents of supervision, as we think it should. Since there have been so few studies, it is possible that further empirical inquiry might show success, or at least success among certain selected subgroups of offenders. But that is not what can be concluded today.

There also has been no research on which aspects of the parole process account for success or failure. Conceivably, any successes might be attributable chiefly to the low standard of proof applicable to parolees who are suspected of new crimes. (If it is easier to re-imprison parolees for alleged new criminal activity, this could help deter or incapacitate, irrespective of any effects of monitoring parolees' noncriminal behavior in the community.) The possibility is a worrisome one because, as we pointed out in Chapter 6, a low standard of proof—whatever its usefulness as an inducement to law-abiding behavior—risks penalizing the innocent. To test the potential influence of this factor, one would need to investigate how parole outcomes are influenced by different parole board policies regarding revocation for new crimes. Needless to say, this has not been attempted.

Could outcomes be improved by changing supervision practices? There is much about today's supervision methods that seems pointless or archaic. Some conditions of parole, such as the common requirement that the parolee support his dependents,[26] have little or no perceptible relation to criminal behavior. Periodic visits between parole agent and parolee tend to be an empty formality. Treatment programs are seldom available to parole agents who wish to refer their charges to treatment. These are matters that could be changed. Parole agents could be given more programs for their clients; silly parole conditions could be dropped; routinized visits could be phased out.

Such changes would make parole supervision *seem* more rational. But even the most sensible-seeming programs may fail when evaluated empirically. On the current state of the evidence, we cannot say whether any of these improvements would, in fact, lead to success.

This leads to the question of whether it is worth experimenting further. Should one try to eliminate present irrationalities, put more

---

there may be other features (such as the sanctions imposed on parole violators) that also affect success or failure. The most useful test of effectiveness remains the test that has (as noted in the text) so seldom been tried: comparing parolees' performance with that of similar groups of ex-prisoners who have been released without *any* supervision.

resources into the supervision process, and then test empirically whether supervision succeeds when thus improved? The answer depends on the moral issue to which we turn next: whether parole supervision can be squared with requirements of justice, even if it were made to work.

IS SUPERVISION JUST? —
DESERT CONSTRAINTS

Supervision, whatever its aim and effects, is part of the offender's punishment, for it is an intrusion visited on him by the state for having been convicted of a crime. We must therefore ask whether supervision can alter the severity of punishment in ways prohibited by the principle of commensurate deserts. Conventional supervision fails this test of justice, as the following illustration suggests.

Suppose the durational standards provide that a specified felony is ordinarily to be penalized by eighteen months' actual confinement in prison. It is proposed that, upon release, there will be parole supervision of, say, an additional two years. Suppose, further, that the principal condition of supervision is that parolees are to make *bona fide* efforts to seek and hold jobs. (We choose this condition because it seems on its face more sensible than many of the parole conditions in use today; there is at least some empirical evidence of links between unemployment and crime.)[27] To ensure that the condition is observed, parolees would also be required to report their address and employment status to their parole agents; and the agent would be required to verify employment with the employer. Violation of this condition could, at the parole board's discretion, result in revocation of parole and reimprisonment for up to the full unexpired balance of the two-year supervision period.

In this illustration, the supervision *per se* does not enhance severity by much. Compared to the one-and-a-half years' initial confinement, the parole conditions hardly seem onerous: the parolee must merely make reasonable efforts to find and keep a job, and the surveillance by the parole agent is limited to verifying employment status. Thus, if the initial imprisonment is approximately what is deserved, the addition of these conditions would not create any large excess of severity above the deserved amount of punishment. Any excess could, moreover, be compensated for in the durational standards, by providing an appropriately scaled-down period of original imprisonment.

The conclusion differs for the revocation sanction, however. Suppose, in our illustration, that the parolee holds a job briefly, quits or is fired, and then does not try to find work. As that would constitute a violation of his parole conditions, he could be revoked and reimprisoned for part or all of the unexpired portion of his two-year parole period. As a result, he could serve a total of nearly three-and-a-half years in confinement. This is more than *twice* the penalty paid by another parolee who was convicted of the same crime but who complied with the parole conditions. So large an increase in severity will breach the commensurate-deserts constraints, if we are looking to what is deserved for the original offense.

Concededly, an individual violator may not serve the full two added years in prison. The parole board, in the exercise of its discretion, may re-parole most imprisoned violators after a few weeks or months, and retain for long periods only those they consider the worst risks. But the problem of disproportionate severity remains as long as the *potential* exists for severe punishment of violators.

One could not rectify this difficulty by scaling down the initial period of confinement. Even with such adjustments, it would still be true that the revoked parole violator and the non-violator would serve strikingly unequal total amounts of prison time—although their original criminal conduct was equally serious and although the violator's subsequent violation was not itself criminal. Nor would it help if experimental evidence were to show that the supervision worked— that is, was effective in reducing recidivism rates among parolees. For the commensurate-deserts principle is, as we said,[28] a constraint of justice that applies even to those punishments that do succeed as crime-control techniques. The fact that the supervision works is no reply to charges that it is unfair.

The foregoing objections hold not only under the Desert Model, but under the Modified Desert Model as well, since the latter permits only a modest amount of variation from deserved severity. Revocation, as the foregoing illustration indicates, may lead to long reconfinements that deviate by large amounts from the requirements of desert.

Thus far we have spoken only of whether the revocation sanction could be deserved for the *original* offense. But might not the sanction be defended instead as a penalty that is merited for the parole violation itself—in our illustration, for the refusal to comply with the employment condition? It is true that failing to seek a job is not a punishable act when committed by an ordinary citizen. But if this requirement is imposed as part of one's punishment for a crime, why shouldn't the flouting of it deserve some extra punishment?

Even on this view of parole revocation, however, the penalty would be excessive. Were parole violations seen as akin to criminal acts—as actions in themselves deserving of punishment—they still would not merit severe penalties unless the conduct was *seriously* reprehensible. Yet how blameworthy can technical parole violations be? No substantial injury is done or is made imminent by the act itself, as is typical of serious crimes. The parole violator is not "getting away" with much less punishment than he deserves for his original crime—as can occur in prison escapes, for example—since he has been made to pay so much of the price of that crime already through his stay in prison before being released on parole. Of course, it is difficult to give a definitive rating to such conduct in the absence of a fuller theory of what constitutes seriousness.[29] But on these common-sense grounds alone, we would be skeptical of claims that a parole violation is so blameworthy in itself as to deserve the long durations of reconfinement that parole revocation potentially entails.

COULD SUPERVISION BE REFORMED?— REDUCING THE SANCTIONS

If the severity of the revocation sanction creates the problem, could supervision be salvaged by scaling down that sanction? A few jurisdictions have been moving in this direction. The new California law, as originally enacted, limited the duration of reconfinement for parole violations to six months; but a recent amendment has raised this amount to one year.[30] Oregon has restricted the period of reconfinement to six months, except for offenders convicted of the most serious crimes.[31] Some proposals would impose still lower limits. The Federal criminal code revision bill, as approved by the Senate in early 1978, ordinarily would limit reimprisonment to ninety days;[32] the Hart-Javits proposal, also dealing with the Federal system, would allow only fifteen days.[33]

Could supervision, with reduced sanctions, meet our criteria of justice? And could it be effective? The answer depends on which of the two models, Desert or Modified Desert, one adopts.

On a Modified Desert Model. Let us begin with the Modified Desert Model, as it involves less difficulty. Here, modest back-up sanctions would be permissible. Even if such sanctions cause the total amount of punishment inflicted on an offender to deviate somewhat from what he deserves for his criminal conduct, this model expressly allows such deviations, provided their extent is limited.

What qualifies as a "modest" sanction will, of course, be debatable. Should the maximum penalty for parole violations be closer to the six-month limit that Oregon has for most cases? Or closer to the Hart-Javits bill's proposed fifteen days? That depends on how much deviation from deserved severity the Modified Desert Model is assumed to allow, and that does not lend itself readily to quantification.* Repeated applications of the sanction will also be a problem. Recurring doses of short-term confinement ("jail therapy") have characterized some existing supervision programs,[34] and these may add up to considerable painfulness. Limits are thus needed on the frequency with which the sanction may be visited on a parolee.

What about effectiveness? There are two questions of effectiveness involved. The first is whether moderate sanctions are enough to induce most parolees to comply with their parole conditions. This would have to be tested empirically; but some degree of success would not surprise us, since the permitted sanctions would still be substantial inconveniences, even if not so severe as today's revocation penalties.

The second, and more troublesome, question is the impact on recidivism, even if parolees *did* comply. Through the traditional revocation sanction, parolees who seemed headed for new crimes could be taken out of circulation. This involved prediction, not cure—identifying which kinds of post-release behavior might indicate an enhanced risk of recidivism. When one limits the power to reconfine parole violators, however, the task becomes the harder one of changing behavior, not just forecasting it. Consider employment requirements for parolees, for example. One could no longer adopt the strategy of ascertaining whether joblessness is predictive of criminality, and then removing from the streets those parolees who fail to find jobs. Since parolees could not be returned to prison for long, the employment requirements would have to be capable of reducing their rate of recidivism while they continued to reside mainly in the community. Generally speaking, such techniques have lagged behind prediction methods.[35]

Despite our lack of optimism, however, we cannot say that the prospects of success are *so* bleak as to make experimentation pointless. Opportunity for such experimentation already exists in those jurisdictions, such as Oregon, that have begun to restrict their revocation sanctions. Parolees' performance under such systems could be compared with that of prisoners released unsupervised, with a waiver or discharge from parole.**

*In deciding this issue, attention must be paid to the special pains of being taken out of the community, even for brief periods. The shock of re-entry into prison, and the severing of new community ties, may increase the severity of even a brief return to confinement.

**This research should examine not only the effect of supervision on recidivism rates, but also inquire into costs. Parole supervision is unquestionably an

How can one ensure that the necessary research will be undertaken? Traditional parole has existed for over three-quarters of a century with little serious inquiry about its effectiveness.[36] If one establishes a system of "reformed" supervision with limited sanctions, the same thing could happen unless precautions are taken. To ensure that testing occurs, we suggest a time limit: authority to operate the system should be made to expire within a specified number of years (say, five). During that time, careful empirical evaluations should be undertaken. If they show some success, the authority to supervise should be continued; otherwise, it should not.

Were the system put through such a testing process, we venture to guess that, if it survives, it will emerge with smaller dimensions than it has today. Perhaps supervision (with the limited sanctions that the Modified Desert Model requires) will be found effective for some categories of offenders. But we would be surprised if this elaborate and costly process needs to be imposed on all ex-prisoners.

On a Desert Model. Parole supervision becomes harder to support on the Desert Model, even with scaled-down sanctions. First, there are problems of justifying the penalties. In the Modified Desert Model, it was not necessary to show that the sanctions for parole violations were themselves deserved; the sanctions merely had to meet that model's requirement of being "modest." A Desert Model, however, imposes tighter constraints. Since no deviations from the commensurate-deserts principle are allowed, parole sanctions would have to satisfy that principle. But how could this be done? The sanctions could not be justified as part of the deserved punishment for the original offense if they imposed on violators *any* added amount of punishment not suffered by non-violators whose crimes were of equal seriousness. Treating the parole violations as deserving of punishment in themselves—as culpable refusals to abide by the terms of a properly authorized sentence—is equally problematic, since ordinarily only *crimes* are punishable acts.*

---

expensive process, but little is known about how expensive it is, where the greatest areas of expense lie, and how much money could be saved through improved procedures. With such data, one could judge whether parole—even if it has some impact on recidivism rates—is effective enough to make it worth the expense.

*One could create a new crime of infringing conditions of parole. But requiring violators to be prosecuted would make the supervision system so cumbersome and costly as, in our view, to reduce the likelihood of its being effective to near-zero.

Alternatively, one could retain an administrative proceeding to determine guilt for the violation, and argue that the rigorousness of the fact-finding process may properly vary with the severity of the penalties. When the authorized sanctions are modest (as they would be in "reformed" parole), the procedures might

Second, there are problems of conflicting missions for the supervising agency. Why supervise at all? In order, we assumed, to keep ex-prisoners law abiding. The offender's non-criminal conduct in the community is being regulated, not because it is deemed worthy in itself of the criminal law's attention, but because controlling such conduct may help forestall later acts by the parolee that are substantive crimes. The parolee may be required to seek a job, for example, not because joblessness is an evil which the criminal law is directly concerned with, but because joblessness is thought linked with future crime. What strategy for penalizing parole violators would best serve this preventive aim? That would have to be determined by experience, but it may be that a selective strategy is the most effective: intervening most vigorously when the circumstances of the violation suggest a particularly high risk of recidivism, while taking less action with other violations.

Any such policy of selectivity would conflict, however, with the conception of parole violations one would have to adopt under a Desert Model. If violations are to be treated as reprehensible acts deserving of punishment, the parole agency should emphasize even-handedness, not selectivity. Instead of seeking information on which enforcement strategy keeps parolees away from subsequent criminality, the agency should as a matter of justice impose equal penalties on parole violators whose infractions are equally serious, however that is judged. This conflict, it should be noted, would *not* exist in the Modified Desert Model, for there the parole sanction would be treated as a deviation from desert—permitted so long as kept within specified bounds. If selective application of the sanction best promoted the aim of preventing recidivism by parolees, this tactic would not be ruled out.

---

on this theory be less formal than a criminal trial. The analogy that might be drawn is that of prison discipline, discussed in Chapter 5: extending an inmate's stay in prison through an administrative proceeding, if he commits acts of disruptive behavior in prison.

But the analogy to prison discipline is questionable. In the prison-disciplinary case, one's choice is restricted. The Desert Model requires severe punishment for serious criminal conduct; and imprisonment is (for the reasons discussed in Chapter 3) the only available severe punishment. If there is to be imprisonment, one must have sanctions to maintain order in the prison. To the extent it is not possible to rely on new prosecutions to maintain a modicum of order in the institution, one may have to resort to administratively imposed sanctions of some kind, with appropriate limits on severity. Parole sanctions do not fit this logic, since the measure they enforce (the parole supervision itself) is not a necessity under the Desert Model. There is an alternative that would dispense with the need for such sanctions: abolish the supervision altogether.

Could there be ways of resolving the conflict? Theoretically, there might be,* but in practice it will be difficult to maintain fine distinctions among the different features of a single supervision system. Just as traditional supervision was plagued by conflicts between its policing and helping missions,[37] supervision under a Desert Model would be troubled by tensions between preventive and punitive missions.

CONCLUSIONS: THEIR DEPENDENCY ON MORAL ASSUMPTIONS

The foregoing suggests that the acceptability of parole supervision varies with the assumed penal philosophy. On a Desert Model, which we favor, supervision would best be eliminated. On a Modified Desert Model, supervision could be retained if its sanctions were reduced substantially, and if it survived a careful evaluation of effectiveness.

The dependency of the conclusions on the assumed aims of punishment becomes still more apparent if one considers more strongly utilitarian penal philosophies. Suppose, for example, someone were to assume that the primary criterion for an appropriate punishment should be its efficiency in diminishing future crime, and that desert should be treated as a less important constraint. In that event, one no longer could object to potentially severe revocation sanctions as undeserved. The primary question would shift from one of justice to one of effectiveness; that is, does parole supervision work? As we saw earlier in this chapter, the scanty research that has been done to date does not yet confirm that supervision can succeed. There would still need to be a testing period, when supervision is scrutinized for effectiveness. But since the limitations of the Modified Desert Model would no longer apply, the revocation sanctions might be the more severe ones that present law permits; and the character of those sanctions, in turn, might alter the impact on recidivism.

Another concern would remain, however. In the preceding chapter, we argued against revoking and reimprisoning parolees for new crimes. The argument was based not on commensurate-deserts, but on a broader principle of procedural fairness: that an individual should not be punished for an alleged new crime unless the state has been required (if the charge was contested) to prove guilt beyond a reasonable doubt. Someone who did not subscribe to a desert-oriented sentencing philosophy might still accept this principle, since

---

*Possibly, the selection of programs for supervisees could be made on rehabilitative grounds, while the policy of punishing violators would be governed by a strict desert rationale.

it relates not to the amount of punishment for those found guilty but to the criteria and methods of deciding guilt. If so, such a person might wish to eliminate potentially severe penalties for technical violations of parole, because these can so easily be used for the ulterior purpose of penalizing parolees suspected of new crimes.[38]

The question of abolition, reform, or retention of parole supervision is thus in important part a moral issue, which depends on the extent to which one believes that punishments ought to be deserved and depends also on one's views about the need for strict requirements of proof.

A CAVEAT ON DISCRETIONARY SENTENCING SYSTEMS

Our analysis here, like our discussion of the early time-fix in Chapter 4, assumes the existence of explicit standards governing the duration of imprisonment for different crimes. Abolishing supervision may produce undesired results if such standards are absent. This is illustrated by the Maine statute. The new law eliminates supervision but leaves the sentencing judge with almost unfettered power to decide how long his custodial sentences are to be.[39] Whatever the actual state of the evidence on the effectiveness of supervision, some Maine judges may *think* that it is a useful measure in controlling recidivism by ex-prisoners. To the extent this is their belief, the elimination of supervision may lead them to impose longer sentences; and to the extent judges' beliefs on this subject differ, this may lead to disparate sentences.[40]

This illustrates again that reforming the punishment process must begin with developing standards on whether and how long convicted offenders are to be imprisoned. When writing those standards, the specific reforms of which we have spoken—the early time-fix and the change in the status of supervision—can be included. But the value of the latter reforms depends on the standards' existence, the kind of rationale the standards follow, and on how carefully the standards are drawn.

IMPLICATIONS FOR PROBATION

Probation, like parole, involves supervising an offender in the community, and imprisoning him if he violates specified conditions of release. It thus raises questions similar to those just discussed, to wit:

—When a probationer is suspected of a new crime and has his probation revoked in a proceeding having fewer safeguards than a criminal trial, is that a fair way of determining guilt?

—When a probationer has his probation revoked and is imprisoned for technical violations that are not crimes, does this violate desert constraints?

It is therefore fair to ask whether our conclusions about parole supervision should carry over to probation. This cannot be resolved here, however, for there are important differences between the two forms of supervision.

When someone has been convicted of serious criminal conduct, the principle of commensurate deserts can be satisfied simply by imprisoning him for a period that comports with the gravity of his conduct, and then releasing him unconditionally. Parole supervision thus is not essential to a fair system of punishment; to the extent it either fails to reduce recidivism, or fails to meet the limitations of the Desert or Modified Desert models, it can be dropped.

Less serious conduct, however, does not deserve imprisonment. With prison ruled out, the offender would have to undergo his penalty while living in the community. When an offender is punished in the community, there must be a monitoring technique to ascertain that he is abiding by the terms of his penalty; and, if he flouts those terms, there would have to be a back-up sanction of some kind. Monitoring and back-up sanctions are features of probation. Simple elimination of *all* the features of probation is thus not a viable alternative, as it was with parole supervision. One faces the more difficult task of devising fair community-based punishments.[41]

Before any definite conclusions about probation are reached, there ought to be an inquiry in at least as much depth as we have attempted here for parole. It should examine the role that probation now plays, and the role that an altered system of community punishments should play in a more desert-oriented system.

✳ *Chapter 8*

Services to Ex-Prisoners

Even if parole supervision is eliminated or restricted, there remains the question of services for ex-prisoners. When prisoners are released, should help be made available to them in obtaining credentials, finding jobs, locating housing, and the like? If so, what kinds of services should be offered and who should provide them? If other needy persons also want the same services, what priority should be given to ex-prisoners' claims? If an ex-prisoner does not wish the services, should he be under any compulsion to accept them?

Provision of services has been one of the supposed functions of parole supervision, but the parole agent seldom has helping resources at his disposal. Moreover, the agent's helping and policing functions tend to conflict, as Elliot Studt found in her study of parole supervision in California.[1] If the parolee has, say, a drinking problem, he will be reluctant to ask for help from a parole agent having the power to re-imprison him for alcohol-related parole violations.

THE AIM OF THE SERVICES: ALLEVIATION OF SUFFERING

Parole supervision, as we saw, has crime control as its primary aim: the criterion for judging its effectiveness is whether it can (while complying with applicable desert constraints) reduce recidivism rates among those supervised. Services, in our view, should be judged by a different standard—their usefulness in helping former prisoners establish a tolerable existence for themselves on returning to the community.[2]

Being imprisoned frays many of the prisoner's ties to the outside world. When released, he faces the problem of reestablishing those ties, and that will be made harder by the stigma of his criminal record. Furlough and work-release may ease this process somewhat by providing the prisoner with a "halfway-out" status before he leaves prison. But it will still be a difficult transition. As Elliot Studt notes:

> The parole period begins with an abrupt change in the individual's way of life. With minimal preparation the offender moves from a subservient, deprived, and highly structured institutional life into a world that bombards him with stimuli, presents complicated problems requiring immediate solution, and expects him to assume responsibilities to which he has long been unused. All the roles he must assume after release are problematical. . . . The expectations, norms, and cues appropriate to an institutional inmate . . . have little pertinence for behavior in the free world. This abrupt introduction to the tasks of status-passage constitutes a crisis for the individual, inducing major disorientation and requiring strenuous adaptive maneuvers. . . .[3]

The aim of the services should be to facilitate this transition by alleviating the pains of readjustment to community life, and assisting the individual to overcome the disadvantages of being an ex-prisoner.

This, it should be noted, is a social-service goal. While it may be hoped that such services will also make ex-prisoners less inclined to offend, the objective should be to reduce suffering.* Suppose, for example, it is proposed to offer ex-prisoners help in locating housing when they leave prison. Although it would be preferable if this service were to reduce recidivism, that hope may not be borne out, for housing conditions may not be linked directly with criminality. The service still should be offered, irrespective of its effects on crime, as long as it succeeds in easing the offender's return to the community.

PRISONERS' VS. OTHERS' CLAIM TO SERVICES

Resources for social services are limited. Why should ex-prisoners be entitled to any of them, when other needy persons who have not committed crimes are in competition for such services?

---

*This social-service aim is distinct from the idea of rehabilitation, as the latter term has been defined in Chapter 3 and as it has traditionally been used by penologists. Rehabilitation has crime control as its aim; it consists of programs designed to reduce recidivism among participants. Services, on the other hand, are measures designed to help clients themselves, irrespective of the effects on crime. The criterion of success is whether the help enhances the quality of the ex-offender's *own* life.

The fact that an individual is an ex-prisoner should not make him less eligible for assistance. It is implicit in what we have said already about the aims of punishment, that penalties should be of discrete, not unlimited, durations. On a Desert Model, offenders would deserve penalties whose duration and restrictiveness are commensurate with the gravity of their criminal conduct. On a Modified Desert Model, such penalties may be slightly altered to achieve other aims. But at the end of the prescribed period, the individual should be entitled to lead a normal existence. The imposition of second-class status on ex-prisoners for an indefinite period, by permanently assigning them low priority for social services, is inconsistent with this notion of discrete punishments.

But why have *special* help for ex-prisoners? We believe this is called for because the experience of being imprisoned has created special disabilities. If one assumes that the ex-prisoner should be entitled to resume a normal life after having paid his penalty, efforts must be made to help him overcome the problems of transition he faces when he returns to the community.

Providing services to ex-prisoners will not be popular. That makes it tempting to ascribe traditional rehabilitative aims to the service programs, so that one can claim that other citizens will benefit (because offenders will be induced to commit fewer new crimes). But such assertions are hazardous. If the services are claimed to be rehabilitative, they will be judged by that standard. Then, if empirical studies show that the programs do not succeed in reducing recidivism rates, pressures will be all the stronger to eliminate assistance. It is better to acknowledge the programs' social-service aim and press for them on that basis; the initial resistance may be greater, but the dangers of eventual disappointment less.

SERVICE NEEDS OF EX-PRISONERS

The services that are needed will vary with the type of ex-prisoner and with the environment to which he expects to return. However, a number of researchers have catalogued the problems most frequently encountered.[4] Not surprisingly, the most pressing needs are material: financial aid, housing, employment, and the like.

Finances. Parolees now leave the institution with very little money. Most have available only "gate money" and meagre savings from institutional work. A 1976 survey[5] found that gate money ranges from nothing (in four states)[6] to somewhat over $100: most jurisdictions award a maximum of between $50 and $100, but many releasees do not receive the maximum.[7] The survey also examined how long gate money would last; using a model that *over*estimated the time, it found that in 30 jurisdictions the funds would last less than a week; in 16, two weeks; and that only one state provided sufficient funds for a month.[8] With the exception of those few inmates enrolled in work-release programs,[9] savings from institutional work are insignificant.[10]

Loans are available to releasees in several jurisdictions, but typically involve small sums and have restricted eligibility criteria.[11] Releasees can sometimes qualify for state or county assistance programs, but rarely are they entitled to aid under the more generous Federal welfare programs. In addition, the families of prisoners may be terminated from Federal assistance should the prisoner return to them.[12]

Status Clearance. Studt found that parolees face "status clearance" problems. Many lack identification papers, such as drivers' licenses, social security cards, and the like. Others face legal or economic encumbrances from the past, such as accrued obligations for child support, income tax claims, and unclear marital status.[13]

Housing. Housing is often difficult to obtain, due to both lack of funds and landlords' resistance to having ex-offenders as tenants. The Citizens' Inquiry reported that the New York City Housing Authority did not accept convicted felons in public housing projects, and many neighborhood housing projects have had similar exclusions. If the parolee's family has been living in public housing during his incarceration, his return may jeopardize their tenancy.[14]

Employment. Finding and keeping a job is a major problem. While statistics are difficult to obtain, one study found that ex-offenders were three times more likely to be unemployed than workers in the general population, and less likely to be employed on a full-time basis.[15] Many parolees have unimpressive employment records and marginal skills; this is made worse by their status as ex-offenders, which not only makes employers suspicious, but may cause formal exclusion from job opportunities through bonding or licensing requirements,[16] or public employment rules.[17]

Psychological Problems. In addition to the material needs of ex-offenders, Rosemary Erickson and her associates found that many releasees experienced special psychological and social stresses. About one-fourth of the sample mentioned problems of meeting people, trouble dealing with family or relatives, or special difficulties with drugs or alcohol.[18]

Each jurisdiction should undertake an in-depth study of the needs of its ex-prisoners. Unless the needs in the particular geographic area are known, it will not be possible to provide services that are responsive.

MEETING THE NEEDS

The services for releasees should be those designed to help ex-prisoners cope with the foregoing problems. They should include: (1) provision of financial support during the initial period after the offender leaves prison; (2) job-placement and job-training services; (3) "status clearance" services such as assistance in obtaining credentials; (4) aid in locating housing; and (5) psychological counselling.

When should assistance be provided? Many authorities report that the period of greatest stress is the weeks and months immediately following release.[19] Priority should be given to providing assistance during this difficult early period. More specific answers about timing depend on the particular needs involved. A few are quite short-term and could be met through furlough or other prerelease programs[20] — status clearance is one example. Most services, however, would probably have to continue for a time after release.

How can such needs effectively be met? Here, several questions would have to be explored: (1) How should success be measured? (2) What should the basic helping techniques be? (3) What are the problems of applying those techniques to ex-prisoners' special problems? (4) What are the costs? The answers will vary with the types of assistance involved. In the area of job training, for example, the measure of success is apparent—increased employment for ex-offenders; and basic job-training techniques have already been developed. However, there is little systematic information on the types of job skills especially useful to ex-offenders, the methods of training best suited to this group, or the means of combating the more subtle forms of job discrimination.[21] Absent these specifics, data on costs is also lacking. Such questions have received little attention up to now, perhaps because the provision of services was so largely eclipsed by the crime-control aims of parole supervision.

Ex-prisoners should have a voice in selecting the services offered. Otherwise the services are unlikely to be helpful or even utilized by their intended clientele.

WHO SHOULD PROVIDE THE SERVICES?

Many prisoners will not know where to obtain social services. Local service agencies may be unaccustomed to coping with ex-prisoners' special problems, and reluctant to deal with convicted persons.[22] It thus would be helpful to have an agency that specializes in offering help to ex-prisoners. The agency could have programs of its own, and also act as a broker or resource manager, channeling to prisoners the services offered by community housing, employment, welfare, and social-service bureaus. The agency would have caseworkers who would inform their clients of the available resources, steer them to the program of choice, and follow up to ensure that the ex-prisoner does receive the service.

Could these tasks be assumed by existing parole agencies? Traditional parole has had a service-providing function, however limited that has been. And, although agents now receive little training in locating and arranging services, specialized training could be provided.[23] How well suited parole agents would be to the task, given such training, can be determined only by experience.

ANY COMPULSION TO ACCEPT SERVICES?

If an ex-prisoner does not wish to accept the services offered, should there be any penalty for refusal? We think not, for both moral and practical reasons.

In Chapter 2, we assigned a high value to personal autonomy—to maximizing each individual's liberty, consistent with the liberty of others. This, we think, requires observance of John Stuart Mill's well-known principle that state compulsion should be used upon competent adults only to prevent them from doing injury to others, and not to prevent self-injury.[24] Compulsory help is barred no matter how beneficial the services are or how unwise an individual would be to refuse them, because a competent adult is entitled to freedom of choice on matters concerning his own life.

This principle, we believe, should apply to the ex-prisoner. Since we are speaking of services designed to benefit the offender himself rather than to protect others from injury at his hands, it would be *he* who suffers if he refuses to participate. Because the risk is that of self-injury, he should not be compelled to accept the services.[25] *

*In a useful article on Mill's principle, the philosopher Gerald Dworkin has suggested that, in certain exceptional cases, compulsory help might be consistent with the idea of personal autonomy. Individuals valuing their own personal freedom, he suggests, might reasonably give their consent to a limited species of

There are also practical impediments to making the services compulsory. It has been said that compulsion tends to vitiate the help offered. Those coercively assisted will resist passively. The helper with a captive clientele loses the incentive to ascertain and respond to the clients' actual needs.[26] The truth of dictum may vary with the kind of help offered. Services that depend on mutual trust, such as counselling or psychiatric assistance, seem apt to fail without clients' active participation. But certain more rudimentary species of help—such as medical services or training in elementary job skills—might be beneficial even on a nonvoluntary basis. The duration of the compulsion might also make a difference. Some writers on helping programs within prisons have suggested, for example, that clients be required to observe or participate on a trial basis for a brief period and then be given the choice about whether to stay or drop out.[27]

Even compulsory services of the latter kind, however, will be difficult to administer to releasees. In a closed setting such as a prison, the authorities control their charges in any event. Participation in work or training programs, if made compulsory, can be enforced through any of a variety of inducements the authorities have at hand. But once the offenders reenter the community, the resources of control are less. Traditionally, parole supervision provided some continuing control; but under the recommendations of the preceding chapter, supervision may be eliminated or else restricted to certain subclasses of offenders.

How, then, could participation in helping programs, if made compulsory, be policed? One might, conceivably, create a system of "mini-supervision" for that special purpose, but the complications are apparent. Suppose that ex-offenders are directed to participate

---

intervention to prevent self-injury, where: (1) the intervention is designed to protect the individual from the consequences of decisions made under unusual pressures when he is not his "usual self"; (2) those consequences would be irreversible; and (3) the intervention is of sufficiently short duration so that he would soon be free to decide again what is in his best interests and to discontinue the proffered service.

On this view, however, it would still be doubtful that ex-prisoners should be compelled to accept services, even during a brief "demobilization" period after release. For what irreversible consequences would be involved? The most obvious concern would be ruled out: that the ex-prisoner, "disoriented" during his first few days in the community and without outside assistance, might commit a new crime and suffer the punishment for it. To prevent that from occurring, the services would have to succeed *as rehabilitation*; that is, they would have to be capable of reducing recidivism. Service programs, we said, would not be designed to meet this crime-prevention test, and many would be unable to meet it. The other consequences of refusing help would not characteristically be so drastic and irreversible.

in specified helping programs following release. Further administrative requirements would then have to be imposed in order to monitor their participation, such as requiring releasees to keep authorities regularly informed about their places of residence. Violation of these requirements would call for the imposition of a sanction. But if the aim is help, the sanction would have to be mild (otherwise, the injury done to the individual could exceed the expected beneficial effects of the program). To impose even the mildest sanction, one must in some fashion reassert control over the violator. Assuming this is not done through the harsh measures of arrest and detention, a system of summonses or similar techniques would be required. That, in turn, would raise the question of what is to be done with those who ignore the summonses. As this system of enforcement proliferates, the agency offering the services is likely to find its resources and energies increasingly absorbed by administering the policing system, rather than providing the services.

Our own view, therefore, is that the services should be voluntary. They should be offered to any released prisoner who feels he needs them, but he should be free to reject them. Participation should not be made a condition of release, nor should there be penalties (even mild ones) for refusal.

How useful will a program of voluntary services be? Many released prisoners will not take advantage of them, or will drop away after a brief involvement. But some may participate and benefit. The extent of participation, and the extent to which it is beneficial, can be ascertained only by trying.

Part IV

The Politics of Reform

※ *Chapter 9*

Implementing the Reforms:
Which Decisionmakers?
Dual or "Real" Time?

We have explained the substance of our proposals. There should be express standards for duration of confinement, which look largely to the gravity of the offender's criminal conduct. The time-fix should occur early—at or shortly after imposition of sentence. Parole supervision should (depending on which theoretical model is assumed) either be eliminated or have its sanctions reduced.

Now we must consider what kind of decisionmaking process, and which decisionmakers, are needed to implement these reforms. Should the durational standards be set by the legislature or some other agency? Should the release date in the individual case be fixed by the trial judge or the parole board? Ought the parole board continue to exist at all, and if so, what should its role be? Should there be, as there now are, two species of sentencing time: lengthy purported sentences and shorter actual confinements? Or should there be a single reckoning of time, with prison sentences expressed in real durations? These questions concern the "politics" of reform: the bureaucratic and political realities encountered when moving from a traditional parole system to the rather different scheme our proposals envision.

MUST THE LEGISLATURE SET
THE STANDARDS?

It is sometimes assumed that if there are to be standards for length of stay in prison, the legislature must set them. (Under California's newly adopted system of "determinate" sentences, the legislature does set the standards;[1] and the same holds for the new Indiana and Illinois sentencing laws.)[2] So tenacious has been the assumption that the legislature must be the standard-setter, that debates over limiting sentencing discretion have tended to focus on the supposed merits and demerits of *legislatively* prescribed norms.[3] The legislature is not, however, the only agency that could set the standards. This function could, instead, be performed by a specialized rule-making body; by the courts; or possibly by the parole board.[4]

In the past, legislatures have showed little interest in sentencing issues, preferring to leave them to courts and parole boards. Their chief involvement has been the setting of statutory maximum punishments. But such maxima usually were so high as to be controlling in none but the most aggravated cases.[5] Occasionally they also set mandatory minimum penalties for crimes considered particularly noxious, as New York did in 1973 for drug offenses (with unhappy results, according to a recent study.)[6] Writing specific penalty standards has thus not been a traditional legislative function.

Some claim, nevertheless, that democratic theory compels one to choose the legislature as the standard-setter. In a representative system of government, the argument runs, the body that represents popular interests should write the rules on matters of public concern; therefore, if there are to be standards on how much to punish offenders, the legislature would be the appropriate body to set them.[7]

This claim, we think, does not stand analysis. In a representative system, the legislature need not be the only agency that sets rules or standards; it may delegate its rulemaking powers, with respect to particular subject matters, to a variety of specialized bodies. This has been common practice in the United States. Congress has given substantive rulemaking authority to numerous regulatory agencies (and the rulemaking powers of some of these bodies, such as the Federal Trade Commission, are broadly defined). State legislatures have conferred similar authority upon state banking, insurance, and other regulatory commissions.

These agencies have had differing degrees of success in carrying out their rulemaking responsibilities; and the desirability of such delegations as a matter of policy may vary with the subject matter involved. But no breach of the *principle* of representative government is involved when an agency other than the legislature, acting under authority conferred by the latter, makes rules for a particular specialized area. The legislature always retains the power to overrule the agency's regulations or retract its rulemaking authority, thus assuring the representative body's ultimate supremacy.[8]

Should the setting of standards for punishments, then, be under-taken by the legislature, or delegated to another, more specialized body? There are two major reasons for preferring the latter. First, drafting standards is a laborious, time-consuming undertaking. Under a Desert Model, crimes will have to be assigned the appropriate grad-ations of seriousness; the different seriousness-gradations will have to be assigned their presumptive penalties; and guidelines will have to be established governing aggravation and mitigation. Under a Modi-fied Desert Model, the rules may be even more complex, since con-siderations other than desert enter the picture. Once established, the standards will call for continued review and revision. Experience will be needed to determine whether the standards work best with gener-alized or more detailed offense descriptions, and with fewer or more numerous penalty gradations.[9] Guidelines on aggravation and mitiga-tion likewise will require change and elaboration through experience, given the difficulty of specifying in advance the numerous contingen-cies that can render an offense more or less blameworthy than usual. Inevitably, there will be mistakes and omissions in the standards, as well as unanticipated problems encountered in their application, that will necessitate alterations.

Given the numerous other demands on its time, the legislature does not seem well suited to these tasks. An overburdened legislative body—which must each year levy taxes, allocate a budget among conflicting constituencies, and debate new state programs—is apt to have little time, interest, or staff resources left over for the task of drafting the sentencing standards with the requisite care, or for the task of evaluating the impact of standards adopted in a previous session.

Second, the politics of sentencing creates problems in a legislative forum. The standards for punishments, we have assumed, should focus on concerns about justice. How well situated is a legislature for addressing such concerns? Debates about punishment, in a legislative forum, will tend to be influenced by the fact that there are many voters who fear crime and criminals, and relatively few convicted felons who mostly are disenfranchised. Once a legislative body be-gins debating specific penalties, there will be strong incentives to inflate penalties (or give the appearance of doing so) in order to dem-onstrate "tough" attitudes on crime to the electorate. There will be few incentives for giving thought to the *justice* of proposed penal-ties—for considering seriously whether those penalties would treat the unpopular minority of convicts fairly and deservedly. A respon-sible legislature may prefer to have the standard-setting task dele-gated to a specialized body that is somewhat more insulated from such pressures, precisely to allow more reflection on the fairness and commensurability of penalties.[10]

Our doubts about a legislative approach are reinforced by our initial (although still tentative)[11] impressions of systems that have recently adopted sentencing standards by legislation. In Indiana, whose legislature adopted a "determinate" sentencing system in 1977,[12] the legislatively prescribed penalties are extremely high, and the amounts of discretion left to sentencing judges very wide.[13] The California legislature was more parsimonious in its prescribed durations when it initially adopted its sentencing standards in 1976. In the following year, however, the legislature approved amendments that began to lengthen prison terms and restore discretion; and in 1978, just before this book went to press, the legislature went still further in this direction.[14]

Finally, if legislative input is desired, it does not have to take the form of enacting the standards themselves. The legislature could continue to set the maximum permissible penalties for different categories of crimes, leaving another standard-setter with the further task of setting the durational standards within those limits. The legislature could also, as we discuss below, give the standard-setting agency guidance as to the rationale to be followed.

AN ALTERNATIVE TO THE LEGISLATURE: A SENTENCING COMMISSION

The task of setting the standards could be entrusted, instead, to a new agency created for the purpose. It has been proposed that a special rulemaking commission (a "sentencing commission") be established by statute, and empowered to write the standards governing the penalties to be imposed for various crimes.[15]

Such a specialized agency would have some advantages. Because the setting of the standards would be its only function, it could devote time and care to the task—more so than an overburdened legislature. It would also be well-situated for modifying and refining its norms on the basis of experience: it could collect information on various problems encountered in applying the standards and adjust its categories of gravity, its presumptive penalties, and its guidelines on aggravation and mitigation accordingly. (Several of the pending proposals require the sentencing commission to collect data on how judges apply the standards, and call upon the commission to revise the standards periodically on the basis of such information.)[16] A specialized, nonelective body may, moreover, be under somewhat less political pressure than the legislature to adopt posturing stances of "toughness."* Much will depend, of course, on the quality of the appointments to the commission.

When a sentencing commission is established, it could be given the express mandate of adopting the reforms we have urged in earlier chapters: standards that are based primarily on desert; an early time-fix; and a change in the status of parole supervision. One bill, proposed by U.S. Senators Gary Hart and Jacob Javits, was drafted with those objectives specifically in mind.[17]** The Hart–Javits proposal explicitly requires that the sentencing commission's standards comply with the principle of commensurate deserts, and that they take the form of presumptive sentences. It also requires an early time-fix; duration of actual confinement is decided at the time of sentence. Post-release supervision is cut back; it may not exceed 10 percent of the offender's prison term in length and the sanction for noncompliance may not exceed fifteen days' imprisonment.

Thus far, only two states have actually created sentencing commissions. Minnesota and—just before this book went to press—Pennsylvania.[18] In Minnesota, a nine-member commission must, by 1980, prepare guidelines for sentencing that are based on "reasonable offense and offender characteristics," and that "take into substantial consideration" current sentencing and releasing practices and correctional resources. In Pennsylvania, an eleven-member commission will write the guidelines, which must be based chiefly on "the degree of gravity" of the offense. Some other jurisdictions are actively considering sentencing commission proposals, but have not yet enacted them.[19]†

---

*This is, of course, a matter of degree. The commission's policies *could* become politicized; if the members of the commission were appointed by the chief executive, for example, the kind of appointments that official makes could become an issue in his or her own election campaign—as Supreme Court appointments became an issue in the 1968 presidential campaign. We are saying merely that a commission would, in normal circumstances, be likely to feel these kinds of pressures less strongly than the legislature itself.

**While this bill did not pass in the Senate, it is useful for the purposes of illustration, and we will refer to it throughout this chapter. It is set forth in full in Appendix III.

†The U.S. Senate, in early 1978, approved a proposed new Federal Criminal Code that creates a sentencing commission, but differs from the Hart-Javits bill in that it specifies neither a rationale for the commission to follow, nor the form the standards should take. This proposed legislation then went to a subcommittee of the House Judiciary Committee, which approved a quite different bill: there would be no sentencing commission, and the U.S. Judicial Conference would be called upon to write advisory sentencing guidelines for use by judges. Because of these and other divergences between the Senate and House versions, the proposal died for the 1978 legislative session.

"REAL TIME" SENTENCES AND ELIMINATION OF PAROLE RELEASE?

If a sentencing commission is established, what should happen to the parole board's power to release offenders from prison prior to expiration of sentence? One suggestion[20] has been to eliminate this power altogether.

Parole now creates a dual system of time. The judge sets a purported sentence of imprisonment of so many years. This sentence does not determine the prisoner's time in confinement, but merely sets an outside limit on the total amount of imprisonment and post-confinement supervision the offender may suffer. Later, the parole board decides the actual duration of confinement, and this usually is much shorter than the judicial sentence; the prisoner who receives a six-year "prison sentence," in many jurisdictions, can expect to be paroled after two or so years.

What if one were to replace this dual system with single reckoning of "real time" in prison? The prisoner, in such a scheme, could not be paroled, and the judge's sentence would determine the actual time he serves. (Strict limits would also have to be placed on the amount of deductions from the sentence for good behavior in prison. Were "good-time" deductions large, there would still be two species of time: the purported sentence and the actual time-in-confinement after the deductions.)

The Hart–Javits bill proposes "real-time" sentences: a sentence of so many months or years would mean that amount of incarceration, subject only to a small adjustment (no more than 15 percent) for good or bad behavior in prison. The sentencing judge would determine the duration of confinement in individual cases, pursuant to the sentencing commission's standards. The parole board would lose its early-release powers.[21]

While this approach involves a radical reallocation of decisionmaking responsibility, it has its attractions, at least before we consider the difficulties of implementation. It would bring appearances in sentencing closer to reality. When the sentencing commission prescribes a presumptive sentence of so many months for a given type of felony, this would be what it seems: a directive that such felons ordinarily serve that much time in prison. When the judge, carrying out these standards, imposes a prison sentence on a particular felon, that would also be what it seems: a sentence to actual imprisonment for the prescribed time.

Attractive as this approach seems, however, serious misunderstandings can arise when one tries to move to "real time." The appearance of a shift toward leniency can be created, even when there has been no real change in the quantum of punishment. Suppose the practice in a jurisdiction has been to give those convicted of a certain felony an average sentence of six years, and to parole them, in most cases, after about two. Suppose a "real-time" scheme were enacted; and the sentencing commission were to adopt the previous average time served (two years) as its new presumptive sentence. Despite the absence of any actual change in the average stay-in-prison, it will *seem*—to those accustomed to sentences expressed in the old manner—as a dramatic reduction: from six years to two! Clarifications will be difficult to disseminate, as these would require detailed comparisons between the old and new systems.

We do not mean to suggest that the commission should always carry forward the old averages of time-served into its new standards. Some categories of crimes may deserve increased imprisonment, just as some may warrant decreases. But even in the instances where the commission opts for increases in actual confinement, appearances will still mislead. Were the commission, in the previous illustration, to *raise* time served by 50 percent (from two years to three), this would still look like a large sentence reduction (from the previous average sentence of six years to a new presumptive sentence of half that amount).

As far as can be ascertained, the public has little clear awareness of how sentencing and parole operate. Popular impressions about sentence lengths (that is, both about judges' average sentences and about average stays in prison) tend to be wide of the mark, both in the direction of over- and underestimation.[22] Given public concerns about crime, any change in the manner of computing sentences is likely to create alarm if it seems to permit convicted felons to leave prison much sooner.

This makes it essential that the sentencing commission avoid creating the appearance of greater leniency than is actually true of its policies. Yet this, as we just saw, would be precisely the impression created by an overnight shift to "real time." Even if the commission is somewhat more insulated from political "heat" than the legislature, it would still find it difficult to confront wide public consternation about its policies.

Is "real time," then, as simple and forthright as it appears? Perhaps it might be, had there never been any other system—that is, had sentences always been expressed in time served, and had the public become acclimated to the lower numbers that such a system would require. But one is not working with a clean slate. People have become accustomed to a dual system of reckoning time, with the long purported sentences that such a system permits. Here, a rapid shift to real-time sentences may heighten confusion, not alleviate it.

Eliminating parole release creates another problem: that of securing compliance with the durational standards. Through parole, responsibility for deciding actual time in prison has been concentrated in a small, specialized agency: the parole board. Were the board to adopt standards, only a few officials (namely, its hearing examiners or individual members) would be called upon to carry them out. Were the parole board's releasing powers eliminated, however, the responsibility for applying the durational standards in individual cases would devolve upon sentencing judges. This is a far more numerous and diverse group, who would have time-fixing as only one of many judicial duties. The magnitude of this shift can be illustrated by the Federal system. The U.S. Parole Commission now has standards for parole release, which are applied by a limited number of hearing examiners who are full-time employees of the commission, and who have the setting of parole dates as their main responsibility. Were release by such an administrative body eliminated, over 500 Federal judges would become responsible for interpreting and applying the durational standards.

This shift from a few specialists to a more numerous group, who could devote less of their time, could complicate the task of compliance. It will be difficult enough to ensure that sentencing judges abide by the commission's standards in their "in-out" decisions (whether to imprison or impose a lesser penalty such as a fine or probation). The standards that concern the duration of actual confinement are apt to be still more complex and controversial. If judges fix durations in individual cases, this will create the doubly difficult task of ensuring that the many trial judges throughout the jurisdiction (none of them hitherto accustomed to dealing with actual time in prison) abide by the standards in their decisions.[23] *

---

*One might devise a variety of mechanisms to monitor judges' compliance, but none would be easy to operate. One possibility would be appellate review of sentences. But to require the appellate courts to police trial judges' compliance with the sentencing standards would create a large new caseload for the appellate courts; and that caseload would be all the more formidable if duration of actual confinement were fixed by judges instead of by the parole board.

Another possibility would be to create an advisory body that would assist judges in applying the standards. The agency might review sentences after they are imposed for the purpose of referring them back for reconsideration if they seem inconsistent with the standards. California gives an advisory review function to its new Community Release Board. It remains to be seen, however, whether judges would be prepared to accept such a body's advice; to the extent they do not accept it, the problem of noncompliant decisions would persist.

The Hart-Javits bill tried to write safeguards to deal with these problems. To ensure that the sentencing commission reduces sentence durations to reflect the fact that it will be dealing with real time, the bill sets limits on length of sentences; imprisonments in excess of five years may be resorted to only for specified crimes of the most heinous nature. To help ensure compliance with the standards, the bill contains strict appellate review provisions: all sentences are reviewable as a matter of right.[24] The adequacy of even these provisions is debatable, however. The five-year limit, for example, might still allow large upward shifts in duration for many felony categories; and there also may be difficulty getting this kind of limit enacted.* The broadly drawn appellate review provisions may also be hard to enact, given the size of appellate courts' present caseloads and trial judges' sensitivities about their independence.

Information about actual experience with eliminating parole release is not yet available. The states that to date have abrogated the parole board's releasing power are those that either have provided no sentencing standards at all (Maine); or else have legislatively prescribed sentencing norms (California, Illinois, and Indiana).[25] Data on those states' experience has not been developed.[26]**

Of the two states that have recently created sentencing commissions, one calls for abolition of parole release when the commission's sentencing guidelines become effective; the other retains parole release.[27] Minnesota opts for abolition: an individual sentenced to prison would have to serve the full sentence which the court imposes pursuant to the commission's guidelines, less reductions for good behavior.[28]† Pennsylvania, on the other hand, chooses retention: its new sentencing commission is authorized to set guidelines only for judges' maximum and minimum sentences, and the parole board keeps its power to release offenders from prison before expiration of their maximum terms.

*The legislature, which creates the sentencing commission, is itself accustomed to the long purported sentences of the dual system, and may not readily perceive why such time limits would be needed in a real-time system. The legislature would also encounter the political problem mentioned already: any unambiguously worded instruction to the commission that the latter scale down its sentences—to compensate for the elimination of parole release—could be misinterpreted by the public as a call for briefer imprisonments, even if no reduction in actual time-in-confinement were intended.

**In the latter three states, it will be difficult to distinguish the effects of eliminating parole release from the effects of choosing the legislature as the body that sets the standards. It should also be noted that several of these jurisdictions allow substantial deductions from the sentence for good behavior in prison, and thus do not truly have "real-time" sentences.

†However, the parole board will still be able to award work release prior to expiration of sentence.

Other jurisdictions—most notably the federal system[29]*—are now debating whether to eliminate parole release, but have not yet resolved the issue.

THE PAROLE BOARD AS STANDARD-SETTER: THE OREGON SYSTEM

Given these problems of eliminating parole release, what would be the consequences of retaining it? Parole release has not, historically, purported to perform the tasks recommended in this report. Instead of stressing commensurate-deserts, parole boards have publicly espoused a rehabilitative and predictive philosophy. Instead of adopting standards, they claimed that every case was unique and had to be decided on its own merits. Instead of fixing time early, they deferred the release decision.

Nevertheless, it should be borne in mind that parole, however one may disagree with its traditional ideology, has performed the important practical function of scaling down time. Legislatures have been accustomed to authorizing, and judges to imposing, lengthy durations of confinement that participants in the process seldom expect to be carried out, that could not regularly be carried out given limitations of prison resources, and that would be disproportionately severe were they carried out. It has fallen to parole boards to reduce these terms to more manageable levels.

The parole board would be capable, moreover, of becoming the vehicle for implementing the reforms we propose. It could be required to set standards for duration of confinement. It could be directed to base those standards primarily on a desert rationale. And it could be required to fix release dates early. The new Oregon statute (set forth in Appendix IV) takes this approach, and its provisions are worth describing.[30]

In Oregon, the judge decides whether to impose a prison term or a lesser sentence such as a fine or probation. If he opts for prison, he specifies that the sentence will run for so many months or years. That time period operates, however, only as an outer limit. The parole board has been free to release the offender on parole at any time prior to the expiration of sentence.[31] The new statute increases the judge's power somewhat by authorizing him to specify a minimum

---

*The bill passed by the U.S. Senate in January 1978 creates a presumption in favor of nonparoleable "real-time" sentences. The version recommended by the House Judiciary Committee's subcommittee, however, retains the U.S. Parole Commission's present powers over actual duration of imprisonment, along with that agency's responsibilities to write guidelines for its parole release decisions.

term of up to one-half of the sentence, which must be served in prison before release on parole.[32] But such minimum terms still are not the rule in Oregon, and even when imposed the parole board (by a vote of four of the five members) can order the offender's release prior to expiration of the minimum.[33] Thus the parole board remains primarily responsible for deciding the length of stay in prison.

The new law requires the parole board (after receiving the recommendations of a joint advisory commission, consisting of judges and parole officials)[34] * to set standards that prescribe specific ranges of duration-of-imprisonment before release on parole.[35]

The statute prescribes the rationale that the board must follow in setting those standards,[36] and that rationale gives primacy to desert. The statutory language states that the standards shall be designed to achieve the following aims: (1) the imposition of "punishment which is commensurate with the seriousness of the prisoner's criminal conduct"; and (2) deterrence and incapacitation,[37] but only to the extent that pursuit of those latter aims is "not inconsistent" with the requirements of commensurateness. The statute goes on to state that the board, in setting its standards, must give "primary weight" to the seriousness of the prisoner's present offense and his criminal history. (This directive to give "primary" rather than exclusive weight to the seriousness of the criminal conduct would seem to permit the board to adopt a Modified Desert Model instead of a strict Desert Model, if it wished.)

The new law mandates an early time-fix. The board must, no later than six months after the offender's entry into prison, set an "initial release date." This date ordinarily determines the duration of confinement. The prisoner may be held beyond his initial release date only in three types of cases: (1) where the board has found the prisoner has committed "serious" disciplinary violations in prison; (2) where there is a psychological or psychiatric diagnosis that the prisoner has developed a "present severe emotional disturbance"; and (3) where the board finds the prisoner's parole plan is "inadequate" (but then, the delay may not exceed three months).[38]

Under this procedure, the defendant learns his date not at the moment of sentence, but shortly after he arrives in prison—to give the parole board the chance to review his file and act. The delay, however, would be comparatively brief. By statute, it could not ex-

---

*This advisory commission consists of the five members of the parole board, five judges appointed by the chief justice of the state, and the governor's legal counsel (who has a tie-breaking vote). It gives representatives of the state's judiciary an important input into the drafting of the standards, while leaving the ultimate responsibility to the parole board.

ceed six months; and the Oregon parole board's rules require more prompt notification in most cases.[39] Thus the defendant would be informed at the beginning of his imprisonment of its duration, rather than the much later time that was characteristic of the traditional indeterminate sentence.

In retaining dual time and keeping the parole board as standard-setter, the Oregon approach may be better able to avoid some of the pitfalls described earlier. The agency developing the durational standards would be one that has long been accustomed to reckoning in real time-in-prison: the parole board. The board's continued exposure to prisoners and prisons ought to give it some sense of the severity of imprisonment, as well as an awareness of the limitations of prison space.

By retaining parole release, Oregon's scheme would avoid the shift to seemingly lower sentences that adoption of "real time" would involve. Were the board to base its prescribed durations on previous averages for time served, it could express its norms in the same numbers as before. (Only if the board *reduced* time-served would it have to use lower numbers.) Thus, there will not be the problem of having to explain away an apparent time-reduction when no real one has occurred. Publication of the standards would, of course, make the board's practices more visible—and thus evoke questions from those who would prefer a different policy on time-served than the board's. But at least debates over the board's policies could be conducted without the false impressions of leniency that a shift to real time could create.[40] *

*Would it be possible to preserve "dual time" through mechanisms other than preserving parole release? That could be done, for example, through having large deductions from the sentence for good behavior in prison: time served would, as in Indiana and California, be the judge's sentence minus accumulated good-time credits of up to, say, one-third or one-half the sentence. But this seems to us a *less* satisfactory solution than Oregon's. It still involves a new way of reckoning sentences—a shift from paroleable sentences to nonparoleable ones that are subject to the new deductions, with all the confusion and suspicion that any shift in time-reckoning tends to create. More serious still is the question of how much good-time can be lost. If prisoners face potential loss of large amounts of good time—as in Indiana, where the entire 50 percent good time deduction can be taken away for a disciplinary violation—the scheme loses its early time-fix and violates desert constraints, for the reasons discussed already in Chapter 5. If, on the other hand, the real sanctions are much smaller—as is true in California with its provisions for vesting of good time—their small size becomes difficult to reconcile with the large apparent sanctions. If one creates a system that has a 33 or 50 percent good-time deduction, and if the prison authorities seek stiff penalties in the supposed interests of discipline, how does one explain vesting and other provisions that limit the *actual* sanction for any single violation to a few weeks' or months' extra confinement? If the statute on its face makes so much of the sentence depend on conduct in the prison, it will

Procedures such as Oregon's might also make the task of maintaining compliance with the durational standards less complicated. Time-fixing decisions in individual cases would be made by parole board members or hearing examiners—who should be more familiar with the standards' content, since the board itself would have drafted them. The process of reviewing release decisions to determine compliance should also be less cumbersome, since that would involve the decisions of only a few decisionmakers, in frequent contact with one another, rather than those of numerous trial judges spread throughout the state. This assumes, however, that the board is prepared to police compliance vigorously; if not, the fact that the board is reviewing decisions of its own agents, without an outside monitor or reviewing body, could make it more difficult to detect misapplications of the rules when they do occur.*

The Oregon system has yet to be evaluated. First, the parole board's standards under the new statute need scrutiny. How well do those standards comply with the statutory mandate that a desert rationale govern primarily? How much discretion do the standards leave to parole decisionmakers in individual cases? To what extent are the prescribed durations longer, or shorter, than the previous averages of time served? How, if at all, will the board's policies be affected by the election of a new (and allegedly more conservative) governor?** The implementation of the standards also need examination. How well does the parole board adhere to its own rules when it makes release decisions in individual cases? Does the system really have an early time-fix—or does it frequently occur that the initially-established release date is subsequently altered? What are the standards' actual impact on duration of confinement? To what extent does plea-bargaining alter or dilute the standards' impact?

Questions such as these will be addressed in a new LEAA-funded study of Oregon's experience,[41] in which we are participants—but

---

make it more difficult to present a public case for restricted actual sanctions. The Oregon statute, by contrast, *purports* to make duration of confinement depend primarily on the seriousness of the offender's criminal conduct, rather than on his behavior inside the prison. There, it will be easier to reconcile restrictions on administratively imposed sanctions for prison misbehavior with the statutory aim of having commensurate punishments.

*Another problem of having the same agency draft and apply the standards is that the drafters can become preoccupied with administrative convenience, at the expense of the merits of the standards. The fact that, in Oregon, the standards must first be considered by an advisory body that includes persons other than parole board members may help guard against this risk.

**The state's chief executive appoints the members of the parole board to staggered, four-year terms, and the governorship changed hands in the November 1978 elections.

the answers are as yet unknown. All we can say is that Oregon's approach *seems* to have certain advantages. Whether these advantages will materialize, and what other disadvantages emerge, remains to be seen.

The Oregon approach requires a parole board that is willing to structure its own discretion and move away from traditional theories of parole. That state's parole board had already been experimenting with guidelines on its own initiative;[42] it worked closely with the legislature in drafting the statute; and has moved quickly since enactment to write new durational standards.[43] In a jurisdiction where the board has resisted efforts to structure its discretion, the provisions of such a statute could be nullified through board inaction or noncooperation. Moreover some jurisdictions have inadequately staffed boards or have used their boards as a place for patronage appointments, and thus may lack the necessary skills and personnel for the standard-setting task.

In that event, there is a variant of the Oregon approach which has been suggested by the American Bar Association-sponsored Committee on the Legal Status of Prisoners.[44] The Committee's report recommends elimination of the parole board and the creation of a new "independent releasing authority" having essentially the same responsibilities as the Oregon statute gives the parole board. This agency is required to prescribe standards governing release of prisoners, and to decide individual offenders' release dates early (within three-and-one-half months of entry into prison). Such a new agency may be more sympathetic and suited to the standard-setting task it is given. Yet, as in the Oregon statute, release prior to expiration of sentence is retained.

WHAT ABOUT "IN-OUT" DECISIONS?

A further question raised by Oregon's procedure is what is to be done with judges' "in-out" decisions—that is, decisions whether to confine or impose a lesser sentence. As the drafters of the Oregon statute did not wish to put judicial sentences under parole board control, they left this critical decision unregulated. It is essential, however, that there also be standards for this decision, because disparity cannot be alleviated by durational standards alone if judges' choices between custodial and noncustodial dispositions remain a matter of individual discretion.*

---

*In some jurisdictions, judges not only decide "in vs. out," but can also affect the duration of confinement through the setting of minimum periods of imprisonment that the parole board cannot alter. Where this is so, it will become

To resolve this problem, a two-tier system for setting standards could be created. The parole board would continue to govern durations of actual confinement, and be required (in the manner of the Oregon statute) to set standards for its release decisions. A new mechanism (such as a sentencing commission)[45] would be established to regulate judges' choices—principally, their choice of imprisonment vs. a lesser penalty. In combination, both the "in-out" and durational aspects of sanctions would be regulated, without eliminating parole release, with the attendant difficulties.

Pennsylvania is beginning to move toward this two-tier solution. Under its newly-enacted sentencing commission law, the commission will set guidelines for the sentencing decisions which judges now are empowered to make. Under companion legislation on which the House Judiciary Committee has been holding hearings, the parole board would be required to set guidelines for its parole release decisions.[46] To help prevent inconsistencies between the two sets of norms, it has been suggested that the two standard-setting bodies be required to consult regularly.[47]

One might, alternatively, begin with such a two-tier system, and then shift gradually to a system where one agency sets the norms. These possibilities, and the advantages of a gradual transition, are explored below.

THE STATUS OF PAROLE SUPERVISION

The new Oregon statute did not address parole supervision. Our proposals on the subject could, however, be accomplished through the following changes.

Limitation of Sanctions. A Modified Desert Model, we explained, would allow supervision with limited sanctions (subject to effectiveness requirements). The parole board, after releasing the offender from prison pursuant to its durational standards, would place him under supervision for a prescribed period. If that period were less than the unexpired portion of the sentence, the offender could simply be discharged from parole when his supervision ends. If a parole violation occurred during the supervision period, the parole board could reimprison him, but only briefly. If a new crime were com-

---

even more important to set standards for judges' decisions, since parole standards alone will not have the degree of influence over duration that they have in Oregon, where the parole board has the last word on release from prison. (A commission regulating judicial sentences will, of course, have its own authority restricted if the state has adopted *legislative* mandatory minima.)

mitted, the revocation process would not be invoked at all; instead the offender would be prosecuted and, if convicted, sentenced on the basis of the new conviction.

One might wish to write the limits on the severity of reconfinements into the statute. Oregon has not done that. The parole board has written regulations on its own initiative, however, that begin to restrict duration of reimprisonments for technical parole violations.[48]

Abolition. A Desert Model, we suggested, would call for the elimination of supervision. Even without any supervision, however, the parole board or a similar administrative agency could be given the function of releasing offenders prior to sentence expiration, and of setting standards for those release decisions. Such a proposal has in fact been made by the A.B.A.'s Committee on the Legal Status of Prisoners. According to the Committee's report:

> On the date of release established by the releasing authority, the prisoner should be released from confinement without further conditions or supervision. The correctional authority should provide counseling and other assistance to released prisoners on a voluntary basis for at least one year after release.[49]

In such a system, the offender would be freed from state control at the moment the board releases him from prison, although his judicial sentence may still have time to run. His status would be akin to that which now exists when the parole board orders a parolee discharged from supervision; the discharged parolee likewise is under no further state control, although his sentence has not yet expired.[50]

The choice between keeping or eliminating supervision is distinct, it should be noted, from the choice of whether or not to have parole release prior to expiration of defendants' judicial prison terms. The California system, for example, eliminates the parole board's releasing authority, but adds on a *separate* term of parole supervision after the prison sentence has expired.[51]

A GRADUAL TRANSITION TO "REAL TIME"

Despite its practical advantages, a system that retains "dual" time carries an important cost. It gives continued apparent legitimacy to prodigal conceptions of time. David Rothman has pointed out that our otherwise highly time-conscious culture has historically thought of prison time in huge quantities, and this has made it harder to justify the more modest actual confinements that fairness and realism require.[52] As long as the system continues to impose five- and ten- and fifteen-year purported prison sentences for common felonies— even if actual times-in-confinement are much shorter—it will give credibility to inflated notions of time.

For that reason, we think the long-run objective should be the creation of a system that speaks in terms of moderate real sentences, and banishes the long fictional prison terms. But the transition to real-time should be undertaken gradually and carefully. The Oregon scheme of parole release standards may be the safest place to begin, because it incorporates the substance of our proposed reforms without the misunderstandings that sudden adoption of a novel time-reckoning could create.

If real-time is introduced, it should be done *gradually*. This might be accomplished, for example, through a slow phase-out of parole release. The board's standard-setting functions would be transferred over time to the sentencing commission; and its function of applying those standards in individual cases, to sentencing judges. Any such phase-out should be done, however, in such a manner as to minimize the hazards of which we have spoken. The following are suggested precautions.[53]

Authority to Set Durational Standards. When the sentencing commission is first created, it should be empowered only to set standards for the sentencing decisions that judges *now* make: the "in-out" choice of a custodial vs. noncustodial sentence; the decision about the maximum term, when custody is invoked; and the decision about a minimum term (to the extent the latter is to be allowed). The parole board, at the outset, should retain its power to release offenders prior to sentence expiration; and, in the manner of the Oregon system, the board should be required to adopt standards for its release decisions.

This would allow the sentencing commission's performance in writing its initial standards to be evaluated, before it is given the further task of setting the standards for actual duration of confinement. How do the commission's initial standard-setting efforts compare, it should be asked, with those of the parole board? To what extent has the commission shown itself capable of writing standards that are conceptually consistent and reasonably specific?

Authority to Fix Durations in Individual Cases. Even when and if the parole board ceases to write the durational standards, it should still be retained for a time as the agency that *applies* those standards. Parole release would thus continue to exist—only now, the sentencing commission would set the releasing standards, which the parole board would carry out in individual cases. It would not seem advisable to transfer to sentencing judges the power to fix actual time in confinement, until there has been an opportunity to evaluate their performance in applying the sentencing commission's standards for their "in-out" decisions. How much resistance have judges shown to restrictions on their discretion in deciding between incarceration and a lesser sentence? How well have they understood and applied the "in-out" standards? How well has appellate review of noncomplying sentences succeeded? Unless these questions have been satisfactorily answered, eliminating the parole board as the time-fixer may *reduce* the opportunity to control disparity.

Introduction of Real-Time. A shift to "real-time" sentences would generate less misunderstanding if it were done in stages. The standard-setter (that is, the parole board, at first; the sentencing commission later, when it takes over the board's standard-setting powers) could, over a period of years, shorten sentences and increase the portion of sentence served in prison before release. One might, for a given felony, begin with a six-year sentence, in which release occurs at one-third; then have a four-year sentence, in which it occurs at one-half; and so forth until one ends with a two-year "real-time" sentence. This would mean that there would not, at any one time, be a drastic apparent reduction in sentence; it would give the public more opportunity to become accustomed to the new way of reckoning sentencing time.

This three-step process is only one method of phasing-in "real-time" sentences, and other variants are possible.* What is critical is

---

*Our suggested three-step process for phasing in real time would eventually remove the parole board from the release decision. Conceivably, however, real time could be introduced through precisely the reverse tactic—of *enlarging* the parole board's authority.

Suppose one were to shift from judges to the parole board the former officials' power to set maximum sentences. Under such a system, the judge would continue to decide whether the offender is to go to prison or receive a lesser sentence. When the judge opts for a prison sentence, however, it would become the parole board's responsibility to set two dates: (1) the date of expiration of the maximum term (formerly the judge's responsibility, now transferred to the board); and (2) the date of actual release from imprisonment (the board's traditional responsibility). There also would be Oregon-type requirements calling upon the board to adopt standards for setting those dates, based on a Desert or Modified Desert model, and mandating that the dates be fixed early.

With such a system in place, the board could begin to introduce "real time." It could do this by gradually shortening the maximum sentences and increasing not the particular technique, but an introduction of real-time sentencing in a manner that is both gradual and designed to keep to a minimum the dangers we have described above.

PRACTICAL CHARACTER OF THE CHOICE

In so highly charged an issue as crime and punishment, it will always be a gamble deciding which agency or agencies should be given responsibility for change. Beyond the rather elementary points mentioned in this chapter, the reformer will need a sophisticated knowledge of the bureaucratic and political realities of his or her locality.

There are, we believe, vital issues of principle that concern how much punishment should be inflicted, and for what purposes. The choice of decisionmaking agencies, however, is a choice of means. It was, in part, historical accident that set the prevailing pattern, where judges decide whether offenders go to prison, and parole boards primarily decide how long they remain there. Whether and in what manner that pattern is to be altered should depend on which agencies seem best able, in the particular jurisdiction, to achieve the substantive reforms we have proposed earlier in this book. We perceive nothing that compels *a priori* a choice of one of these agencies over another. Judges are not necessarily the only suitable time-fixers; parole boards are not necessarily obsolete. The question must be regarded as a *practical* one, of which agency or agencies could write standards of the desired kind, and could apply those standards properly in individual cases—and, above all, of how one can keep to a minimum the formidable hazards attendant on reform.

---

the proportion of the term that had to be served before release, until the release date and the sentence-expiration date merged in a single date that would constitute both the end of the sentence and the end of the offender's stay in prison. Thus the proposal would: (1) permit a gradual phase-in of real time; while (2) retaining a small, specialized body—already familiar with dealing in actual durations of imprisonment—to draft and apply the standards.

Such a system bears superficial resemblance to the old California system, in which the parole board also fixed the maximum duration of sentence as well as the release date. But the differences are important: there would be standards, a just-deserts orientation, and an early time-fix, whereas the old California system was characterized by standardlessness, a supposed rehabilitative philosophy, and long delays before fixing release dates.

 *Chapter 10*

Conclusions: Abolish Parole?

Traditional parole has had four main features. We would change each.

- The decision concerning when to release prisoners, it was assumed, should be made by assessing their needs for treatment and likelihood of offending again. Our assumption is different. Durations of confinement should, as a requirement of justice, depend chiefly on the degree of blameworthiness of the offender's criminal conduct.

- The decision fixing the date of release from prison, it was believed, should be deferred until the offender had served a substantial portion of his sentence. We recommend that the decision take place early—at or shortly after imposition of sentence—subject to subsequent adjustments only for prison overcrowding situations and (to a limited extent) for prison disciplinary infractions.

- The ex-prisoner, it was thought, was to be supervised in the community, in order to reduce his likelihood of returning to crime. We are skeptical about both the fairness and efficacy of supervision as it has historically operated. On what we have called the Desert Model, supervision should be eliminated entirely. On the alternative Modified Desert Model, supervision could be retained— but only if it met requirements of effectiveness and if the severity of sanctions for parole violations were substantially scaled down. In either case, however, there should be a system of voluntary social services when prisoners leave the institution.

- Prisoners were released on condition that they not commit further crimes; and if suspected of new criminal activity, they could be reconfined through an administrative, parole-revocation proceeding having less stringent evidentiary requirements and lower standards of proof than a criminal trial. We think this separate procedure for trying new criminal conduct, with its reduced safeguards, entails unacceptable risks of penalizing the innocent.

Nevertheless, we urge caution before abolishing the parole board as the agency for deciding release from prison. The board performs the vital function of scaling down lengthy judicial sentences into shorter and more realistic periods of actual confinement. The parole board's mission can be redefined. It is capable (as the Oregon system exemplifies) of becoming the vehicle for the substantive reforms we have urged, such as durational standards based primarily on desert and an early time-fix. Unless precautionary steps are taken—and we have described what some of these might be—eliminating the parole board's releasing power could have considerable ill-effects, both in generating pressures to increase time served in prison and in making it more difficult to secure compliance with the durational standards.

One final caution. Our recommendations in this book depend on two major assumptions: (1) that there are to be explicit standards governing durations of confinement; and (2) that those standards are parsimonious in prescribing imprisonment, particularly lengthy terms.

In systems where these assumptions do not obtain, our recommendations will not necessarily be useful, and could be harmful. If the time-fixer is allowed wide discretion about how much time to prescribe, eliminating or restricting parole supervision may merely lead some time-fixers to opt for longer confinements. If a penal system routinely resorts to lengthy durations of imprisonment, requiring an early decision on the release date may only eliminate such slim hopes for mercy as might otherwise exist.

In short, it would be better to ignore our recommendations entirely than accept a part of them without the emphasis on standards and on moderate durations, around which all our other arguments turn.

Appendices

Appendix I

Reconsideration of Long Prison Terms?

We have urged that long terms of confinement be invoked sparingly: that is, only for the most heinous of crimes. For these latter cases, usually involving acts of violence, what should the time-fixing procedure be?

Our general recommendation in Chapter 4 was that release dates be fixed early (at sentence or shortly after), subject to later change only for acts of prison indiscipline and for prison overcrowding. Were this recommendation applied to the minority of very serious cases receiving the longest confinements, two kinds of problems might arise.

First, emotions evoked by the event. Heinous crimes are the most likely to evoke strong feelings on the part of the public and of officials involved in the case. Such feelings tend to run highest at or near the moment of conviction, when details of the crime are fresh in people's minds. Arguably, this may not be the most propitious moment for a considered and dispassionate judgment of the case. And the time-fixer's attitudes could matter, even under our proposals: although the presumptive duration would be regulated by standards, some discretion will remain to impose an enhanced term on account of aggravating circumstances.

Second, problems of visualizing long terms. Beyond a certain point —three or four years, or whatever—it becomes increasingly difficult to visualize time stretching into the future. If the time fix is early, and the time-fixer has discretion to choose, say, between a five and a seven-and-a-half year term, he or she may have trouble grasping the difference. Both seem simply to be long stays.

These concerns might militate in favor of an altered procedure for the very serious crimes: namely, having a "second look" later in the offender's term. The time-fixer would be required to set a probable release date early. After a specified fraction of the term had elapsed, however, the prisoner could petition for a review of the case. At that time, the time-fixer would be required to reassess the facts of the case and the term imposed, in the light of the applicable standards and either confirm the original release date or set an earlier one.

Such a procedure might have the advantage of allowing the case to be considered in a calmer atmosphere, when it has lost some of its notoriety and a more detached assessment of the crime can be made. Review of the decision might also make the time periods involved seem more real. Long stretches of *past* time are somewhat easier to comprehend, as one has milestones to compare. The difference between five and seven-and-a-half years, for example, may be brought into sharper relief by reference to other events transpiring at the time.

There are potential disadvantages also: of replicating some of the ills of indeterminacy of sentence. If the initial time-fix is subject to later alteration, the time-fixer may be tempted, in his first decision, to resolve all doubts in favor of lengthier terms since he or she knows that "mistakes" can be corrected later. Defendants convicted of the most serious crimes may thus, to the extent the time-fixer has discretion, be kept long in ignorance of their actual release dates.

Whatever the merits of this "second look" procedure, it should be reserved—if used at all—for the most serious crimes. Other, less heinous offenses would not generate such strong feelings, nor would their punishments be so long; these, in any event, should be handled by the early time-fix procedure we recommended in Chapters 4 and 5.

"Punitive" Supervision

In our analysis of parole supervision in Chapter 7, we assumed that it was a measure aimed at preventing crimes by those supervised. Based on this assumption, we imposed an effectiveness criterion: that there be empirical evidence that supervision is capable of reducing recidivism rates among parolees.

Is this assumption necessary? Why should there not be purely "punitive" supervision—intended solely as a deprivation, irrespective of any effect on parolees' future criminal behavior? Released offenders might conceivably be barred from certain activities (or required to perform certain others) simply because this is an unpleasantness which is part of their deserved punishment. To analyze this possibility, let us consider two distinct versions of it: "mild" and "onerous" supervision, respectively.

"Mild" Punitive Supervision

In this version, most of the punishment would still be experienced through the offender's initial imprisonment—with supervision adding relatively little to the penalty. Suppose offenders convicted of a given crime were deemed to deserve six severity points, on a hypothetical severity scale of ten. Suppose the rule is that five of the severity points would be served through a specified period of imprisonment; and the sixth point would be served by requiring offenders, after their return to the community, either to refrain from doing something they like or to do something they dislike. Were any ex-prisoner to violate this requirement, he would receive a sanction, such as intermittent confinement or a short stint in jail, of the moderate degree of unpleasantness needed to serve out the "unused" severity point. (This example assumes there exists a severity scale that can measure the comparative painfulness of different types of sanctions. Such a scale does not now exist; but let us suppose, for the sake of argument, that one were possible.)

What is wrong? One cannot object on grounds of desert, since the severity of the supervision, and of its back-up sanction, have been carefully scaled so as to ensure that the total penalty comports with the gravity of the crime. The difficulty is, rather, that this elaborate mechanism of supervision seems to have no point. If the only object is to inflict deserved punishment, that could be achieved simply by imprisoning offenders slightly longer, and releasing them outright.

Imprisonment has its own major drawbacks, of course: it is expensive, and—as customarily practiced in American prisons—it is dangerous for those who are confined. These disadvantages are not, however, significantly alleviated through such a scheme of "mild" punitive supervision. Since most of the punishment would still be administered through defendants' initial stay in prison, the expense and the danger to prisoners would remain largely present. By adding the appendage of punitive supervision to the corpus of imprisonment, one has only complicated the penal system.

"Onerous" Punitive Supervision

What, however, if the supervision were made more severe? Consider, again, offenders who are convicted of a crime that is deemed to deserve six severity points on a hypothetical severity scale of ten. Suppose that considerably more drastic constraints were imposed on ex-prisoners' behavior in the community—for example, that these constraints were to amount in themselves to three severity points.* In that event, one could reduce the duration of the initial imprisonment considerably, saving expense and, perhaps, reducing the dangers to those punished.

Is this kind of sanction desirable? It is, evidently, quite different from parole supervision as customarily practiced. Not only is the aim different (purely punitive, instead of preventive), but the degree of

---

*In this scenario, there could even be a substantial period of reconfinement, were the individual to violate the conditions of his release. Supposing the initial three severity points were served through a one-and-a-half year stay in prison. Were the prisoner, shortly after his release, to violate the terms of his supervision, he would still "owe" nearly three remaining severity points. Conceivably, he could be made to serve these by being returned to prison to complete his punishment there.

intrusion into the supervised offender's life would have to be escalated considerably.

While this kind of measure lies somewhat beyond the scope of our present study,* we have reservations about it. Such measures would, in the first place, leave a disturbing amount of discretion to enforcing agents. The degree to which purportedly "onerous" supervision is actually unpleasant would depend in large part on day-to-day judgments of the individual agents assigned to supervise their charges. And those judgments—of how closely to scrutinize the parolee, and of which violations to report or overlook—will be extremely difficult to review and control. The actual onerousness of the sanction will thus depend on the inclination of the agent, on whether he is friendly or hostile. While the problem of differences in enforcement styles exists also for lesser community penalties applicable to non-serious offenses, it is more worrisome here. The greater the purported severity of the sanction, the greater the potential disparity between rigorous and relaxed enforcement.

Still more disturbing would be the potential intrusiveness of enforcement. Noninstitutional punishments ought not to interfere with the privacy of unconvicted third persons.[1] Onerous conditions of supervision, such as strict limits on parolees' everyday activities, are particularly likely to involve such intrusions. Supervisees would be under the strongest temptations to violate such conditions, since they are being asked to undergo privations that are so much greater than those suffered by others with whom they are living. (Great as the deprivations of imprisonment are, they are at least suffered in common with other inmates; the prisoner may be able to bracket off his stay in prison as separate from his normal existence—as time to be endured while he looks forward to returning to ordinary life. Substantial deprivations inflicted on the offender while he is in the community are so galling, because he may be the only sufferer among his family and associates.) Given the strength of such temptations, there would have to be the most determined effort to enforce the conditions. That, however, would require enforcement agents to exercise close surveillance that would place under scrutiny whole groups of persons among whom the offender moves in the community, including those quite unaware of his status as an ex-convict.

We assume it is desirable to have community-based sanctions for non-serious offenses—but these would not be severe. Onerous community sanctions, applicable to serious crimes, are a different story.

*We have not, for example, studied "split" sentences, in which a judge sentences an individual to probation for several years, on condition that he serve so many months of the sentence in the county jail.

David Rothman and Willard Gaylin have noted that "Prisons, at least, have confined the despotism of the state behind walls. . . . We must not deinstitutionalize offenders at the price of institutionalizing the rest of us."[2] A penal system in which some offenders are subject to strict controls while they live among their fellow citizens could create a degree of official presence in people's ordinary lives, a sense of omnipresent authority, that is undesirable in a free society.

※ *Appendix III*

The Hart-Javits Bill

This proposed legislation, introduced by Senators Gary Hart and Jacob Javits as S. 204 in the 1977 session of the U.S. Senate, would: (1) create a sentencing commission to set standards for criminal sentences; (2) require the commission to follow a desert rationale in formulating its standards; (3) eliminate parole release and substitute "real-time" sentences; (4) require a scaling-down of sentence durations to reflect the shift to real time; and (5) restrict the duration of post-release supervision to 10 percent of the sentence, and limit the duration of reconfinements for parole violations to 15 days. We are not suggesting it is ideal legislation, and there are specific provisions we would write differently.[1] It is set forth, rather, to illustrate the discussion in Chapter 9.

95th CONGRESS 1st Session   **S. 204**

IN THE SENATE OF THE UNITED STATES

January 12 (legislative day, January 10), 1977

Mr. Hart (for himself and Mr. Javits) introduced the following bill: which was read twice and referred to the Committee on the Judiciary

---

A BILL

To establish the Federal Sentencing Commission; and for other purposes.

Be it enacted by the Senate and House of Representatives of the United States of America in Congress assembled, That this Act may be cited as the "Federal Sentencing Standards Act of 1977."

FINDINGS; PURPOSE

SEC. 2. (a) The Congress finds that the present system of punishing persons convicted of Federal crimes fails to achieve fairness or consistency, or to protect the public, and that such system—

(1) results in the imposition of penalties that are frequently either unduly lenient or unduly severe:

(2) permits unwarranted, and unreviewable, disparity in sentences;

(3) operates without consistent and understandable rationale or standards; and

(4) undermines public confidence in the equity, impartiality, and effectiveness of Federal criminal justice.

(b) It is the purpose of this Act—

(1) to establish a method of promulgating standards for criminal sentences that will help deter crime and punish convicted criminal offenders fairly and equally;

(2) to establish in such standards the principle that the severity of a sentence should be commensurate with the gravity of the offense;

(3) to reduce the disparity between sentences imposed upon persons convicted of the same crime by requiring that such sentencing standards shall consist of presumptive sentences of varying severity for criminal offenses of varying degrees of gravity, with limited variations allowed for special aggravating and mitigating circumstances; and

(4) to allow each convicted offender sentenced to imprisonment to know at the time that such sentence is imposed the actual duration of his confinement, but also to maintain appropriate incentives for good institutional behavior.

DEFINITIONS

SEC. 3. For purposes of this Act, the term—

(1) "Parole Commission" means the United States Parole Commission in the Department of Justice established in section 4202 of title 18, United States Code;

(2) "Commission" means the Federal Sentencing Commission established in section 4;

(3) "criminal offense" means a category, or any subcategory thereof, established under section 6, of crimes punishable under any statute of the United States;

(4) "convicted offender" means any person who is convicted of or pleads guilty to a crime punishable under any statute of the United States;

(5) "imprisonment" means the requirement that any convicted offender live in any prison, jail, or other institution of confinement;

(6) "presumptive sentence" means a definite and specific penalty, established by the Commission, as provided in section 6, for a criminal offense of a particular gradation of gravity;

(7) "rule" means any rule, regulation, or schedule proposed or adopted by the Commission;

(8) "sentencing judge" means any judge of the United States, as defined in section 451 of title 28. United States Code, presiding at a trial in which any defendant is convicted of or pleads guilty to any criminal offense for which a presumptive sentence is in effect; and

(9) "sentencing standards" means the schedules, rules, and regulations for sentencing convicted offenders which the Commission establishes in accordance with the provisions of this Act.

FEDERAL SENTENCING COMMISSION

SEC. 4. (a) (1) There is established a commission to be known as the Federal Sentencing Commission. The Commission shall be composed of five members appointed by the President of the United States, by and with the consent of the Senate.

(2) Members of the Commission shall serve for terms of five years, except that of the members first appointed —

    (A) one shall be appointed for one year;

    (B) one shall be appointed for two years;

    (C) one shall be appointed for three years;

    (D) one shall be appointed for four years; and

    (E) one shall be appointed for five years.

The member appointed under subparagraph (E) shall be or have been a member of the Parole Commission or its predecessor, the United States Board of Parole.

(3) Any person appointed to fill a vacancy occurring other than by the expiration of a term of office shall be appointed (A) only for the unexpired term of the member he succeeds, and (B) in the same manner as in the case of the original appointment.

(4) Members of the Commission shall receive compensation equivalent to the compensation paid at level IV of the Executive Schedule (5 U.S.C. 5315).

(b) (1) The Commission shall have an Executive Director who shall be appointed by the Commission. The Executive Director shall be paid at a rate not to exceed the rate of basic pay in effect for level V of the Executive Schedule (5 U.S.C. 5316).

(2) With the approval of the Commission, the Executive Director may—

    (A) appoint and fix the pay of such additional personnel as he deems necessary, and

    (B) procure temporary and intermittent services to the same extent as is authorized by section 3109(b) of title 5, United States Code, but at rates for individuals not to exceed the daily equivalent of the annual rate of basic pay in effect for grade GS–15 of the General Schedule (5 U.S.C. 5332).

(3) In carrying out its responsibilities under this Act, the Commission shall, to the fullest extent practicable, avail itself of the assistance, including personnel and facilities, of other agencies and departments of the United States Government. The heads of such agencies and departments may make available to the Commission such personnel, facilities, and other assistance, with or without reimbursement, as the Commission may request.

(c) The Commission is abolished six years after the date of enactment of this Act unless, prior to that time, the Congress adopts a concurrent resolution disapproving the abolition of the Commission.

DUTIES OF COMMISSION; ADMINISTRATIVE PROVISIONS

SEC. 5. (a) The Commission shall—

(1) prescribe rules to carry out the provisions of sections 6, 7, 8, 9, 11, and 12 in accordance with the provisions of subsection (b);

(2) collect from each district court of the United States such detailed information (which each such court shall assist in providing) relating to sentencing practices in each such court as the Commission shall by rule require; and

(3) review the information collected pursuant to paragraph (2) in accordance with the provisions of subsection (c).

(b) (1) Not later than eighteen months after the date of enactment of this Act, the Commission shall publish in the Federal Register proposed rules to carry out the provisions of sections 6, 7, 8, 9, 11, and 12. Not earlier than sixty days, but not later than ninety days, after the date of publication of such proposed rules, the Commission shall hold public hearings to afford interested persons a reasonable opportunity to present data, views, or arguments concerning such proposed rules, in an oral presentation, or in writing prior to the hearing. The Commission shall consider fully all submissions respecting such proposed rules, revise such proposed rules on the basis of such submissions to the extent appropriate and consistent with the policy of this Act, and issue a concise statement of the principal reasons for adoption, and the reasons for overruling any considerations urged against adoption. All such procedures shall be consistent with the applicable provisions of sections 553 (b) and (c) of title 5, United States Code.

(2) The Commission, before adopting any such proposed rule under this section, shall transmit such proposed rule and such statement to the Senate and the House of Representatives.

(3) (A) If the Senate and the House of Representatives do not, through agreement to a concurrent resolution, disapprove the proposed rule within forty-five calendar days after receipt thereof, then the Commission may adopt such rule and it shall thereupon become effective. The Commission may not adopt any rule which is disapproved under this subparagraph.

(B) For purposes of this paragraph, the term "Calendar days" does not include any calendar day (i) on which both Houses of the Congress are adjourned sine die, or (ii) during a recess by either House of three or more days.

(C) If such proposed rule consists of a schedule of presumptive sentences as provided in section 6, a schedule of aggravating or mitigating circumstances as provided in section 7, or a schedule of sanctions as provided in section 9 (a), any such resolution of disapproval must disapprove such schedule as a whole.

(c) Each year, during the two-year period after the date on which the first rules adopted as provided in subsection (a) become effective, the Commission shall review the information collected as required by subsection (a) (2) and shall reassess such rules accordingly. If the Commission finds, on the basis of such review, that modification of such rules is desirable, the Commission may modify such rules in accordance with the procedures set forth in subsection (b). At the end of such two-year period, the Commission shall conduct such a review at least once every three years, unless the Commission is sooner abolished as provided in section 4. The Commission shall publish the results of all such reviews.

(d) The Commission shall transmit a report to the Congress each year. Each such report shall contain a detailed statement with respect to the activities of the Commission in carrying out its duties under this Act, and any recommendations for legislative or other action by the Congress which the Commission considers appropriate.

PRESUMPTIVE SENTENCES

SEC. 6. (a) The Commission shall establish, in accordance with the provisions in section 5, a schedule —

(1) setting forth gradations of gravity of criminal offenses;

(2) prescribing an appropriate gradation of gravity for each criminal offense;

(3) prescribing a presumptive sentence for each gradation of gravity.

(b) The severity of each presumptive sentence prescribed as provided in subsection (a) (3) shall be commensurate with the gravity of the criminal offense to which such presumptive sentence is assigned.

(c) (1) For the purpose of subsections (a) and (b), the Commission, in determining the gravity of a criminal offense, shall assess the degree of harm or risk of harm of the type of criminal conduct involved in such criminal offense and the degree of culpability of a perpetrator engaging in that type of conduct.

(2) For the purpose of subsections (a) and (b), the Commission may establish, solely for purposes of this Act, subcategories of any criminal offense and assign different gradations of gravity to such subcategories, if it finds that such subcategories have distinct degrees of gravity. Whenever the Commission establishes such subcategories, it shall also prescribe the criteria that each sentencing judge must use to determine the applicable subcategory for the criminal conduct engaged in by such convicted offender. For purposes of this Act, such subcategory shall be considered to be the criminal offense of which the criminal offender was convicted.

MITIGATING AND AGGRAVATING CIRCUMSTANCES

SEC. 7. (a) The Commission shall establish, in accordance with the provisions of section 5, a schedule and rules —

(1) prescribing variations from any presumptive sentence established under section 6 or account of mitigating or aggravating circumstances;

(2) specifying which types of circumstances shall qualify as mitigating or aggravating circumstances that justify a variation from such presumptive sentence; and

(3) specifying, with respect to each such type of mitigating or aggravating circumstance, a particular amount or a maximum permitted amount of variation from such presumptive sentence.

(b) If a sentence of imprisonment is prescribed as the presumptive sentence, no variation on account of aggravating circumstances prescribed by the Commission under subsection (a) shall increase the duration of such imprisonment by more than 50 per centum.

(c) For the purpose of subsection (a), the Commission —

(1) shall not consider as an aggravating or mitigating circumstance, the anticipated effect on the future behavior of the convicted offender, or of any other person, of imposing a sentence more or less severe than the presumptive sentence; and

(2) may specify as a mitigating or aggravating circumstance, any particular acts or circumstances surrounding the commission of a criminal offense which renders the degree of harm or risk of harm of the criminal conduct, or the degree of culpability of the offender in engaging in such conduct, greater or less than the gradation of gravity prescribed for such criminal offense under section 6.

(d) Notwithstanding the provisions in subsection (c), the Commission shall establish rules, consistent with the provisions of this section, which shall —

(1) prescribe as an aggravating circumstance the fact that a convicted offender has previously been convicted of a serious offense in section 8 (b), and

(2) require the imposition of a sentence more severe than the presumptive sentence in any case in which such aggravating circumstance is present.

SENTENCES OF IMPRISONMENT

SEC. 8. (a) The Commission shall —

(1) prescribe a presumptive sentence of imprisonment under section 6 only for serious criminal offenses; and

(2) prescribe, with respect to serious criminal offenses, no presumptive sentence in excess of five years of actual imprisonment, except as otherwise provided in subsection (c).

(b) A criminal offense is serious for purposes of subsection (a) if, as determined under section 6 (c) (1), it entails a substantial degree of harm or risk thereof and a high degree of culpability on the part of the person who commits such criminal offense. In determining whether the harm or risk thereof is substantial, the Commission shall consider whether the conduct—

(1) involves the infliction, risk, or threat of substantial bodily injury; or

(2) involves the infliction or risk of substantial harm (other than of bodily injury), including but not limited to the substantial abuse of a public office, a public or private trust, or of government processes, or the deprivation of a substantial portion of the livelihood of a victim of such criminal offense.

(c) Subsection (a) (2) shall not apply to the criminal offenses of murder, manslaughter, forcible rape, aircraft hijacking, kidnapping, or treason, or any attempt or aiding or abetting of such offenses.

SENTENCES OTHER THAN IMPRISONMENT

SEC. 9. (a) The Commission shall establish, in accordance with the provisions in section 5—

(1) a schedule of penalties other than imprisonment, to be assigned as presumptive sentences for criminal offenses for which imprisonment may not be prescribed as the presumptive sentence under section 8; and

(2) a schedule specifying the (A) terms and conditions applicable to such penalties, and (B) sanctions which may be applied by any sentencing judge to any convicted offender who violates such terms or conditions.

(b) For the purpose of subsection (a) (1), such penalties may include—

(1) intermittent confinement for days, evenings, or weekends, or portions thereof;

(2) supervision in the community;

(3) a fine or forfeiture;

(4) a curfew or travel restrictions; or

(5) community service.

(c) For the purpose of subsection (a) (2) (A), the terms and conditions of such penalties prescribed by the Commission may include the duration, scheduling, and place of any intermittent confinement; the amount or method of calculating or determining any fine or forfeiture; and the nature, type and extent of any supervision, curfew, travel restriction, or community service.

(d) For the purpose of subsection (a) (2) (B), no sanction that is imposed on a convicted offender for failing to comply with such terms and conditions may result in the imprisonment of such convicted offender for more than one year.

(e) The Attorney General shall, after consulting with the Commission, establish or designate an office within the Department of Justice that shall be responsible for implementing and carrying out any penalties under this section which are prescribed by the Commission and imposed upon convicted offenders by any sentencing judge.

MAXIMUM SENTENCES

SEC. 10. No presumptive sentence prescribed by the Commission under section 6 for a criminal offense, including any variation thereof on account of aggravating circumstances prescribed by the Commission under section 7, may exceed in severity the maximum punishment for such offense prescribed by any other statute of the United States.

ABOLITION OF PAROLE; EARLY RELEASE FOR GOOD BEHAVIOR

SEC. 11. (a) Whenever the Commission prescribes imprisonment as a penalty under section 6, 7, or 8, the Commission —

(1) shall consider that such penalty refers to the period of time which convicted offenders must actually serve in confinement, except as otherwise provided in subsection (c); and

(2) may by rule prescribe that the release of convicted offenders from imprisonment shall be followed by a period of supervision in the community to aid the transition of such offenders to the community, and prescribe the terms and conditions of such supervision and the sanctions which may be applied to any convicted offender who fails to comply with such terms and conditions, except that —

(A) the duration of any such supervision shall not exceed 10 per centum of the convicted offender's sentence of imprisonment; and

(B) no sanction for noncompliance with the terms and conditions of such supervision shall result in the imprisonment of a convicted offender for more than fifteen days.

(b) After the date on which the schedule established pursuant to section 6 becomes effective, the Parole Commission shall have no authority under section 4203 of title 18, United States Code, to grant parole to any prisoner except that the Parole Commission shall have the authority —

(1) to grant parole to any otherwise eligible prisoner who was sentenced before that date; and

(2) to administer any supervision in the community authorized by the Commission under subsection (a) (2).

(c) (1) Notwithstanding the provisions of subsection (a), the Commission may establish rules pursuant to which —

(A) each imprisoned offender is entitled to a deduction from the term of his imprisonment, if he has not committed a serious disciplinary infraction while imprisoned; or

(B) any imprisoned offender who has committed such a serious disciplinary infraction may be penalized by an addition to the term of his imprisonment.

(2) If the Commission establishes rules as provided in paragraph (1), it shall, after consulting with the Attorney General, the Director of the Bureau of Prisons of the United States Department of Justice, and other appropriate officials, (A) prescribe the procedures for determining whether an imprisoned offender

has committed a serious disciplinary infraction, and (B) define what constitutes a serious disciplinary infraction for purposes of this subsection.

(3) No rule established as provided in paragraph (1) shall permit—

(A) any deduction from the term of any convicted offender's imprisonment, pursuant to paragraph (1) (A) in excess of 15 per centum of the duration of such term if such term is three years or less, or 10 per centum of the duration of such term if such term is more than three years; or

(B) any addition to the term of any convicted offender's imprisonment, pursuant to paragraph (1) (B), in excess of 10 per centum of the duration of term.

(d) Whenever the Commission, in accordance with section 5 (c), amends its schedule and rules under section 6 to reduce the severity of any presumptive sentence, or under section 7 in such a manner as could reduce the severity of any penalty imposed thereunder, the Commission may establish rules—

(1) prescribing that any such amendment shall apply retroactively to convicted offenders who were sentenced as provided in this Act prior to the effective date of such amendment and who still are undergoing punishment; or

(2) directing sentencing judges to reduce or terminate the punishment of such convicted offenders, consistently with the Commission's rules under paragraph (1).

DUTIES OF SENTENCING COURTS

SEC. 12. (a) (1) Each sentencing judge shall impose on any convicted offender the presumptive sentence assigned to the criminal offense of which he was convicted, except if a variation from the presumptive sentence is permitted or required by the Commission's rules under section 7, such judge shall vary such presumptive sentence only as provided in section 7.

(2) If the sentencing judge (A) varies any presumptive sentence, based upon the existence of any aggravating or mitigating circumstance, or (B) refuses, upon request by the defendant or the United States, to vary any presumptive sentence, such judge shall disclose the variation or refusal in open court, and make a statement for the record of the justification therefor, including a description of any such aggravating or mitigating circumstances and all other information, evidence, or other factors considered by the judge, in accordance with the rules which the Commission shall prescribe under this Act.

(b) The Supreme Court of the United States shall have the power, after consulting with the Commission, to prescribe rules of practice and procedure pursuant to section 3772 of title 18, United States Code, with respect to the imposition of sentences under this Act and under the rules of the Commission, except that the Supreme Court may delegate such power to the Commission, subject to such terms and conditions as the Supreme Court may prescribe.

APPELLATE REVIEW

SEC. 13. The convicted offender or the United States may appeal any sentence imposed under section 12 to the appropriate United States court of appeals solely on the ground that—

(1) the sentencing judge imposed such sentence in violation of a rule established by the Commission under this Act or of a provision of this Act; or

(2) any rule established by the Commission and related to such sentence is invalid, because (A) the Commission did not comply with the provisions in section 5 with respect to such rule, or (B) the presumptive sentence, aggravating or mitigating circumstances, or other parts of the sentencing standards adopted by the Commission are arbitrary and capricious.

✻ *Appendix IV*

The Oregon Parole Reform Law

This statute was enacted in the 1977 session of the Oregon Legislature as Chapter 372 of that year's session laws. It retains the parole board as the agency primarily responsible for deciding the duration of imprisoned offenders' confinement. However, it (1) requires the parole board (after receiving the recommendations of a joint advisory commission consisting of judges and parole board members) to set explicit standards governing such standards; (2) requires that these standards be based on a primarily desert-oriented rationale; and (3) requires the board to use an early time-fix. (The statute does not alter the status of parole supervision.) As any legislation actually adopted, it is the product of compromise; some of its provisions (e.g., §4(1) empowering judges to set minimum sentences, and §3(2) dealing with consecutive sentences) are not ones we would personally advocate. It is set forth, not as an "ideal" statute, but for the purposes of illustrating the discussion in Chapter 9.

In early 1978, the Oregon Parole Board issued a new set of standards under this statute, which are set forth in Chapter 254 of the Oregon Administrative Rules.

Chapter 372

Be It Enacted by the People of the State of Oregon:

SECTION 1. (1) There is hereby established an Advisory Commission on Prison Terms and Parole Standards consisting of 11 members. Five members of the commission shall be the voting members of the State Board of Parole.

Five members of the commission shall be circuit court judges appointed by the Chief Justice of the Supreme Court. The legal counsel to the Governor shall serve as an ex officio member of the commission and shall not vote unless necessary to break a voting deadlock. The Administrator of the Corrections Division shall act as an advisor to the commission.

(2) The term of office of each of the members appointed by the Chief Justice is four years. Before the expiration of the term of any of those members, the Chief Justice shall appoint a successor whose term begins on July 1 next following. A member is eligible for reappointment. If there is a vacancy for any cause, the Chief Justice shall make an appointment to become immediately effective for the unexpired term.

(3) Notwithstanding the term of office specified by subsection (2) of this section, of the members first appointed by the Chief Justice:

(a) One shall serve for a term ending June 30, 1978.

(b) One shall serve for a term ending June 30, 1979.

(c) One shall serve for a term ending June 30, 1980.

(d) Two shall serve for a term ending June 30, 1981.

(4) A member of the commission shall receive no compensation for his services as a member. However, all members may receive actual and necessary travel and other expenses incurred in the performance of their official duties under ORS 292.495.

(5) The chairman of the State Board of Parole and a judge elected by the judicial members shall serve in alternate years as chairman of the commission. The chairman and a vice chairman shall be elected prior to July 1 of each year to serve for the year following. The commission shall adopt its own bylaws and rules of procedure. Six members shall constitute a quorum for the transaction of business. An affirmative vote of six members shall be required to make proposals to the board under this Act.

(6) The commission shall meet at least annually at a place and time determined by the chairman and at such other times and places as may be specified by the chairman or five members of the commission.

(7) The State Board of Parole shall provide the commission with the necessary clerical and secretarial staff support and shall keep the members of the commission fully informed of the experience of the board in applying the standards derived from those proposed by the commission.

(8) The commission shall propose to the State Board of Parole and the board shall adopt rules establishing ranges of duration of imprisonment and variations from the ranges. In establishing the ranges and variations, factors provided in sections 2 and 3 of this Act shall be considered. The rules adopted and any amendments thereto which may be adopted shall be submitted to the Sixtieth Legislative Assembly. The Sixtieth Legislative Assembly may amend, repeal or supplement any of the rules.

SECTION 2. (1) The commission shall propose to the board and the board shall adopt rules establishing ranges of duration of imprisonment to be served for felony offenses prior to release on parole. The range for any offense shall be within the maximum sentence provided for that offense.

(2) The ranges shall be designed to achieve the following objectives:

(a) Punishment which is commensurate with the seriousness of the prisoner's criminal conduct; and

(b) To the extent not inconsistent with paragraph (a) of this subsection:

(A) The deterrence of criminal conduct; and

(B) The protection of the public from further crimes by the defendant.

(3) The ranges, in achieving the purposes set forth in subsection (2) of this section, shall give primary weight to the seriousness of the prisoner's present offense and his criminal history.

SECTION 3. (1) The commission shall propose to the board and the board shall adopt rules regulating variations from the ranges, to be applied when aggravating or mitigating circumstances exist. The rules shall define types of circumstances as aggravating or mitigating and shall set the maximum variation permitted.

(2) When a prisoner is sentenced to two or more consecutive terms of imprisonment, the duration of the term of imprisonment shall be the sum of the terms set by the board pursuant to the ranges established for the offenses, subject to variations established pursuant to subsection (1) of this section.

(3) In no event shall the duration of the actual imprisonment under the ranges or variations from the ranges exceed the maximum term of imprisonment fixed for an offense, except in the case of a prisoner who has been sentenced under ORS 161.725 as a dangerous offender, in which case the maximum term shall not exceed 30 years.

SECTION 4. (1) In any felony case, the court may impose a minimum term of imprisonment of up to one-half of the sentence it imposes.

(2) Notwithstanding the provisions of sections 2 and 5 of this Act:

(a) The board shall not release a prisoner on parole who has been sentenced under subsection (1) of this section until the minimum term has been served, except upon affirmative vote of at least four members of the board.

(b) The board shall not release a prisoner on parole who has been convicted of murder defined as aggravated murder under the provisions of ORS 163.095, except as provided in ORS 163.105.

SECTION 5. (1) Within six months of the admission of a prisoner to any state penal or correctional institution, the board shall conduct a parole hearing to interview the prisoner and set the initial date of his release on parole pursuant to subsection (2) of this section. Release shall be contingent upon satisfaction of the requirements of section 6 of this Act.

(2) In setting the initial parole release date for a prisoner pursuant to subsection (1) of this section, the board shall apply the appropriate range established pursuant to section 2 of this Act. Variations from the range shall be in accordance with section 3 of this Act.

(3) In setting the initial parole release date for a prisoner pursuant to subsection (1) of this section, the board shall consider reports, statements and information received under ORS 144.210 from the sentencing judge, the district attorney and the sheriff or arresting agency.

(4) Notwithstanding subsection (1) of this section, in the case of a prisoner whose offense included particularly violent or otherwise dangerous criminal conduct or whose offense was preceded by two or more convictions for a Class A or Class B felony or whose record includes a psychiatric or psychological diagnosis of severe emotional disturbance, the board may choose not to set a parole date.

(5) After the expiration of six months after the admission of the prisoner to any state penal or correctional institution, the board may defer setting the initial parole release date for the prisoner for a period not to exceed 30 additional days pending receipt of psychiatric or psychological reports, criminal records or other information essential to formulating the release decision.

(6) When the board has set the initial parole release date for a prisoner, it shall inform the sentencing court of the date.

SECTION 6. (1) Prior to the scheduled release on parole of any prisoner and prior to release rescheduled under this section, the board shall interview each prisoner to review his parole plan, his psychiatric or psychological report, if any, and the record of his conduct during confinement.

(2) The board shall postpone a prisoner's scheduled release date if it finds, after hearing, that the prisoner engaged in serious misconduct during his confinement. The board shall adopt rules defining serious misconduct and specifying periods of postponement for such misconduct.

(3) If a psychiatric or psychological diagnosis of present severe emotional disturbance has been made with respect to the prisoner, the board may order the postponement of the scheduled parole release until a specified future date.

(4) Each prisoner shall furnish the board with a parole plan prior to his scheduled release on parole. The board shall adopt rules specifying the elements of an adequate parole plan and may defer release of the prisoner for not more than three months if it finds that the parole plan is inadequate. The Corrections Division shall assist prisoners in preparing parole plans.

SECTION 7. The board shall adopt rules consistent with the criteria in section 2 of this Act relating to the rerelease of persons whose parole has been revoked.

SECTION 8. (1) Notwithstanding the provisions of ORS 179.495, prior to a parole hearing or other personal interview, each prisoner shall have access to the written materials which the board shall consider with respect to his release on parole, with the exception of materials exempt from disclosure under paragraph (d) of subsection (2) of ORS 192.500.

(2) The board and the Administrator of the Corrections Division shall jointly adopt procedures for a prisoner's access to written materials pursuant to this section.

SECTION 9. The board shall state in writing the detailed bases of its decisions under sections 4 to 6 of this Act.

SECTION 10. (1) Whenever any person is convicted of a felony, the Corrections Division shall furnish a presentence report to the sentencing court. If a presentence report has previously been prepared by the Corrections Division with respect to the defendant, the division shall furnish a copy of that report, and a supplement bringing it up to date, to the sentencing court. The reports shall contain recommendations with respect to the sentencing of the defendant, including incarceration or alternatives to incarceration whenever the Corrections Division officer preparing the report believes such an alternative to be appropriate. All recommendations shall be for the information of the court and shall not limit the sentencing authority of the court.

(2) The commission shall propose to the board and the board shall adopt rules establishing a uniform presentence report form for use pursuant to subsection (1) of this section.

Section 11. ORS 137.079 is amended to read:

137.079. (1) A copy of the presentence report and all other written information concerning the defendant that the court considers in the imposition of sentence shall be made available to the district attorney, the defendant or his counsel a reasonable time before the sentencing of the defendant. All other written information, when received by the court outside the presence of counsel, shall either be summarized by the court in a memorandum available for inspection or summarized by the court on the record before sentence is imposed.

(2) The court may except from disclosure parts of the presentence report or other written information described in subsection (1) of this section which are not relevant to a proper sentence, diagnostic opinions which might seriously disrupt a program of rehabilitation if known by the defendant, or sources of information which were obtainable with an expectation of confidentiality.

(3) If parts of the presentence report or other written information described in subsection (1) of this section are not disclosed under subsection (2) of this section, the court shall inform the parties that information has not been disclosed and shall state, for the record the reasons for the court's action. The action of the court in excepting information shall be reviewable on appeal.

Section 12. ORS 137.120 is amended to read:

137.120. (1) Each minimum period of imprisonment in the penitentiary which prior to June 14, 1939, was provided by law for the punishment of felonies, and each such minimum period of imprisonment for felonies, hereby is abolished.

(2) Whenever any person is convicted of a felony, the court shall, unless it imposes other than a sentence to serve a term of imprisonment in the custody of the Corrections Division, sentence such person to imprisonment for an indeterminate period of time, but stating and fixing in the judgment and sentence a maximum term for the crime, which shall not exceed the maximum term of imprisonment provided by law therefor; and judgment shall be given

accordingly. Such a sentence shall be known as an indeterminate sentence. The court shall state on the record the reasons for the sentence imposed.

(3) This section does not affect the indictment, prosecution, trial, verdict, judgment or punishment of any felony committed before June 14, 1939, and all laws now and before that date in effect relating to such a felony are continued in full force and effect as to such a felony.

Section 13. ORS 138.040 is amended to read:

138.040. The defendant may appeal to the Court of Appeals from a judgment on a conviction in a district or circuit court, including a judgment where the court imposes a sentence which is cruel, unusual or excessive in light of the nature and background of the offender or the facts and circumstances of the offense. Upon an appeal, any decision of the court in an intermediate order or proceeding may be reviewed. A judgment suspending imposition or execution of sentence or placing a defendant on probation shall be deemed a judgment on a conviction and shall not be subject to appeal after expiration of the time specified in ORS 138.071 except as may be provided in ORS 138.050 and 138.510 to 138.680. If in the judgment of the appellate court the punishment imposed by the sentence appealed from is cruel, unusual or excessive, the appellate court shall direct the court from which the appeal is taken to impose the punishment that should be administered.

Section 14. ORS 138.050 is amended to read:

138.050. A defendant who has pleaded guilty or no contest may take an appeal from a judgment on conviction where it imposes a sentence that is cruel, unusual or excessive in light of the nature and background of the offender or the facts and circumstances of the offense. If the judgment of conviction is in the circuit court or the district court, the appeal shall be taken to the Court of Appeals; if it is in the justice of the peace court or municipal court or city recorder's court, the appeal shall be taken to the circuit court of the county in which such court is located. On such appeal, the appellate court shall only consider the question whether an excessive, cruel or unusual punishment has been imposed. If in the judgment of the appellate court the punishment imposed is excessive, unusual or cruel, it shall direct the court from which the appeal is taken to impose the punishment which should be administered.

Section 15. ORS 144.035 is amended to read:

144.035. (1) In hearings conducted by the State Board of Parole, the board may sit together or in panels.

(2) Each panel shall consist of at least two members. The chairman of the board from time to time shall make assignments of members to the panels. The chairman of the board may participate on any panel and when doing so shall act as chairman of the panel. The chairman of the board may designate the chairman for any other panel.

(3) The chairman shall apportion matters for decision to the panels. Each panel shall have the authority to hear and determine all questions before it. However, if there is a division in the panel so that a decision is not unanimous, the chairman of the board shall reassign the matter and no issue so reassigned shall be decided by fewer than three affirmative votes.

(4) The provisions of subsections (1) to (3) of this section shall not apply to a decision to release a prisoner sentenced under subsection (1) of section 4 of this 1977 Act. In such cases, the board shall release the prisoner only upon affirmative vote of at least four members of the board.

Section 16. ORS 144.345 is amended to read:

144.345. Whenever the State Board of Parole considers an alleged parole violator and finds such person has violated one or more conditions of parole and the evidence offered in mitigation does not excuse or justify the violation, the board may revoke parole.

SECTION 17. The board shall comply with the rulemaking provisions of ORS chapter 183 in the adoption, amendment or repeal of rules pursuant to sections 2, 3, 6 to 8 and 10 of this Act.

SECTION 18. ORS 144.175, 144.180 and 144.221 are repealed.

Notes

CHAPTER 1: POSING THE QUESTION

1. Some indication of the use of parole in the United States is provided by the Uniform Parole Reports. In 1974, 61 percent of all felons released from prison were released on parole—nearly 74,000 individuals. Uniform Parole Reports, *Newsletter* (Davis, Cal.: National Council on Crime and Delinquency, March 1976), at Table 6. (The table is based on information from 49 states, the District of Columbia, Puerto Rico, and the Federal government.)

2. Jessica Mitford, *Kind and Usual Punishment* (New York: Knopf, 1973), at 294; Statement of Ernest van den Haag in 95th Cong., 1st Sess., Subcomm. on Criminal Laws and Procedures, Comm. on the Judiciary, U.S. Senate, *Hearings on S. 1437 etc.*, June 1977, Part XIII, at 8915, 8921.

Other advocates of abolition include: U.S. Attorneys General Griffin Bell and Edward Levi; Senator Edward Kennedy; Richard McGee, the former corrections director of California; the Citizens' Inquiry on Parole (in its study of New York parole); David Fogel, the former Executive Director of the Illinois Law Enforcement Commission; and David Stanley of the Brookings Institution (in a study of parole in six jurisdictions). Statement of Honorable Griffin Bell in *Hearings on S. 1437 etc.*, *supra* this note, at 8593, 8595; Address by Hon. Edward Levi before the Governors' Conference on Employment and the Prevention of Crime, Milwaukee, Wisconsin, February 2, 1976; Richard McGee, "A New Look at Sentencing: Part I," *Federal Probation* June 1974, at 3–8; and "Part II," September 1974, at 3–11; Citizens' Inquiry on Parole and Criminal Justice, *Prison Without Walls: Report on New York State Parole* (New York: Praeger, 1975); David Fogel, *We Are The Living Proof . . . : The Justice Model for Corrections* (Cincinnati: Anderson, 1975); and David T. Stanley, *Prisoners Among Us* (Washington, D.C.: The Brookings Institution, 1976).

3. Maine Revised Statutes, Title 17–A, chs. 47–53.

4. California, Indiana, and Illinois have abolished parole release; in the typical case, the board no longer determines duration of confinement. California abolished the Adult Authority and created a "Community Release Board" to administer parole supervision (supervision for one year for most offenders was continued), review the administration of good time, advise on pardons and commutations, and parole those few inmates sentenced to life terms. In Indiana, parole release is eliminated, but the parole board still will set periods of supervision up to a maximum of one year. In Illinois, the Parole and Pardon Board was abolished and a "Prisoner Review Board" was created; the board will determine release dates for inmates sentenced under the old code, review the administration of good time, advise in matters of executive clemency, and administer "mandatory supervised release" (inmates are released to supervision for a term of one, two, or three years, depending on the felony classification of the commitment offense). See California Penal Code §§ 1170, 3000, and 3040; Indiana Code §§ 35–50–1–1 to 35–50–6–6; and Illinois Statutes, Chapter 38 §§ 1003–3–1 to 1008–2–4.

5. See, e.g., State of Connecticut, Legislative Commission to Study Alternate Methods of Sentencing Criminals, *Report Presented to the Connecticut General Assembly* (Hartford, Conn.: October, 1977). See also Mark G. Neithercutt, "Parole Legislation," *Federal Probation*, March 1977, at 22; and Stephen Gettinger, "Three States Adopt Flat Time; Others Wary," *Corrections Magazine*, September 1974, at 16–17.

6. See Uniform Parole Reports, *supra* note 1, at table 3. In 1974, for the 47 states for which information is presented, the range in numbers paroled was from only 10 in one jurisdiction to 5,058 in another.

7. See, e.g., Don M. Gottfredson *et al.*, "Making Paroling Policy Explicit," 21 *Crime and Delinquency* 34 (1975); Don M. Gottfredson *et al.*, *Classification for Parole Decision Policy: Final Report* (Washington, D.C.: National Institute of Law Enforcement and Criminal Justice, 1978); Joseph E. Scott, "The Use of Discretion in Determining the Severity of Punishment for Incarcerated Offenders," 65 *Journal of Criminal Law and Criminology* 214 (1974); Anne M. Heinz *et al.*, "Sentencing by Parole Board: An Evaluation," 67 *Journal of Criminal Law and Criminology* 1 (1976); State of Connecticut, Commission on Parole Evaluation Techniques and Rehabilitation, *Staff Report*, (Hartford, Conn.: September, 1975); and Robert O. Dawson, "The Decision to Grant or Deny Parole," 1966 *Washington University Law Quarterly* 243 (1966).

8. See, e.g., Stanley, *supra* note 2, chs. 5, 6, 7.

9. See, e.g., Vincent O'Leary and Kathleen J. Hanrahan, *Parole Systems in the United States* (Hackensack, N.J.: National Council on Crime and Delinquency, 1976), at 1–25, and in greater detail, 82–344.

10. *Id.*, at 32–33, and 82–344. For citation in footnote: *id.*, at 33.

11. *Id.*, at 82–344. A few jurisdictions (e.g., Oregon and the U.S. Parole Commission) have recently moved to an early decision on the date of parole release. Soon after the admission to the institution, the inmate is notified of the period of time he can expect to serve before parole. Oregon Administrative Rules § 254–30–005; U.S. Parole Commission Rules § 2.12 in 42 *Federal Register* 39808, 39811 (1977).

12. In Georgia and Texas, however, parole hearings are the exception; most parole decisions are made on the basis of the inmate's institutional file. A third state, North Carolina, provides hearings only for those inmates thought to merit parole consideration after a review of the file. *Id.*, at 31.

13. One study of New York parole found that hearings ranged from 4 to 25 minutes, with the majority between 6 and 12 minutes. Citizens' Inquiry, *supra* note 2, at 86.

14. See note 7, *supra*.

15. See, e.g., Gottfredson *et al.*, "Making Paroling Policy Explicit," *supra* note 7.

16. See, e.g., Gottfredson *et al.*, *Classification for Parole Decision Policy: Final Report, supra* note 7, ch. 5.

17. For a description of the method of developing such guidelines, see Don M. Gottfredson, Leslie T. Wilkins, and Peter B. Hoffman, *Guidelines for Parole and Sentencing* (Lexington, Mass.: Lexington Books, 1978).

18. Parole guidelines are becoming more common. Oregon, Minnesota, and New York are using guidelines, and Florida has just enacted legislation that would require their use. Oregon Administrative Rules §§ 254–30–030 thru 254–30–055 (1978); Minnesota Department of Correction Rules § 7–104 (1977); New York State Division of Parole Rules §§ 8005, 8010 (1978); Fla. Session Laws, 1978, ch. 78–417.

At present, there is no national information on the use of guidelines. A study now in progress will address this question. That study will survey recent changes in legislation, policy, or court decisions that affect parole discretion, particularly release discretion. Preliminary findings suggest that in addition to the boards listed above, Maryland is using guidelines, and the following states are developing guidelines: Alaska, Kentucky, Missouri, Washington, and Wisconsin. Vincent O'Leary and Lawrence F. Travis, National Parole Institutes, National Council on Crime and Delinquency (in progress). (Preliminary findings were made available to the authors by Lawrence Travis, letter on file with the Graduate School of Criminal Justice, Rutgers University.)

19. For information on parole conditions, see, e.g., Resource Center on Correctional Law and Legal Services, *Survey of Parole Conditions in the United States* (Washington, D.C.: Commission on Correctional Facilities and Services, American Bar Association, December, 1973); and William C. Parker, *Parole* (College Park, Md.: American Correctional Association, 1975).

20. See Elliot Studt, *Surveillance and Service in Parole—A Report of the Parole Action Study* (Washington, D.C.: National Institute of Corrections, reprinted 1978).

21. O'Leary and Hanrahan, *supra* note 9, at 73–78.

22. The requirements of due process at revocation were determined by the Supreme Court in Morrissey v. Brewer, 408 U.S. 471 (1972), and Gagnon v. Scarpelli, 411 U.S. 778 (1973). A summary of these requirements can be found in Chapter 6, *infra*.

23. For a breakdown of the number of jurisdictions that credit street time, see Chapter 6, note 6, *infra*.

24. Two boards, the Federal Parole Commission and the Oregon Parole Board, have issued guidelines governing duration of reconfinement in revocations. See Chapter 7, text at notes 16 and 17, *infra* for a brief description.

25. M. Kay Harris, "Disquisition on the Need for a New Model for Criminal Sanctioning Systems," 77 *West Virginia Law Review* 263, 297 (1975).

26. See notes 17 and 18 *supra*, concerning use of parole guidelines; and concerning improved procedures, note 11 *supra*, and O'Leary and Hanrahan, *supra* note 9, at 31–72.

27. See, e.g., Robert Martinson, "What Works?—Questions and Answers About Prison Reform," *The Public Interest*, Spring 1974, at 22–54; and, in more detail, Douglas Lipton, Robert Martinson, and Judith Wilks, *The Effectiveness of Correctional Treatment: A Survey of Treatment Evaluation Studies* (New York: Praeger, 1975); and David F. Greenberg, "The Correctional Effects of Corrections: A Survey of Evaluations," in David F. Greenberg, ed., *Corrections and Punishment* (Beverly Hills, Cal.: Sage Publications, 1977), at 111–148.

28. See, e.g., Harris, *supra* note 25, at 299.

29. *Id.* at 301.

30. Studt, *supra* note 20, ch. 5.

31. Stanley, *supra* note 2, at 190.

32. See, e.g., Andrew von Hirsch, *Doing Justice: The Choice of Punishments* (New York: Hill and Wang, 1976), chs. 8 and 15.

CHAPTER 2: GENERAL ASSUMPTIONS

1. See Andrew von Hirsch, *Doing Justice: The Choice of Punishments* (New York: Hill and Wang, 1976), ch. 1; see also American Bar Association, Joint Committee on the Legal Status of Prisoners, "Tentative Draft of Standards Relating to the Legal Status of Prisoners," 14 *American Criminal Law Review* 377, 417–420 (1977).

2. One commentator has described the position of sentencing judges as follows:

... the judge has no guide except a statutory mandate such as not less than one year nor more than fifteen years. He can do as he pleases within the limits. If he chooses he can focus on the crime alone without considering the criminal. He can act without a pre-sentence investigation. He can be guided by a theory of rehabilitation, retribution or deterrence—or by no theory. He can give a wholly emotional response ... without making any effort to find a rational basis for any facet of his decision. He can announce his decision without findings, without reasons, without relating what he does with what he has done before, and without relating his decision to the relevant questions of other judges. His discretionary power is so much at large that review by an appellate court would usually be futile.

Kenneth Culp Davis, *Discretionary Justice: A Preliminary Inquiry*, (Chicago: University of Illinois Press, 1971), at 137–38. For a similar description of the traditional parole process, see Chapter 1 *supra*, text at note 25.

3. See, e.g., *Doing Justice, supra* note 1, ch. 4; Marvin E. Frankel, *Criminal Sentences* (New York: Hill and Wang, 1972); Anthony Partridge and William B. Eldridge, *The Second Circuit Sentencing Study: A Report to the Judges of the Second Circuit* (Washington, D.C.: Federal Judicial Center, 1974); L. Paul Sutton, *Criminal Sentencing: An Empirical Analysis of Variations in Sentences Imposed in Federal District Courts*, Ph.D. dissertation, State University of New York at Albany (Ann Arbor, Mich.: University Microfilm, 1975).

4. Frankel, *id.*, at 10.

5. See, e.g., Zebulon R. Brockway, "The Ideal of a True Prison System for a State," in *Transactions of the National Congress on Penitentiary and Reformatory Discipline*, October 1870 (Albany, N.Y.: Weed, Parsons & Co., 1871), at 38; American Correctional Association, "Declaration of Principles," in *Manual of Correctional Standards* (Washington, D.C.: American Correctional Association, 1959), at xxi.

6. American Law Institute, *Model Penal Code: Proposed Official Draft* (Philadelphia: American Law Institute, 1962), § 7.01(1).

7. Erving Goffman, *Asylums* (Garden City, New York: Anchor Books, 1961); and see, e.g., David Rothman, "Decarcerating Prisoners and Patients," 1 *Civil Liberties Review* 8 (1973); Gresham M. Sykes, *The Society of Captives* (Princeton: Princeton University Press, 1958); and Donald Clemmer, *The Prison Community* (New York: Holt, Reinhart and Winston, 1940).

8. See, e.g., *Doing Justice, supra* note 1, at 5.

9. See Note, "The Parole System," 120 *University of Pennsylvania Law Review* 282, 286–300 (1971); and Fred Cohen, *The Legal Challenge to Corrections*, A consultant's paper prepared for the Joint Commission on Correctional Manpower and Training (Washington, D.C.: March, 1969).

CHAPTER 3: THE PURPOSES OF PUNISHING—THE DESERT AND MODIFIED DESERT MODELS

1. For citation in footnote: These definitions are taken from Andrew von Hirsch *Doing Justice: The Choice of Punishments* (New York: Hill and Wang, 1976), at 11, 19, and 38.

Further refinement of the definition of "rehabilitation" is found in a recent paper by John Monahan. He points out that in speaking of rehabilitation, one is: (1) speaking only of forms of *planned* intervention—as opposed to the spontaneous reform of the offender while undergoing punishment; and (2) referring to efforts to reduce the probability of recidivism *below* what other, nonprogram influences (such as aging, or the effects of deterrence) could account for. See John Monahan, "The Role of Rehabilitation and Special Deterrence in the Criminal Justice System," Preliminary Report to the Panel on Research on Rehabilitative Techniques, Committee on Research on Law Enforcement and Criminal Justice, National Academy of Sciences, Washington, D.C. (November, 1977) (unpublished).

2. Leon Radzinowicz, *Ideology and Crime* (New York: Columbia University Press, 1966), chs. 2 and 3; David Rothman, "Decarcerating Prisoners and Patients," 1 *Civil Liberties Review* 8 (1973).

3. See, e.g., Johannes Andenaes, "The General Preventive Effects of Punishment," 114 *University of Pennsylvania Law Review* 949 (1966).

4. For philosophical discussions, see, e.g., J.D. Mabbott "Punishment," 48 *Mind* 152 (1939); C.W.K. Mundle, "Punishment and Desert," 4 *Philosophical Quarterly* 216 (1954); K.G. Armstrong, "The Retributivist Hits Back," 70 *Mind* 471 (1961); H.J. McCloskey, "A Non-Utilitarian Approach to Punishment," 8 *Inquiry* 249 (1965); Herbert Morris, "Persons and Punishment," 52 *The Monist* 475 (1966); H.L.A. Hart, "Prolegomenon to the Principles of Punishment," in his *Punishment and Responsibility* (New York: Oxford University Press, 1968); Joel Feinberg, *Doing and Deserving* (Princeton: Princeton University Press, 1970); Claudia Card, "Retributive Penal Liability," in *Studies in Ethics*, Monograph No. 7, American Philosophical Quarterly Monograph Series (Oxford: Basil Blackwell, 1973); John Kleinig, *Punishment and Desert* (The Hague: Martinus Nijoff, 1973); Joel Kidder, "Requital and Criminal Justice," 15 *International Philosophical Quarterly* 235 (1975); *Doing Justice, supra* note 1; Richard Wasserstrom, "Some Problems with Theories of Punishment," in J.B. Cederblom and William L. Blizek, eds., *Justice and Punishment* (Cambridge, Mass.: Ballinger, 1977); Herbert Fingarette, "Punishment and Suffering," 50 *Proceedings of the American Philosophical Association* 6 (August 1977); Don E. Scheid, *Theories of Legal Punishment*, Ph.D. dissertation, Department of Philosophy, New York University, June 1977 (unpublished); Hugo A. Bedau, "Retribution and the Theory of Punishment," 75 *Journal of Philosophy* 601 (1978).

For discussions in the legal and penological literature, see Norval Morris, *The Future of Imprisonment* (Chicago: University of Chicago Press, 1974), ch. 3; M. Kay Harris, "Disquisition on the Need for a New Model of Criminal Sanctioning Systems," 77 *West Virginia Law Review* 263 (1975); Martin R. Gardner, "The Renaissance of Retribution—An Examination of *Doing Justice*," 1976 *Wisconsin Law Review* 781 (1976); Frederic R. Kellogg, "From Retribution to 'Desert,' " 15 *Criminology* 179 (1977).

5. For a critique of attempts to be "neutral" on the different aims of punishment, see Andrew von Hirsch, Book Review (of O'Donnell, Churgin and Curtis, *Toward a Just and Effective Sentencing System*) 7 *Hofstra Law Review* No. 1 (1979) (in press).

6. *Doing Justice, supra* note 1, ch. 8.

7. For citation in footnote: *Id.*; and Kleinig, *supra* note 4.

8. The following discussion of the commensurate-deserts principle is drawn from *Doing Justice, supra* note 1, chs. 8 and 11.

9. *Id.*, ch. 6.

10. *Doing Justice, supra* note 1, at 129—130.

11. See, e.g., Citizens' Inquiry on Parole and Criminal Justice, *Prison Without Walls: A Report on New York Parole* (New York: Praeger, 1975), at 175.

12. *Doing Justice, supra* note 1; Kleinig, *supra* note 4.

13. *Doing Justice, supra* note 1, ch. 9.

14. *Doing Justice* devotes a chapter to raising some of the issues, but does not suggest answers. *Id.*

15. See, e.g., Thorsten Sellin and Marvin Wolfgang, *The Measurement of Delinquency* (New York: Wiley, 1964); Peter H. Rossi *et al.*, "The Seriousness

of Crimes: Normative Structure and Individual Differences," 39 *American Socio-logical Review* 224 (1974); Charles F. Wellford and Michael Wiatrowski, "On the Measurement of Delinquency," 66 *Journal of Criminal Law and Criminology* 175 (1975); Charles W. Thomas, Robin C. Cage, and Samuel Foster, "Public Opinion on Criminal Law and Legal Sanctions: An Examination of Two Concep-tual Models," 67 *Journal of Criminal Law and Criminology* 110 (1976): Dale K. Sechrest, "Comparisons of Inmate's and Staff's Judgments of the Severity of Offenses," 6 *Journal of Research in Crime and Delinquency* 41 (1976); Robert M. Figlio, "The Seriousness of Offenses: An Evaluation of Offenders and Non-Offenders," 66 *Journal of Criminal Law and Criminology* 189 (1975); and Arnold Rose and Arthur Prell, "Does the Punishment Fit the Crime? A Study in Social Validation," 61 *American Journal of Sociology* 247 (1955); Richard F. Sparks, Hazel G. Genn and David J. Dodd, *Surveying Victims: A Study of the Measurement of Criminal Victimization* (Chichester: Wiley, 1977), ch. 7.

16. Wolfgang has suggested that research on perceptions of seriousness be used for that purpose, Marvin E. Wolfgang, "Seriousness of Crime and a Policy of Juvenile Justice," in Short, ed., *Delinquency, Crime, and Society* (Chicago, University of Chicago Press, 1976), at 267–286.

17. Marvin Wolfgang is currently conducting a study of scaling seriousness of crime, using a large (30,000 households) representative sample. Approxi-mately 200 different offenses are being analyzed, including some that did not appear in the original Philadelphia study, such as a greater number of white-collar crimes, political corruption and bribery, corporate crime, and environ-mental offenses. The study is being conducted at the Center for Studies in Crim-inology and Criminal Law, University of Pennsylvania.

18. Marc Riedel, "Perceived Circumstances, Inferences of Intent and Judg-ments of Offense Seriousness," 66 *Journal of Criminal Law and Criminology* 201 (1975); *Doing Justice, supra* note 1, footnote at 82; Andrew von Hirsch, "Proportionality and Desert: A Reply to Bedau," 75 *Journal of Philosophy* 622 (1978); Chapter 9 *infra*, note 10.

19. Chapter 6 *infra*, text at notes 38 and 39.

20. See, Chapter 6, *infra*, note 39.

21. Compare *Doing Justice, supra* note 1, ch. 11, with Kleinig, *supra* note 4, ch. 7.

22. Norval Morris seems to suggest this view in his 1976 lecture, "Punish-ment, Desert and Rehabilitation," reprinted in 95th Congress, 1st Sess., Sub-comm. on Criminal Laws and Procedures, Comm. on the Judiciary, U.S. Senate, *Hearings on S. 1437 etc.*, June 1977, Part XIII, at 9306–9339.

23. This difficulty is recognized by Norval Morris in the just-cited essay, where he advocates that desert be used only to set upper and lower limits on the amount of punishment. To justify the unequal punishment of the equally deserving, he is forced to argue that equality of treatment is not one of the essential requirements of justice. *Id.*

24. The presumptive sentence device is recommended both in *Doing Jus-tice, supra* note 1, ch. 12, and Twentieth Century Fund, Task Force on Criminal Sentencing, *Fair and Certain Punishment* (New York: McGraw-Hill, 1976).

25. Twentieth Century Fund, *supra* note 24.

26. *Doing Justice, supra* note 1, chs. 12 and 16.

27. The U.S. Parole Commission has developed methods of "feeding back" decisions in individual cases, for use in reviewing its dispositional standards. While the Commission uses a somewhat different conceptual model from ours, these techniques could well be worth borrowing with appropriate modifications. See Don M. Gottfredson, Leslie T. Wilkins, and Peter B. Hoffman, *Guidelines for Parole and Sentencing* (Lexington, Mass.: Lexington Books, 1978), Appendix B.

28. See, e.g., the point system now used by the Oregon Parole Board in its parole release guidelines, Oregon Administrative Rules §§ 254–30–030 and 031, and Exhibits A and B thereto.

29. For fuller discussion, see *Doing Justice, supra* note 1, ch. 13.

30. *Id.*, chs. 13 and 16.

31. *Id.*, ch. 13.

32. Albert W. Alschuler, "Sentencing Reform and Prosecutorial Power: A Critique of Recent Proposals for 'Fixed' and 'Presumptive' Sentencing," 126 *University of Pennsylvania Law Review* 550 (1978); and, e.g., F.E. Zimring, "Making the Punishment Fit the Crime," *Hastings Center Report*, December 1976, at 13–17.

33. James Q. Wilson, "The Political Feasibility of Punishment," in J.B. Cederblom and William L Blizek, eds., *Justice and Punishment* (Cambridge, Mass.: Ballinger, 1977), at 107, 115–116.

34. At the time this book went to press, no evaluations of the effects of determinate penalty systems had been completed. However, a number of such evaluations are now underway. See, e.g., Chapter 9 *infra*, note 11.

35. Arthur Rosett and Donald R. Cressey, *Justice by Consent: Plea Bargains in the American Courthouse* (Philadelphia: J.B. Lippincott, 1976), ch. 7.

36. See, e.g., *Doing Justice, supra* note 1, at 106; and James Vorenberg, "Narrowing the Discretion of Criminal Justice Officials," 1976 *Duke Law Journal* 651, 680–82 (1976); but see, Alschuler, *supra* note 32, at 575–76.

37. Gottfredson, Wilkins, and Hoffman, *supra* note 27, at 136. The authors state:

> It seems that there may be little conflict between two apparently quite different options in model building. We know that the weightings and methods for deriving equations do not seem to make much difference to the power of prediction. Indeed, we have noted that simple weights of either unity or zero (applied to the individual items making the scores) generally provide the results equal to more sophisticated methods. We know also that equations that have different sets of items included provide equally good predictive performance—there is no particular set of items or weights which is clearly optimal in terms of predictive power. Clearly, one of the reasons for this is that the predictive items are also correlated with each other. It is, therefore, highly probable that equations could be found that reflected only the just-deserts theory, and that, at the same time, proved equally as predictive of success or failure as did equations that utilized items that were not justified by this theory. In operational terms, this could mean that the distinction between a predictive mode and a just-deserts mode could be moot! Despite the very different considerations and

highly significant theoretical and philosophical differences, the application could converge in one equation! For those who argue in favor of a strict desert model, this may be a philosophically *tidy* solution. Clearly, those who would advocate the just-deserts approach could not find any reasonable grounds to reject a set of guidelines merely because the means for quantifying the prior criminal record happened to be predictive.

38. See text *supra* at notes 19 and 20.

CHAPTER 4: THE CASE FOR AN EARLY TIME-FIX

1. "Indeterminacy" has been used to refer to a variety of sentencing structures. It is sometimes used to refer to a system in which the judge sets a minimum and maximum term within the statutory limits and the parole board determines the release date; in other instances, it refers to systems—such as California's, under its old law—in which the judge does not decide sentence duration, and the parole board fixes not only the moment of parole release but also the maximum duration of state control.

2. Vincent O'Leary and Kathleen Hanrahan, *Parole Systems in the United States* (Hackensack, N.J.: National Council on Crime and Delinquency, 1976), at 82–344.

3. As mentioned in Chapter 1, some parole boards have adopted guidelines that specify the period of confinement that should ordinarily be served by different categories of offenders (see ch. 1, *supra* note 18). Some other boards, while not having formal guidelines, may have some known "rules of thumb," e.g., that certain categories of offenders will be released at first eligibility. Either guidelines or rules of thumb may enable the inmate to predict when most people in his category are likely to leave prison. But even then, he cannot predict whether his own case will follow the norm, or fall in the minority of cases when the board chooses to go outside its guidelines or its usual practices.

Some jurisdictions have implemented "contract parole" programs for certain categories of offenders. While these programs are generally rehabilitative in aim, they do provide the inmate involved with a more definite idea of when he will be released. For description and discussion, see, e.g., American Correctional Association, "Mutual Agreement Programming," in Carter, Wilkins, and Glaser, eds., *Correctional Institutions*, 2nd ed. (Philadelphia: Lippincott, 1977), at 342; Leon Leiberg and William Parker, "Toward Change in Correctional Manpower Services: Mutual Agreement Programming," in Amos and Newman, eds., *Parole* (New York: Federal Legal Publications, 1975), at 363; Steven Gettinger, "Parole Contracts: A New Way Out," *Corrections Magazine*, September 1975, at 3; and James O. Finckenauer and Carol Rauh, "Contract Parole: Some Legal and Rehabilitative Issues of Mutual Agreement Programming for Parole Release," 5 *Capital University Law Review* 175 (1976).

4. Norval Morris, *The Future of Imprisonment* (Chicago: University of Chicago Press, 1974).

5. Richard McGee, "A New Look at Sentencing: Part I," *Federal Probation*, June 1974, at 3–8; and "Part II," September 1974, at 3–11.

6. David Fogel, *We Are the Living Proof . . . : The Justice Model for Corrections* (Cincinnati: Anderson, 1975).

7. David Stanley, *Prisoners Among Us* (Washington, D.C.: The Brookings Institution, 1976).

8. Citizens' Inquiry on Parole and Criminal Justice, *Prison Without Walls: Report on New York State Parole* (New York: Praeger, 1975).

9. Maine Statutes, Title 17–A, chs. 47–53.

10. California Penal Code §§ 1170, 3000 and 3040. These provisions originated in Chapter 1139 of the 1976 session laws. For an analysis of the new California sentencing law, see April K. Cassou and Brian Taugher, "Determinate Sentencing in California: The New Numbers Game," 9 *Pacific Law Journal* 5 (1978).

11. Indiana Penal Code §§ 35–50–1–1 through 35–50–6–6. These provisions were mainly added by P.L. 148 of the 1976 session laws.

12. Illinois Statutes, ch. 38, §§ 1003–3–1 through 1008–2–4. These provisions mainly derive from P.A. 80–1099 of the 1977 session laws.

13. Oregon Revised Statutes §§ 144.110–.125, 144.775–.790. These provisions were added by Chapter 372 of the session laws of 1977.

14. Florida Statutes § 947.16. This was added by Chapter 78–417 of the 1978 session laws.

15. U.S. Parole Commission Rules § 2.12, in 42 *Federal Register* 39808, 39811 (1977).

16. There are some exceptions: for example, parole release continues to be available in California for persons sentenced to life terms. California Penal Code § 3040.

17. Andrew von Hirsch, *Doing Justice: The Choice of Punishments* (New York: Hill and Wang, 1976), chs. 8 and 11; and Chapter 3 *supra*, text at note 21. *Doing Justice* distinguishes: (1) the overall magnitude of the penalty scale from (2) the scale's internal structure (that is, the *relative* amounts of punishment given different crimes). While *Doing Justice* suggests that crime-control aims such as deterrence may be considered to a limited extent in deciding the scale's overall magnitude, they should *not* be considered at all in deciding the internal structure of the scale. The latter should be decided exclusively by reference to the seriousness of the offender's criminal conduct.

18. *Doing Justice, supra* note 17, at 101–2.

19. Such skepticism could lead either to: (1) decriminalizing the conduct entirely; or (2) keeping its criminal status, but reducing its seriousness rating. Here, we are speaking of the second of these.

20. See Laurence H. Tribe, *American Constitutional Law* (Mineola, N.Y.: Foundation Press, 1978), at 477–484.

21. See, e.g., American Law Institute, *Model Penal Code: Proposed Official Draft* (Philadelphia: American Law Institute, 1962), § 7.01 (1)(a).

22. For citation in footnote, see James Q. Wilson, *Thinking About Crime* (New York: Basic Books, 1974), chs. 8 and 10. For an analysis of such effects, see, e.g., Shlomo Shinnar and Reuel Shinnar, "The Effects of the Criminal Justice System on the Control of Crime: A Quantitative Approach," 9 *Law and*

Society Review 581 (1975); Panel on Research on Deterrent and Incapacitative Effects, *Report*, in Blumstein, Cohen, and Nagin, eds., *Deterrence and Incapacitation: Estimating the Effects of Criminal Sanctions on Crime Rates* (Washington, D.C.: National Academy of Sciences, 1978), at 65−75.

23. For a summary of prediction techniques and their problems, see Don M. Gottfredson, "Assessment of Prediction Methods," in Johnson, Savitz, and Wolfgang, eds., *The Sociology of Punishment and Corrections*, 2nd ed. (New York: Wiley, 1970).

24. Morris, *supra* note 4, ch. 3.

25. Andrew von Hirsch, "Prediction of Criminal Conduct and Preventive Confinement of Convicted Persons," 21 *Buffalo Law Review* 717 (1972).

26. As summarized by Gottfredson:

> In a lengthy history of parole prediction studies, a number of consistently reported differentiators have been found. The most useful guides to prediction of parole violation behavior are indices of past criminal behavior . . .
>
> Offenders against persons have been found at least since 1923 to be generally better risks . . . than are offenders against property. . . . In general, the probability of parole violation decreases with age . . .
>
> Histories of opiate drug use or of alcoholic difficulties are unfavorable prognostic signs for parole performance; this has been found for both male and female parolees . . .
>
> The use of aliases has been found, in California's studies to be predictive of unfavorable parole performance among both male and female adult prisoners. When the offender's history reflects a criminal record for others in the person's immediate family, this too is an unfavorable prognostic sign.
>
> Recent studies indicate that a combination of life history information, which provides the main basis for prediction in most studies, when combined with data from personality testing may result in a superior prediction of parole violations. Measures of social maturity have been found helpful in predicting in a number of studies.

Gottfredson, *supra* note 23, at 758−59 (footnotes omitted).

Other reviews of the predictive utility of information have reached similar conclusions. See, e.g., Vincent O'Leary and Daniel Glaser, "The Assessment of Risk in Parole Decision Making," in West, ed., *The Future of Parole* (London: Duckworth, 1972); Daniel Glaser, *The Effectiveness of a Prison and Parole System*, abridged ed. (New York: Bobbs-Merrill, 1969), at 18−29; and Roger Hood and Richard Sparks, *Key Issues in Criminology* (New York: McGraw-Hill, 1970), at 180−81.

27. Gene Kassebaum, David Ward and Daniel Wilner, *Prison Treatment and Parole Survival* (New York: Wiley, 1971), at 224.

28. See, for example, the United State Parole Commission's prediction index, known as the "Salient Factor Score." See U.S. Parole Commission, Research Unit, "Salient Factor Scoring Manual, Revised," *Report 14*, March 1977.

For citation in footnote: see, e.g., John L. Coffee, Jr., "The Repressed Issues in Sentencing: Accountability, Predictability and Equality in the Era of the Sentencing Commission," 66 *Georgetown Law Journal* 975 (1978).

29. John Monahan, "The Prediction of Violent Criminal Behavior: A Methodological Critique and Prospectus," in Blumstein, Cohen, and Nagin, *supra* note 22, at 244–269.

30. Concerning the MMPI, see, e.g., James H. Panton, "Use of the MMPI as an Index to Successful Parole," 53 *Journal of Criminal Law, Criminology and Police Science* 484 (1962); Harrison G. Gough, Ernest A Wenk, and Vitali V. Rozynko, "Parole Outcome as Predicted from the CPI, the MMPI and a Base Expectancy Table," 70 *Journal of Abnormal Psychology* 432 (1965); James L. Mack, "The MMPI and Recidivism," 74 *Journal of Abnormal Psychology* 432 (1969); and Nathan G. Mandel and Alfred J. Barron, "The MMPI and Criminal Recidivism," 57 *Journal of Criminal Law, Criminology and Police Science* 35 (1966). Concerning the California Personality Inventory, see, e.g., Kassebaum, Ward, and Wilner, *supra* note 27; and Gough, Wenk, and Rozynko, *supra* this note.

Panton used a subscale of the Minnesota Multiphasic Personality Inventory (MMPI), and reported success in identifying 80.5 percent of both parole violators and nonviolators; two other studies using the MMPI reached different conclusions. Mack found that "the MMPI, considered alone, is not associated with recidivism to any important extent within such homogeneous populations as the present one, although the existence of a minimal association, of doubtful predictive utility, cannot be ruled out." Mandel and Barron attempted to: (1) test the ability of five psychologists to "blind sort" admission and prerelease MMPI profiles of offenders into recidivist and nonrecidivist categories; and (2) develop a scale for the MMPI that would have predictive value in identifying recidivist values. Both efforts were unsuccessful. With respect to the "blind sort," the authors conclude (at 36):

> We are therefore in agreement with Clark (1948) that "blind" inspectional analysis of MMPI profiles alone does not yield significant differences between groups of the type under consideration and that such analysis is of little or no value in predicting future recidivistic and non-recidivistic behavior in individual cases. This is by no means to say, however, that the interpretation of a single profile in conjunction with the evaluation of other information such as past history, interview and observational data, etc., provides no added predictive value. On the contrary, the authors believe that the use of the MMPI in this way makes a genuine contribution to the accurate prediction in the individual case, but they know of no studies which have corroborated this.

The predictive utility of the California Personality Inventory has also been tested. Kassebaum, Ward, and Wilner used the CPI scores on a subgroup of the parolees in their study in an attempt to explain parole performance. They found that "personality characteristics as measured by the CPI, were not significantly related to parole success." The Gough, Wenk and Rosynko study compared the predictive utility of the California Youth Authority Base Expectancy, the MMPI and the CPI, alone and in combination with each other. The findings indicated, on cross-validation, that the single best predictor was the Base Expectancy Score, but that some increase in predictive ability could be obtained by combining certain of the scales of the CPI with the information of the Base Expectancy.

31. Of those studies cited in the preceding note, only one clearly used personality tests administered both "early" (upon admission to prison) and "late" (prior to the parole decision). It seemed to make no difference whether the early or late information was used. (Mandel and Barron, *id.*) Kassebaum, Ward, and Wilner used CPI scores obtained shortly before parole release, but found no relation with parole success. (Kassebaum, Ward, and Wilner, *supra* note 27.)

32. For review of some of these studies, see Douglas Lipton, Robert Martinson, and Judith Wilks, *The Effectiveness of Correctional Treatment: A Survey of Treatment Evaluation Studies* (New York: Praeger, 1975), at 87; O'Leary and Glaser, *supra* note 26, at 157−59; and Stanley, *supra* note 7, at 53−55.

33. Norval Morris suggests that behavior on partial release might have predictive usefulness, although he does not advocate deciding duration-of-confinement on predictive grounds. Morris, *supra* note 4, at 41−42.

34. The only studies have been treatment rather than prediction studies, which tried to measure whether participation in work release, prerelease or half-way-house programs reduced participants' rate of return to crime. The results were mixed; as one survey concludes:

> This review of programs designed to ease the transition from prison to free community has highlighted two major items:
>
> (1) With minor reservation, the majority of agencies administering the programs report that graduated release is beneficial to the offender and to society, and should be expanded, and
>
> (2) The more rigorous the methodology used with research and experiments undertaken in regard to prerelease, work release, and halfway houses, the more ambivalent or negative are the findings regarding the efficacy of such programs.

National Institute of Mental Health, *Graduated Release*, Crime and Delinquency Topics (1971) at 23; see also Lipton, Martinson, and Wilks, *supra* note 32 at 269−81, 529−31; and David F. Greenberg, "The Correctional Effects of Corrections: A Survey of Evaluations," in Greenberg, ed., *Corrections and Punishment* (Beverly Hills, Cal.: Sage, 1977), at 111, 122−24.

35. See, Paul Meehl, *Clinical Versus Statistical Prediction* (Minneapolis: University of Minnesota Press, 1954); and Harrison Gough, "Clinical vs. Statistical Prediction in Psychology," in Postman, ed., *Psychology in the Making* (New York: Knopf, 1962); and Monahan, *supra* note 29. Monahan reports that statistical prediction methods have not shown "the same superiority over the clinical method in the case of violence as it has with the prediction of other behaviors." He suggests, however, that this finding can be accounted for by the relative lack of study of actuarial methods for predicting violence, rather than any inherent superiority of clinical methods. In his words (at 258):

> There have been few actuarial studies of any sort, and all have relied on data from a single source (the California Department of Corrections).

It would seem that actuarial methods need to be pursued with more vigor before an exception is declared to the general superiority of actuarial over clinical prediction.

36. In the case of prediction of violence, for example, Monahan's review of clinical studies reports; *id.* at 250, that: "the conclusion to emerge most strikingly from these studies is the great degree to which violence is overpredicted. Of those predicted to be dangerous, between 54 and 99 percent were false positives. . . . "

37. Walter G. Bailey, "An Evaluation of 100 Studies of Correctional Outcomes," in Johnson, Savitz, and Wolfgang, eds., *supra* note 23, at 783.

38. James Q. Robinson and Gerald Smith, "The Effectiveness of Correctional Programs," 17 *Crime and Delinquency* 67, 80 (1971).

39. Lipton, Martinson, and Wilks, *supra* note 32.

40. Greenberg, *supra* note 34.

41. See, e.g., Ted Palmer, "Martinson Revisited," 12 *Journal of Research in Crime and Delinquency* 133 (1975).

42. See, e.g., Robert Martinson and Judith Wilks, "Knowledge in Criminal Justice Planning: A Preliminary Report." New York, Center for Knowledge in Criminal Justice Planning, Oct. 15, 1976.

43. See Marvin E. Frankel, *Criminal Sentences* (New York: Hill and Wang, 1972), at 90.

44. See, e.g., Lipton, Martinson, and Wilks, *supra* note 32.

45. Greenberg, *supra* note 34, at 122–24. A brief review of some of these studies is also provided by the National Institute of Mental Health, *Graduated Release, supra* note 34.

46. There are two distinct issues to be considered. The first—which we are discussing in the text—is how long the treatment program will last. We are suggesting that the information needed to estimate its duration may be knowable early. The second issue is whether, if the offender performs poorly in the treatment program, this is grounds for postponing his release. This is an issue of *prediction*: namely, whether a particular item of "late" information (the offender's good or poor performance in the program) is a better forecaster of his returning to crime than early information (e.g., about his criminal history). It should be noted that even if the program can meet tests of effectiveness as a rehabilitative program, it is not necessarily a good predictor, for the tests of success are different. With treatment, the test is: do participants in the program recidivate, as a group, less often than an otherwise-similar group of nonparticipants? With the prediction, the test is: is the *quality* of the offender's performance in the program a useful sign of likelihood of returning to crime? As to the latter question, our analysis regarding prediction—set forth in the text at notes 23–36 and 50–52—would hold.

47. The most comprehensive current survey and analysis of the deterrence literature concludes that current ability to measure the magnitude of deterrent effects is quite limited. Panel on Research on Deterrent and Incapacitative Effects, *Report*, in Blumstein, Cohen, and Nagin, *supra* note 22, at 19–63.

48. See, e.g., Johannes Andenaes, "General Prevention Revisited: Research and Policy Implications," 66 *Journal of Criminal Law and Criminology* 338, 347

(1975); and Franklin E. Zimring and Gordon Hawkins, *Deterrence, Legal Threat in Crime Control* (Chicago: University of Chicago Press, 1973), ch. 4; *Doing Justice, supra* note 17, ch. 7.

49. For citation in footnote: Little research has been conducted on public knowledge of criminal penalties, but a study conducted in California found widespread ignorance. Among the subsamples of the study, however, ignorance of the penalties was not evenly distributed: those who had been incarcerated were correct more often than the general population. Dorothy Miller et al., "Public Knowledge of Criminal Penalties: A Research Report," in *Deterrent Effects of Criminal Sanctions, Progress Report of the Assembly Committee on Criminal Procedure* (California Legislature, Assembly, 1968); and see Berl Kutchinsky, " 'The Legal Consciousness': A Survey of Research on Knowledge and Opinion About Law," in Podogorecki et al., eds., *Knowledge and Opinion About Law* (S. Hackensack, N.J.: Rothman, 1973), particularly at 103–108.

50. As Hood and Sparks note:

> ... the accuracy and reliability of prediction tables depend to a large extent on the identification of factors associated with reconviction. This in turn depends entirely on the quality of information which is available about offenders; and at the moment this is very low, wherever research is based on administrative records routinely kept by correctional agencies. Almost invariably such personal and social data as are available in these records are haphazardly recorded, and are thus likely to be missing or inaccurate for a high proportion of cases. ...

Hood and Sparks, *supra* note 26, at 185.

51. For example, a Canadian study attempted to use information available *after* release to predict arrest at six, twelve, and twenty-four months. Use of those variables predicted marginally better than prerelease variables (a base expectancy score). The author notes, however:

> Post-release information does seem to improve predictive efficiency and is, for the most part, available within five weeks from date of release. However, our study has shown that this information is extremely difficult to obtain; unless it is collected for other reasons, then, perhaps it is not worth collecting such information for the small improvement in predictive ability alone.

Irwin Waller, *Men Released from Prison* (Toronto: University of Toronto Press, 1974), at 176.

52. See Don M. Gottfredson, Leslie T. Wilkins, and Peter B. Hoffman, *Guidelines for Parole and Sentencing* (Lexington, Mass.: Lexington Books, 1978), at 136 and ch. 5.

53. For citation in footnote: the pre-1977 procedures of the U.S. Parole Commission are described in Project, "Parole Release Decisionmaking and the Sentencing Process," 84 *Yale Law Journal* 810, 818–19, 901–02 (1975).

54. Frankel, *supra* note 43, at 97.

55. In addition to Frankel, *id.*, see, e.g., The American Friends Service Committee, *Struggle for Justice* (New York: Hill and Wang, 1971), at 93–96; Jessica Mitford, *Kind and Usual Punishment* (New York: Knopf, 1973) at 86–9; and

E. Barrett Prettyman, "The Indeterminate Sentence and the Right to Treatment," 11 *American Criminal Law Review* 7, 24—25 (1972).

56. Maurice L. Farber, "Suffering and Time Perspective of the Prisoner," in *University of Iowa Studies: Studies in Child Welfare* (1944), vol. 20, at 172—73, 177—78.

57. As will be discussed in Chapter 9, the time-fixing responsibility could be given either to a judge or to an administrative agency such as a parole board. In the latter case, there could still be an administrative appeal, such as the rules of the U.S. Parole Commission provide. U.S. Parole Rules, *supra* note 15, §§ 2.24 through 2.26.

58. Maine Statutes, *supra* note 9.

59. "Determining the Impact of Fundamental Changes in the Law and Implications for the Future: The Evaluation of the Maine Experience" (LEAA Grant No. 76—NI—99—0142, directed by Frederick A. Hussey and John H. Kramer, Pennsylvania State University (planned completion date, early 1979).

CHAPTER 5: THE EARLY TIME-FIX AND PROBLEMS OF THE PRISON

1. Two national surveys conducted by *Corrections Magazine* report increases in prison population across the country and severe overcrowding in several states. See, Steve Gettinger, "U.S. Prison Population Hits All-Time High," *Corrections Magazine*, March 1976, at 9; and Rob Wilson, "U.S. Prison Population Again Hits New High," *Corrections Magazine*, March 1977, at 3. A more recent national survey found that the number of inmates incarcerated on June 30, 1977 exceeded the institutional rated capacity by 21,485. The survey also found regional variation in the extent of crowding. See Andrew Rutherford, *et al.*, *Prison Population and Policy Choices, Vol. I: Preliminary Report to Congress* (Cambridge, Mass.: Abt Associates, 1977), at 18—20, and 104—116. See also, "Overcrowding in Prisons and Jails: Maryland Faces a Correctional Crisis," 26 *Maryland Law Review* 182 (1976); and "Task Force of Top Officials Sees 'Crisis in Corrections' in the Southern States," *Criminal Justice Newsletter* vol. 7, No. 3 (Feb. 2, 1976); U.S. Department of Justice, LEAA, NCJISS, *Prisoners in State and Federal Institutions on December 31, 1976*, National Prisoner Statistics, Bulletin SD—NPS—PSF—4 (Washington, D.C.: U.S. Government Printing Office, February 1978); and U.S. Department of Justice, LEAA, NCJISS, *Prisoners in State and Federal Institutions on December 31, 1977—Advance Report*, National Prison Statistics, Bulletin SD—NPS—FSF—5A (April, 1978).

2. The National Advisory Commission estimates the cost of construction for an institution at $30,000 to $50,000 per inmate, and operating costs at from $1,000 to more than $12,000 per inmate per year. National Advisory Commission on Criminal Justice Standards and Goals, *Corrections* (Washington, D.C.: U.S. Government Printing Office, 1973), at 352—53. More recently, the *mean* construction cost per bed has been calculated at $37,117 for high-security institutions, and $28,480 for mixed-security institutions. Neil M. Singer and Virginia B. Wright, *Cost Analysis of Correctional Standards: Institutional-Based Programs and Parole* (Washington, D.C.: American Bar Association, 1975), Vol. 1, at 4.

Nevertheless, many states are planning construction. See Rutherford, *et al.*, *supra* note 1, at 118−29.

3. See, e.g., Rutherford *et al.*, *supra* note 1, at 9−10.

4. A brief review of the literature on overcrowding and human behavior is provided by Megargee. His study, designed to examine the relationship between population size and disciplinary reports in a prison for male youthful offenders, found "a clear association between restriction on personal space and the occurrence of disruptive and aggressive behavior." However, Megargee did not examine "write-ups" for disruptive and aggressive behavior separately, so no firm conclusion about the relationship between crowding and aggressive behavior can be drawn from his research. Edwin I. Megargee, "Population Density and Disruptive Behavior in a Prison Setting," in Cohen, Cole, and Bailey, *Prison Violence* (Lexington, Mass.: Lexington Books, 1976). See, also, Peter L. Nacci, Hugh E. Teitelbaum and Jerry Prather, "Population Density and Inmate Misconduct Rates in the Federal Prison System," *Federal Probation*, June 1977, at 26. (One early study does not seem to support the contention that overcrowding dramatically increases the discomforts of incarceration. See Donald Clemmer, "Some Aspects of Crowded Prisons," *American Correctional Association Proceedings*, 1957, at 28.)

Evidence of the adverse effects of overcrowding has been presented in recent prison litigation. Federal judges have begun to view prison conditions resulting from overcrowding as constituting "cruel and unusual punishment." See, for example, James v. Wallace, 406 F. Supp. 318 (M.D. Alabama, 1976), in which the court issued an order requiring the prison population to be reduced to design capacity for each facility, and prohibited the acceptance of new inmates (except escapees and revoked parolees) until the population had been so reduced; see also Costello v. Wainwright, 525 F.2d 1239 (5th Cir., 1976), in which the Florida Division of Corrections was ordered to lower the inmate population to "emergency capacity" within one year of the date of the decision, and to "normal capacity" thereafter; Gates v. Collier, 501 F.2d 1291 (5th Cir., 1974); Hamilton v. Schiro, 338 F.Supp. 1016 (E.D. Louisiana, 1970), Finney v. Arkansas Board of Corrections, 505 F.2d 194 (8th Cir., 1974); and McCray v. Sullivan, 399 F.Supp. 271 (S.D. Alabama, 1975).

5. This is a commonly asserted function of parole. See, e.g., Keith Hawkins, "Some Consequences of a Parole System for Prison Management," in West, ed., *The Future of Parole* (London: Duckworth, 1972), at 112−113; M. Kay Harris, "Disquisition on the Need for a New Model for Criminal Sanctioning Systems," 77 *West Virginia Law Review* 263, 305−306 (1975); and the National Advisory Commission, *supra* note 2, at 395.

6. Andrew Rutherford *et al.*, *supra* note 1, at 50−60, 71−78, 185.

7. Could one supplement this argument with one based on the idea of desert itself?

It is true that crowding affects the severity of imprisonment. The more overpopulated a prison becomes, the harsher its conditions. A given period of imprisonment—which would have been deserved for the offense had prison occupancy rates been normal—could thus become disproportionately severe once the prison became sufficiently overcrowded.

The difficulty is that, when one tries to alleviate crowding through shortening terms of imprisonment, it may have the opposite effect. To remedy the crowding, one may have to reduce the prison terms so much as to render them *less* severe than deserved. Therefore, we have based our argument not on desert, but on an obligation of avoiding cruelty that overrides even desert.

8. Obviously, one can debate at what point a sanction becomes unacceptably cruel. Prison abolitionists argue that imprisonment *per se* is so painful as to fall in this category. We are adopting a more conventional view by drawing the line at overcrowded prisons—given the special deprivation that overcrowding entails.

9. These bodies differ somewhat in their recommendations. On the question of minimum square footage for the prisoners' sleeping area, for example, the following standards have been proposed:

National Advisory Commission on Criminal Justice Standards and Goals	80 sq. ft. per inmate
Federal Bureau of Prisons	75 sq. ft. per inmate
National Clearinghouse for Criminal Justice Planning and Architecture	70 sq. ft. per inmate
United Nations Minimum Standards	65 sq. ft. per inmate
American Correctional Association	60 sq. ft. per inmate
Gates v. *Collier*, 390 F. Supp. 482 (N.D. Miss., 1975)	50 sq. ft. per inmate

Rutherford *et al.*, *supra* note 1, at 11.

10. *Id.*, at 159—190. Part of the present difficulty in projecting populations is uncertainty about future sentencing policies. Were durational standards under a Desert Model or Modified Desert Model adopted, that would be better known; but there still could be other areas of continuing uncertainty, such as prosecutors' response to the standards.

11. This function of parole has been mentioned by several authorities. See, e.g., Hawkins, *supra* note 5, at 98—106; Harris, *supra* note 5, at 305; S.H. Gifis, "Decision Making in a Prison Community," 1974 *Wisconsin Law Review* 349, 385 (1974); and Robert Kastenmeier and Howard Eglit, "Parole Release Decision-Making: Rehabilitation, Expertise and the Demise of Mythology," in Amos and Newman, eds., *Parole* (New York: Federal Legal Publications, 1975), at 97—99. In fact, the impact of parole on institutional discipline has been cited as one of the major reasons for the rapid spread of parole in this century. Attorney General's Survey of Release Procedures, *Parole* (1939) (New York: Arno Press, reprinted 1974), Vol. IV, at 34.

12. Peter B. Hoffman, "A Paroling Policy Feedback Method," in William B. Amos and Charles L. Newman, eds., *Parole* (New York: Federal Legal Publications, 1975), at 343, 356—58.

13. See, e.g., Joseph E. Scott, "The Use of Discretion in Determining the Severity of Punishment for Incarcerated Offenders," 65 *Journal of Criminal Law and Criminology* 214, 219 (1974); Anne M. Heinz *et al.*, "Sentencing by a Parole Board: An Evaluation," 67 *Journal of Criminal Law and Criminology* 1,

10−12 (1976); and see Don M. Gottfredson *et al.*, *Classification for Parole Decision Policy: Final Report* (Washington, D.C.: National Institute of Law Enforcement and Criminal Justice, 1978).

In addition, one survey of parole procedure found that in at least four states, inmate conduct may influence parole eligibility: in Colorado, an inmate who attacks another inmate or custodial officer with a deadly weapon is ineligible for parole; Kansas requires a minimum security classification before parole will be considered; New Mexico requires a good conduct record for the six months prior to parole eligibility; and in Wyoming, an inmate who has escaped, attempted escape, assisted in an escape, or assaulted another inmate or member of the staff is precluded from parole by law. Vincent O'Leary and Kathleen Hanrahan, *Parole Systems in the United States* (Hackensack, N.J.: National Council on Crime and Delinquency, 1976), at 32−33.

14. The National Advisory Commission, for example, recommends that criminal conduct by inmates be dealt with through prosecution. See National Advisory Commission, *supra* note 2, § 2.11 and Commentary; see also Commission on Accreditation for Corrections, *Manual of Standards for Adult Correctional Institutions* (Rockville, Md.: Commission on Accreditation for Corrections, August 1977), § 4320 (such cases should be "referred for consideration for criminal prosecution").

15. See the fuller discussion of standards of proof in Chapter 6 *infra*.

In Wolff v. McDonnell, 418 U.S. 549 (1974), the Supreme Court established the minimum procedural rights of inmates at disciplinary hearings where loss of good time credits or solitary confinement were possible penalties. The Court required written notice of the alleged violation, provided sufficiently in advance of the hearing to permit the inmate time to prepare (no less than 24 hours); provision for the inmate to present witnesses and documentary evidence if it "will not be unduly hazardous to institutional safety or correctional goals"; and, written statement by the factfinders as to the evidence relied upon and reasons for the disciplinary action taken. *Id.* at 563−67.

The Court specifically did not provide for confrontation or cross-examination of witnesses, *id.* at 567−69, leaving that matter "to the sound discretion of the officials of state prisons," *id.* at 569. Nor did they provide for assistance of counsel. However,

> Where an illiterate inmate is involved . . . or where the complexity of the issue makes it unlikely that the inmate will be able to collect and present the evidence necessary for an adequate comprehension of the case, he should be free to seek the aid of a fellow inmate, or if that is forbidden, to have adequate substitute aid in the form of help from the staff or from a sufficiently competent inmate designated by the staff. [*Id.* at 570.]

The partial dissents of Justices Marshall and Brennan, and of Justice Douglas, clearly state the problems left unsolved by the Court's ruling. See *id.* at 580−601.

Justices Marshall and Brennan state, for example:

> Today's decision deprives an accused inmate of any enforceable constitutional right to the procedural tools essential to the presentation of any

meaningful defense, and makes the required notice and hearing formalities of little utility. Without the enforceable right to call witnesses and present documentary evidence, an accused inmate is not guaranteed the right to present any defense beyond his own word. Without any right to confront and cross-examine adverse witnesses, the inmate is afforded no means to challenge the word of his accusers. Without these procedures, a disciplinary board cannot resolve disputed factual issues in any rational or accurate way. . . . In such a contest, it seems obvious to me that even the wrongfully charged inmate will invariably be the loser. [*Id.* at 581–82.]

16. See American Bar Association, Committee on the Legal Status of Prisoners, "Tentative Draft of Standards relating to the Legal Status of Prisoners," 14 *American Criminal Law Review* 377, 444–453 (1977).

17. Even in *Doing Justice*, where a Desert Model is otherwise espoused, some possible deviation from desert constraints is suggested for prison disciplinary cases. Andrew von Hirsch, *Doing Justice: The Choice of Punishments* (New York: Hill and Wang, 1976), at 130–131.

18. This has been suggested, for example, by Norval Morris in his *The Future of Imprisonment* (Chicago: University of Chicago Press, 1974), at 39–40.

19. Some indication of current problems in this area is provided by a survey conducted by the American Bar Association. The jurisdictions for which information was ascertainable (44) uniformly reported that institutional rules of conduct are in written form, and all but one jurisdiction reported that the rules are distributed to the inmates. Examination of the rules in some jurisdictions revealed many infractions that were "so vague and indefinite that it [was] difficult to differentiate between what might be permissible conduct and what might constitute a violation."

The survey also found that only 11 of the 44 jurisdictions indicated the sanctions that could be imposed for violation of the rules, suggesting that largely unfettered discretion in imposition of penalties exists for most disciplinary tribunals. American Bar Association, *Survey of Prison Disciplinary Practices and Procedures* (Washington, D.C.: A.B.A. Resource Center on Correctional Law and Legal Services, 1974), at 12–13.

20. It is frequently asserted that there is something akin to presumption of guilt at institutional disciplinary hearings. See, e.g., Richard G. Singer, "Confining Solitary Confinement: Constitutional Arguments for a 'New Penology,' 56 *Iowa Law Review* 1251, 1294–95 (1971); see also Gene Kassebaum, David A. Ward, and Daniel M. Wilner, *Prison Treatment and Parole Survival* (New York: Wiley, 1971), at 53, who state:

We sought to determine the chances an inmate had to be exonerated by the committee by relating the pleas and dispositions in 303 cases that were processed by the Disciplinary Committee during the course of our study; . . . those chances were about two in ten.

The fact that disciplinary committees find few inmates "not guilty" is not surprising when one is reminded that the members of the court consist of the senior staff members in the administrative hierarchy. The actions these men take are highly visible to all persons in the institution. The court can rarely afford to find inmates innocent because such a ruling implies that the reporting staff was wrong. For the morale of the rank-and-file correctional officers, such inferences cannot be permitted.

Our recommendation of an independent hearing body is found also in A.B.A. Committee on Legal Standards of Prisoners, *supra* note 16, at 452–53.

21. Oregon Revised Statutes § 144.125. The statute is set forth in Appendix III, and this provision found in § 6(2) as there set forth.

22. The new rules of the Oregon Parole Board implementing this provision are disappointing, however. The rules establish four degrees of "serious misconduct" each with different amounts of permitted time-extensions. However, the description of these four degrees of misconduct are extremely vague (e.g., "hazard to human life/health" and "hazard to security"). Oregon Administrative Rules § 254–30–055.

23. The Oregon board's current rules do specify a limit, but it is extremely (in our view, unacceptably) high: for the most serious infractions, the extension could be up to a doubling of the time served, subject to a five-year limit. *Id.*

24. For citation in footnote: for a description of *traditional* good-time statutes, see O'Leary and Hanrahan, *supra* note 13, at 33.

25. California Penal Law §§ 2930–2932. For discussion, see April Kestell Cassou and Brian Taugher, "Determinate Sentencing in California: The New Numbers Game," 9 *Pacific Law Journal* 1, 77–84 (1978).

26. McAnany *et al.* have warned that discretionary good-time provisions can result in a *de facto* retention of indeterminacy, with the problems of the parole release decision transferred, largely unchanged, to the disciplinary committee. See Patrick D. McAnany, Frank S. Merritt, and Edward Tromanhauser, "Illinois Reconsiders 'Flat Time': An Analysis of the Impact of the Justice Model," 52 *Chicago-Kent Law Review* 621, 652–56 (1976).

27. Indiana Penal Code §§ 35–50–6–1, 35–50–6–3, 35–50–6–4.

28. *Id.*, § 35–50–6–5.

29. See Todd R. Clear, John D. Hewitt, and Robert M. Regoli, "Discretion and the Determinate Sentence: Its Distribution, Control and Effect on Time Served," 24 *Crime and Delinquency* 428 (1978).

30. For fuller discussion, see, Andrew von Hirsch, "The New Indiana Sentencing Code: Is It Determinate Sentencing?" Paper presented at the colloquium of the Indiana Lawyers Commission, September 20–23, 1978, Indianapolis, Indiana (unpublished).

CHAPTER 6: PAROLE AS A SEPARATE ADJUDICATIVE SYSTEM FOR NEW CRIMES

1. A 1973 survey of parole conditions found that all but one jurisdiction had as a parole condition that the parolee abide by the law. The one jurisdiction without a "law abidingness" condition was New Hampshire. American Bar Association, *Survey of Parole Conditions in the United States* (Washington, D.C.: American Bar Association, Resource Center on Correctional Law and Legal Services, 1973), at 12–3, 17–8.

A more recent survey of parole conditions (1975) found that the law abiding-ness condition had become slightly less common. Four other states—Indiana, Oklahoma, Texas, and West Virginia—omitted this condition. William C. Parker, *Parole*, rev. ed. (College Park, Md.: American Correctional Association, 1975), at 201–204.

2. Information on Federal parole violator warrants suggests that in a large proportion of cases suspected new criminal activity is the reason for initiation of the revocation process. In 1973, 1,321 warrants were issued; 74.3 percent were for law violations. In 1974, 69.3 percent of the 1,397 warrants issued were for law violations. U.S. Department of Justice, Federal Bureau of Prisons, *Statistical Reports: Fiscal Year 1973*, and U.S. Department of Justice, Federal Bureau of Prisons, *Statistical Reports: Fiscal Year 1974*, the latter reported in Michael J. Hindelang *et al.*, *Sourcebook of Criminal Justice Statistics: 1976* (Albany, N.Y.: Criminal Justice Research Center, 1977), Table 6.117.

3. Some indication of the incidence of revocation in lieu of prosecution is provided by the Uniform Parole Reports. A three-year follow-up of male parol-ees released in 1972 showed that 15 percent were returned to prison as parole violators, and that this 15 percent figure was made up as follows: 4 percent "with new minor conviction(s) or in lieu of prosecution"; 3 percent "in lieu of prosecution of a new major offense(s)"; 8 percent with "no new conviction(s) and not in lieu of prosecution" ($N = 19,440$; these national data do not reflect all parolees released in 1972 due to incomplete data from some jurisdictions). Uniform Parole Reports, *Newsletter* (Davis, Cal.: National Council on Crime and Delinquency, December, 1976).

4. Dawson provides a fuller description of these advantages to the parole agency and other criminal justice officials. See Robert O. Dawson, *Sentencing: The Decision as to Type, Length, and Conditions of Sentence* (Boston: Little, Brown, 1969), at 363–64.

5. Dawson, *id.*, at 365; and see Statement of Paul Chernoff and Mark W. Foster in 92nd Cong., 2nd Sess., Subcomm. No. 3 of the Comm. on the Judiciary, U.S. House of Representatives, *Hearings on Corrections, Federal and State Parole Systems* (1972), Part VII–A, at 729.

In Massachusetts, for example, most inmates are eligible for parole after serving one-third of the minimum sentence. However, those offenders who receive a new sentence while on parole must serve two-thirds of the new minimum sentence before eligibility. Vincent O'Leary and Kathleen S. Hanrahan, *Parole Systems in the United States* (Hackensack, N.J.: National Council on Crime and Delinquency, 1976), at 188.

6. The manner of computing the time remaining varies by jurisdiction. In the jurisdictions for which information is available (49), 32 boards report that the time spent under parole supervision, or "street time," is credited toward the sentence; 13 report that it is not; 3 that it may or may not be; and one, that street time is not credited toward the sentence if the parolee has been convicted of a new offense, but is if the parolee is revoked for a technical violation. *Id.*, at 82–344.

7. Patrick M. Reilly, "The Doctrine of Collateral Estoppel in Parole Revocation," 4 *Fordham Urban Law Journal* 609, 620–21 (1976). Some parole boards,

however, seem somewhat more reluctant to resort to revocation for this purpose. It has been reported that under the old law in California, for example, in these cases "[t]he manual requires . . . the evidence to be 'overwhelming' or an admission of guilt must be obtained." Gene Kassebaum, David A. Ward, and Daniel M. Wilner, *Prison Treatment and Parole Survival: An Empirical Assessment* (New York: Wiley, 1971), at 193.

8. O'Leary and Hanrahan, *supra* note 5, compiled from 88–344.

9. The U.S. Parole Commission sometimes has done this, and the Supreme Court has upheld the practice. Moody v. Daggett, 429 U.S. 78 (1976), which involved a parolee convicted and sentenced for two crimes while on parole. The U.S. Parole Commission issued, but did not execute, a parole violator warrant. Instead, the warrant was lodged as a detainer to be executed only after the offender served his new sentence. The parolee claimed he was denied his constitutionally protected right to a prompt revocation hearing. The Supreme Court held that no constitutionally protected right had been violated.

10. See, e.g., David Stanley, *Prisoners Among Us: The Problem of Parole* (Washington, D.C.: The Brookings Institution, 1976), at 109.

11. Elliott Studt notes that the breadth of parole rules serves, among other purposes, to legitimate substantive complaints against parolees in revocation reports. "A list of such rule violations is often used by the agent to 'beef up' a revocation report, when the primary charge seems relatively minor." Elliot Studt, *Surveillance and Service in Parole* (Washington, D.C.: National Institute of Corrections, reprinted 1978), at 145.

On this point, see also John Irwin, *The Felon* (Englewood Cliffs, N.J.: Prentice-Hall, 1970), at 162; and see Nancy Lee and Donald H. Zuckerman, "Representing Parole Violators," 11 *Criminal Law Bulletin* 327, 334 (1974). The authors note:

> . . . even if a parolee is aware of all the rules and tries to comply, he can, at virtually any time, be charged with violating his parole because the conditions are so broad and vague that a parole officer so disposed can always find a violation. . . . Parolees are frequently charged with violations to which the real defense is that whatever occurred (if anything) does not justify revocation of parole.

12. Dawson, *supra* note 4, at 362–63, reports that at the time of his study officials in Michigan and Wisconsin stated that most technical revocations were really cases involving a return to crime by the parolee. Similarly, the Citizens' Inquiry reported that suspected criminal activity was frequently the basis for technical violations. The Citizens' Inquiry on Parole and Criminal Justice, *Prison Without Walls: Report on New York State Parole* (New York: Praeger, 1975), at 132.

13. 408 U.S. 471 (1972).

14. 411 U.S. 778 (1973).

15. 408 U.S. at 485.

16. *Id.* at 437.

17. *Id.* at 489.

18. Gagnon established the following criteria regarding the right of counsel:

... counsel should be provided in cases where, after being informed of his right to request counsel, the probationer or parolee makes such a request, based upon a timely and colorable claim (i) that he has not committed the alleged violation of the conditions upon which he is at liberty; or (ii) that, even if the violation is a matter of public record or is uncontested, there are substantial reasons which justified or mitigated the violation and make revocation inappropriate, and that the reasons are complex or otherwise difficult to develop or present. In passing on a request for the appointment of counsel, the responsible agency also should consider, especially in doubtful cases, whether the probationer appears to be capable of speaking effectively for himself. In every case in which a request for counsel at a preliminary or final hearing is refused, the grounds for refusal should be stated succinctly in the record.

411 U.S. at 790–91.

19. U.S. Parole Commission Rules § 2.21(b), in 42 *Federal Register* 39808, 39815 (1977).

20. Two studies of the California parole system have reported that the typical surveillance activities of parole agents seldom yield evidence of criminal activity. According to Studt, *supra* note 11, at 82–83:

During the course of surveillance observation, the Study's staff was particularly impressed by the fact that the agent's ordinary field activities seemed never to turn up evidence of criminal behavior, except in the case of occasional drug use; and that, actually, it was rare for any facts gathered in routine field visits (with the possible exception of a complaint from a family member) to result in the type of investigation that led to revocation. . . .

A study of 90 reports to the Adult Authority in which revocation decisions could have been made was undertaken to check this observation. . . .

The findings . . . revealed that in only 3 of the 90 cases was positive information about antisocial behavior acquired through surveillance activities in the field; in all 3 of these cases the parolee was either under the influence of drugs at the time of the agent's visit or volunteered that he had reverted to using. The agent's ineffectual efforts to find the parolee over some period of time accounted for another 10 cases; and in an additional case the lack of a monthly report in the mail initiated the investigation. Except for one other case, in which the parolee walked into the parole office during a psychotic episode, the rest of the investigations were triggered by information outside the parole organization.

Takagi found that of 1,023 emergency reports prepared by parole agents, 71.2 percent were based on information compiled by law enforcement agencies; 14.1 percent were based on the findings of chemical testing for narcotics; 9.4 percent were based on information supplied by the parolee's family, employer, or friends; 2.9 percent were based on information collected by the agent himself, and 2.4 percent resulted from the parolee's voluntary admission of illegal activities. Paul Takagi, *Evaluation Systems and Adaptations in a Formal Organization:*

A Case Study of a Parole Agency, Ph.D. Dissertation, Stanford University, 1967 (Ann Arbor: University Microfilms), at 109—10.

A description of the parole practices of three other jurisdictions supports the California findings and suggests that parole officers seldom uncover evidence of criminal activity of parolees. According to Dawson, *supra* note 4, at 343:

> The instances in which initial suspicion of parole violations arises from direct observation by the parole officer are few in comparison to instances in which suspicion is aroused from a report by police or other persons. The principal role of the parole officer is to verify information received from other sources. . . . The police are the parole officer's major source of information concerning parole violation and virtually his exclusive source concerning serious new offenses committed by parolees.

21. Maine Statutes, Art. 17—A, § 1254(1), which states, "An imprisoned person shall be unconditionally released and discharged upon the expiration of his sentence. . . ."

22. In re Winship, 397 U.S. 358 (1970).

23. Morrissey v. Brewer, 408 U.S. 471 (1972).

24. Comment, "Does Due Process Require Clear and Convincing Proof Before Life's Liberties May Be Lost?" 24 *Emory Law Journal* 104, 122—24 (1975) (footnotes omitted).

25. Johnson v. Louisiana, 406 U.S. 356 (1972); Apodaca v. Oregon, 406 U.S. 404 (1972).

26. A survey of parole practices found that at final revocation hearings the hearing body consists of the full board in 14 jurisdictions; two members to a majority of the board in 23 jurisdictions; at least one member in 7 jurisdictions; hearing officer(s) in 6 jurisdictions, and "others" in 2 jurisdictions. O'Leary and Hanrahan, *supra* note 5, at 57.

27. Stanley, *supra* note 10, at 115—16. He also notes (at 116) that

> . . . research in California showed that "nearly 80 percent of the recommendations of parole agents against revocation and over 90 percent of their recommendations for revocation were accepted by the Adult Authority [parole board]."

Id., quoting James Robinson and Paul Takagi, "The Parole Violator as an Organizational Reject," in Carter and Wilkins, eds., *Probation and Parole: Selected Readings* (New York: Wiley, 1970), at 235.

28. Right to counsel was determined by the *Gagnon* decision, *supra* note 18. A survey of parole practices found that when asked *in general* if attorneys were permitted at revocation hearings (as opposed to asking about compliance with the *Gagnon* ruling) 47 boards reported that they permitted attorneys at preliminary hearings, and 25 of those appointed attorneys for indigent inmates; at final hearings, the responses totaled to 50 and 29, respectively. O'Leary and Hanrahan, *supra* note 5, at 55, 58.

29. Cross-examination, as provided by *Morrissey,* is somewhat discretionary. At the preliminary revocation hearing, the parolee has the following right:

> On request of the parolee, a person who has given adverse information on which parole revocation is to be based is to be made available for question-

ing in his presence. However, if the hearing officer determines that an informer would be subject to risk of harm if his identity were disclosed, he need not be subject to confrontation and cross-examination.

Similarly, at the final revocation hearing, the right to confront or cross-examine adverse witnesses can be abridged if "the hearing officer specifically finds good cause for not allowing confrontation." Morrissey v. Brewer, 408 U.S. at 487, 489.

30. In *Morrissey*, the Supreme Court specifically asserted that evidence not admissible at trial is admissible at revocation proceedings:

> We emphasize there is no thought to equate this second stage of parole revocation to a criminal prosecution in any sense. It is a narrow inquiry; the process should be flexible enough to consider evidence including letters, affidavits, and other material that would not be admissible in an adversary criminal trial. [408 U.S. at 489.]

Evidence otherwise excludible in criminal trials under the Fourth Amendment protections against unreasonable search and seizure is usually admissible in revocation proceedings. The Fourth Amendment rights of parolees are at issue in three situations: search by the police; search by the parole officer; and joint search by the police and parole officers. Case decisions have varied, but in general, evidence secured by illegal police search is not admissible at trial, but may be introduced at revocation hearings. Searches by parole officers are usually not subject to Fourth Amendment requirements; evidence gained by parole officer search is admissible at both trial and revocation. Case decisions concerning joint searches have not been uniform.

See, e.g., Case Comment: "Constitutional Law: Warrantless Parole Officer Searches—A New Rationale," 60 *Minnesota Law Review* 805 (1976); Note, "Fourth Amendment Limitations on Probation and Parole Supervision," 1976 *Duke Law Journal* 71 (1976); and Note, "Striking the Balance Between Privacy and Supervision: The Fourth Amendment and Parole and Probation Officer Searches of Parolees and Probationers," 51 *New York University Law Review* 800 (1976).

31. See, e.g., Arthur Rosett and Donald R. Cressey, *Justice by Consent: Plea Bargains in the American Courthouse* (Philadelphia: J.B. Lippincott, 1976).

32. A striking illustration is a recent Washington case, where a parolee was charged with assault and acquitted. The parole board had commenced revocation proceedings based on the same alleged conduct, but then had suspended them pending the outcome of the criminal trial. After the trial, the parole board revoked the offender's parole on the basis of essentially the same evidence as had been used in the trial.

The state court upheld the revocation, despite the prior acquittal on the same charge, on grounds that the applicable standard of proof is lower in the revocation proceeding. Standlee v. Smith, 83 Wash. 2d 405, 518 P.2d 721 (1974).

The case was later overturned by a Federal district court in a habeas corpus proceeding, on grounds that the acquittal served as collateral estoppel against subsequent parole revocation on the basis of such similar evidence. Standlee v. Rhay, 403 F. Supp. 1247 (E.D. Wash., 1975). However, the court limited its holding to cases where the parole board had "acceded" to the prosecution by suspending its revocation proceedings pending the outcome of the criminal trial. In the court's words (403 F. Supp., at 1255):

> It should be noted that the Court's holding will not impair the usual operations of the Parole Board. The Board remains free to exercise its fact-finding powers to revoke under its normal procedures, including the preponderance of evidence burden of proof and lax rules of evidence, except in those cases, as here, where the Parole Board deliberately accedes to the criminal prosecution. In such latter cases the Board may not then reach an inconsistent finding and conclusion.

The Federal court further restricted its holdings to cases where the sole issue in the revocation proceeding "was whether petitioner had committed criminal offenses, and not whether he was guilty of technical parole violations." *Id*. This gives the parole board a method of avoiding such reversals—namely, find the parolee guilty of at least one technical parole infraction as well as of having violated the law-abidingness condition. The Citizens Inquiry report, *supra* note 12, at 132, notes this practice is used in New York:

> It is the practice of the parole board that wherever possible revocation should be based on at least one technical violation, even if there also is a new criminal arrest. This avoids the possibility that a court could order the revoked parolee to be released because the revocation decision was based solely on a new arrest or conviction that was later dismissed or reversed on appeal.

The same practice was reported for California in Kassebaum, Ward, and Wilner, *supra* note 7, at 193.

33. For a discussion of the custody theory of parole, see, e.g., Note, "The Parole System," 120 *University of Pennsylvania Law Review* 282, 286–300 (1971); and Fred Cohen, "The Legal Challenge to Corrections," A Consultant's Paper prepared for the Joint Commission on Correctional Manpower and Training (Washington, D.C.: March, 1969), at 31–34.

34. In Re Winship, 397 U.S. 358 (1970).

35. 397 U.S. at 363–64.

36. 397 U.S. at 372.

37. For a description of possible duration of reconfinement, see Chapter 7 *infra*, text and notes, at notes 16–18.

38. Andrew von Hirsch, *Doing Justice: The Choice of Punishments* (New York: Hill and Wang, 1976), Ch. 10.

39. See, e.g., George Fletcher, *Rethinking Criminal Law* (Boston: Little, Brown, 1978), at 460–466; Stephen A. Schiller, Book Review, 67 *Journal of Criminal Law and Criminology* 356 (1976).

It is important to note that the treatment of prior offenses in *Doing Justice* is one that calls for *reductions*, not increases, in the severities of punishments. The first offender is to get *less* punishment than he would were the presence or absence of a criminal record disregarded in assessing his culpability; and the multiple offender is not to get any more punishment than he would in a desert-based system in which prior criminality were not considered. *Doing Justice, supra* note

38, ch. 10. This translates, in that book's recommended scale of punishments (*id.*, ch. 16), into a system in which crimes involving threatened but not actual violence, such as armed robbery, would get sentences of intermittent confinement for the first offense, and sentences of no more than three years for "multiple recidivist infractions." Were the presence or absence of a prior criminal history ruled out, as the above-cited critics argue it should under a desert model, the net effect would be to make the system a more severe one: if the first and tenth armed robbery had to be punished equally, one could scarcely justify such low sanctions as intermittent confinement ever being applied.

This point, that reductions rather than increases are involved, seems lost on some of the critics. Fletcher, for example, assumes that what is being recommended is *more* punishments for recidivists than could be justified in a system that ignored prior criminality. Much of his criticisms—e.g., his charge that taking prior criminality into account is an authoritarian view—make sense only on this assumption, which is contrary to the position actually being argued for in *Doing Justice*.

40. See, e.g., Don M. Gottfredson, "Assessment of Prediction Methods," in Johnson, Savitz, and Wolfgang, eds., *The Sociology of Punishment and Correction*, 3d ed. (New York: Wiley, 1970), at 758.

41. See, e.g., Albert A. Alschuler, "The Prosecutor's Role in Plea Bargaining," 36 *University of Chicago Law Review* 50 (1968); and Rosett and Cressey, *supra* note 31.

42. For citation in footnote: Albert A. Alschuler, "Sentencing Reform and Prosecutorial Power: A Critique of Recent Proposals for 'Fixed' and 'Presumptive' Sentencing," 126 *University of Pennsylvania Law Review* 550 (1978); Stephen Gettinger, "Plea Bargaining: A Major Obstacle to True Reform in Sentencing," *Corrections Magazine*, September 1977, at 34–5, and Stevens H. Clarke and Gary G. Koch, *The Effect of the Prohibition of Plea Bargaining on the Disposition of Felony Cases in Alaska Criminal Courts: A Statistical Analysis* (Anchorage, Alaska: Alaska Judicial Council, September 1978) (Alaska's efforts to restrict plea bargaining); Note, "Restructuring the Plea Bargain," 82 *Yale Law Journal* 286 (1972) (procedures to follow in plea bargains).

43. Caseload pressure is frequently assumed to be a major factor in the rate of cases that are decided via plea bargaining. A study of caseload and plea bargaining practice in Connecticut suggests, however, that caseload pressure may not be so large a part of the explanation. See Milton Heumann, "A Note on Plea Bargaining and Case Pressure," 9 *Law and Society Review* 515 (1975); and Herbert S. Miller *et al.*, *Plea Bargaining in the United States: Phase I Report* (Washington, D.C.: Georgetown University Law Center, April 1977), at 16–24.

44. See text at notes 38–40, *supra.*

45. For citation in footnote: Indiana Penal Code § 35–50–2–8. For discussion of why such a statute violates desert constraints even under a desert theory that considers prior criminality, see *Doing Justice, supra* note 38, at 86–87.

46. See, e.g., Sol Rubin, *The Law of Criminal Correction* (New York: West, 1973), at 645; Comment, "Parole Holds: Their Effect on the Rights of the Parolee and the Operation of the Parole System," 19 *U.C.L.A. Law Review* 759, 789–795 (1972). For a survey of parole board practice in allowing release pend-

ing the revocation decision, see O'Leary and Hanrahan, *supra* note 5, at 49, 82–344.

47. See, e.g., Temporary Commission on the New York State Court System, *...And Justice For All: Part II* (New York: Temporary Commission on the State Court System, 1973), ch. 6.

48. For discussion of the bail problem and alternatives to bail, see, e.g., Paul B. Wice, *Freedom for Sale: A National Study of Pretrial Release* (Lexington, Mass.: Lexington Books, 1974); Daniel Freed and Patricia M. Wald, *Bail in the United States*, a report prepared as a Working Document for the National Conference on Bail and Criminal Justice (Washington, D.C., May 27–29, 1964); and Wayne H. Thomas, Jr., *Bail Reform in America* (Berkeley: University of California Press, 1976).

CHAPTER 7: PAROLE SUPERVISION

1. This is a description of conventional supervision practices in most jurisdictions. Special programs, designed to increase some aspects of assistance or surveillance for certain groups of parolees, exist in some jurisdictions. See, e.g., David T. Stanley, *Prisoners Among Us* (Washington, D.C.: The Brookings Institution, 1976), at 163–67.

2. This seems to vary, however, by jurisdiction (and agent, see n. 7 *infra*). A study of the Iowa system, for example, reports that rehabilitation received emphasis. See Robert C. Prus, *Revocation Related Decision-Making: A Labeling Approach*, Ph.D. dissertation, University of Iowa (Ann Arbor, Mich.: University Microfilms, 1974); on the other hand, studies of the parole supervision systems of California and New York found that control tended to predominate. Elliot Studt, *Surveillance and Service in Parole* (Washington, D.C.: National Institute of Corrections, reprinted 1978); and Citizens' Inquiry on Parole and Criminal Justice, *Prison Without Walls: Report on New York State Parole* (New York: Praeger, 1975), respectively.

3. A recent survey found that the average caseload size for agencies which provide both parole and probation supervision was 68, and that the average caseload size was 51 in agencies which supervise only parolees. National Criminal Justice Information and Statistics Service, *State and Local Probation and Parole Systems* at (Washington, D.C.: Department of Justice, LEAA, February 1978), at 6. (It is not unusual for parole and probation supervision to be provided by the same agency. Stanley reports that 35 states have officers who do both kinds of supervision, but that six of those states have some officers assigned only to parole. Stanley, *supra* note 1, at 87–88.)

4. Stanley, *supra* note 1, at 84–6.

5. *Id.*, at 93; Charles L. Newman, *Personnel Practices in Adult Parole Systems* (Springfield, Ill.: Charles C. Thomas, 1971), at 60–64.

6. Stanley, *supra* note 1, at 82–84. The author of a survey of parole conditions conducted several years ago characterized parole conditions as follows: "some . . . are moralistic, most are impractical, others impinge on human rights, and all reflect obsolete criminological conceptions. On the whole, they project a percept of a man who does not exist." Nat Arluke, "Parole Rules," in John-

son, Savitz, and Wolfgang, *The Sociology of Punishment and Correction*, 2d ed. (New York: Wiley, 1970), at 699, 702.

7. Studt, *supra* note 2, at 140.

8. Stanley, *supra* note 1, at 95—101.

9. Federal Judicial Center, "Probation Time Study," (1973), quoted in Stanley, *supra* note 1, at 125—26. Time studies in other jurisdictions report similar findings. See, e.g., Arthur P. Miles, *A Time Study of Wisconsin Probation and Parole Agents* (Madison, Wis.: State Department of Public Welfare, Division of Corrections, March 1964); William L. Jacks, *A Time Study of Parole Agents* (Pennsylvania Board of Parole, March, 1961); and Susi Megathalin, *Probation/ Parole Caseload Review* (Atlanta: Georgia Department of Offender Rehabilitation, 1973), reported in Neil M. Singer and Virginia B. Wright, *Cost Analysis of Correctional Standards: Institutional-Based Programs and Parole* (Washington, D.C.: American Bar Association, 1975), Vol. II, at 69.

10. Studt, *supra* note 2, at 136—37.

11. Ch. 6, note 27.

12. See, e.g., Richard Dembo, "Orientation and Activities of the Parole Officer," 10 *Criminology* 193 (1972); Daniel Glaser, *The Effectiveness of a Prison and Parole System*, abridged ed., (New York: Bobbs-Merrill, 1969), at 291—99; and Stanley, *supra* note 1, at 116.

13. James Robinson and Paul T. Takagi, "The Parole Violator as an Organizational Reject," in Carter and Wilkins, eds., *Probation and Parole: Selected Readings* (New York: Wiley, 1970); and see Paul Takagi, *Evaluation Systems and Adaptations in a Formal Organization: A Case Study of a Parole Agency*, Ph.D. dissertation, Stanford University (Ann Arbor, Mich.: University Microfilms, 1967), at 181—85; and Prus, *supra* note 2, at 154—56.

14. Uniform Parole Reports, "1972 Parolees, Three Year Follow-up and Trend Analysis," *Newsletter* (Davis, Cal.: National Council on Crime and Delinquency, December, 1976), at Table 3.

15. For information on New York State, for example, see State of New York, Department of Correctional Services, *Annual Statistical Report: 1975 Data, Inmate and Parole Populations* (Albany, New York: Division of Program Planning, Evaluation and Research, n.d.), at Table D—10, p. 90.

16. U.S. Parole Commission Rules § 2.21 (a), in 42 *Federal Register* 39808, 39815 (1977).

17. See text at note 31, *infra*. Duration of reconfinement is ordinarily 4—6 months. However, it is 6—10 months for offenders originally convicted of crimes of the two highest seriousness gradations. Oregon Administrative Rules § 254—70—042 (1978).

18. The unexpired parole periods of New York parolees revoked in 1975 were:

Unexpired Parole Period	Total	Percent
	2,036	100.0
Less than 3 months	23	1.1
3 months but less than 6 months	151	7.4
6 months but less than 9 months	254	12.5

Unexpired Parole Period (*continued*)

9 months but less than 1 year	298	14.7
1 year but less than 1½ years	503	24.7
1½ years but less than 2 years	245	12.0
2 years but less than 2½ years	180	8.9
2½ years but less than 3 years	82	4.0
3 years but less than 4 years	80	3.9
4 years but less than 5 years	39	1.9
5 years and over	158	7.8
Life	23	1.1

Source: *Annual Statistical Report, supra* note 15, at 76, Table D–4.

19. An example is the study, as reported by Robert Martinson and Judith Wilks, "Save Parole Supervision," *Federal Probation,* September 1977, at 23. James Robison, however, presents information that suggests dischargees are *less* often returned to prison than parolees. And he summarizes the findings of another study in which dischargees had slightly more favorable disposition outcomes than did parolees for about two years, but by three years, the outcomes were virtually the same. James O. Robison, "The California Prison Parole and Probation System: It's Time to Stop Counting," *Technical Supplement No. 2,* A Special Report to the Assembly (April 1969), at 72–74.

20. Don M. Gottfredson, "Some Positive Changes in the Parole Process," Paper presented at the panel on "Successes and Failures of Parole," at the American Society of Criminology meeting, November 1, 1975, Toronto, Canada, at 10–14.

21. Mark Jay Lerner, "The Effectiveness of a Definite Sentence Parole Program," 15 *Criminology* 211 (1977).

In addition, one study not yet available has apparently found positive results for parole supervision. The study was conducted by Howard R. Sacks of the University of Connecticut School of Law and Charles Logan of the Department of Sociology at that university. *News Release,* Department of Correction (Hartford, Connecticut, n.d.), October 1977.

22. Irwin Waller, *Men Released from Prison* (Toronto: University of Toronto Press, 1974).

23. *Id.,* at 190.

24. "Bay Area Discharge Study: Preliminary Summary of Findings" (Sacramento: Department of Youth Authority, Research Division, 1977).

25. For citation in footnote: For a review of caseload research, see, e.g., Mark G. Neithercutt and Don M. Gottfredson, "Case Load Size Variation and Differences in Probation and Parole Performance," in Amos and Newman, eds., *Parole* (New York: Federal Legal Publications, 1975); an earlier review of those studies is found in Stuart Adams, "Correctional Caseload Research," in Johnson, Savitz, and Wolfgang, eds., *The Sociology of Punishment and Correction,* 2d ed. (New York: Wiley, 1970).

26. That condition was reported for 25 jurisdictions in 1975. William C. Parker, *Parole,* rev. ed. (College Park, Md.: American Correctional Association, 1975), at 202–04.

27. Parole conditions relating to employment were found in 33 jurisdictions, as of 1975. For recent evidence as to possible links between employment and recidivism, see John Monahan and Linda Costa Monahan, "Prediction Research and the Role of Psychologists in Correctional Institutions," 14 *San Diego Law Review* 1028 (1977).

28. See Chapter 3, *supra*, text at notes 8–10.

29. See, Chapter 3, *supra*, text at notes 13–18.

30. California Penal Code § 3057. The change was made in the 1978 legislative session by Chapter 582 of the 1978 session laws.

31. See Note 17, *supra*.

32. S. 1437, 95th Cong., 2nd Sess. §§ 2303, 3844(e) (1978). For further discussion of this bill, see Chapter 9 *infra*, note 29.

33. S. 204, 95th Cong., 2nd Sess. § 11(a)(2)(B) (1978). The bill is set forth in full in Appendix III. For further discussion of this bill, see Chapter 9 *infra*, text at notes 17, 21, and 24.

34. See, e.g., National Advisory Commission on Criminal Justice Standards and Goals, *Corrections* (Washington, D.C.: Government Printing Office, 1973), at 407.

35. Chapter 4 *supra*, text at notes 23–29, 37–42, 47–48.

36. See this chapter, text at notes 19–26.

37. See Chapter 8 *infra*, note 1.

38. Chapter 6, *supra*, text at notes 10–12.

39. Maine Revised Statutes, Art. 17–A § 1201. See also Frederick A. Hussey and John H. Kramer, "Issues in the Study of Criminal Code Revision: An Analysis of Reform in Maine and California," in National Institute of Law Enforcement and Criminal Justice, ed., *Determinate Sentencing: Reform or Regression* (Washington, D.C.: Government Printing Office, March 1978), at 111, 116–122.

40. Empirical evidence is not now available on how the elimination of supervision has affected sentencing practice in Maine, but such disconcerting results are a possibility.

A study directed by John Kramer is now nearing completion on the impact of the new Maine sentencing law. See Chapter 4 *supra*, note 59. However, the study does not specifically deal with elimination of supervision and its effects.

41. See, e.g., Andrew von Hirsch, *Doing Justice: The Choice of Punishments* (New York: Hill and Wang, 1976), ch. 14.

CHAPTER 8: SERVICES TO EX-PRISONERS

1. Elliot Studt, *Surveillance and Service in Parole—A Report of the Parole Action Study* (Washington, D.C.: National Institute of Corrections, reprinted 1978).

2. This social service, rather than crime control, aim is also urged in Citizens' Inquiry on Parole and Criminal Justice, *Prison Without Walls: A Report on New York Parole* (New York: Praeger, 1975), at 179.

3. Elliot Studt, *The Reentry of the Offender into the Community* (Washington, D.C.: Office of Juvenile Delinquency and Youth Development, Department of Health, Education and Welfare, 1967), at 3.

4. See, for example, Citizens' Inquiry, *supra* note 2; Rosemary J. Erickson, Wayman J. Crow, Louis A. Zurcher, and Archie V. Connett, *Paroled But Not Free: Ex-Offenders Look at What They Need to Make It Outside* (New York: Behavioral Publications, 1973); Elliot Studt. *Surveillance and Service in Parole*, *supra* note 1; John Irwin, *The Felon* (Englewood Cliffs, N.J.: Prentice-Hall, 1970); and Daniel Glaser, *The Effectiveness of a Prison and Parole System* (New York: Bobbs-Merrill, 1969).

5. Robert Horowitz, *Back on the Street—From Prison to Poverty* (Washington, D.C.: American Bar Association, Transitional Aid Research Project for Ex-Offenders, Commission on Correctional Facilities and Services, June 1976).

6. They are Alaska, Delaware, North Dakota and South Carolina. Each of these states provides clothing and transportation at release. South Carolina included in its 1976/77 budget a provision for gate money. *Id.*, at 3.

7. *Id.* The author notes that there are two reasons for the failure to provide the maximum. First, in some states, "where appropriations fail to keep pace with statutory changes," there are insufficient funds. Second, in many jurisdictions the amount of gate money is left to the discretion of corrections officials.

8. *Id.*, at 6—9. However, at least one state is more generous to ex-prisoners who look for employment. The state of Washington has established a "Stipend Program" for eligible inmates which provides support for up to 26 weeks while a releasee seeks employment. If full benefits are provided, the releasee will receive $1,340 over a six-month period. *Id.*, at 16—17, 23—25, and Appendix B.

9. Most correctional systems have only a small proportion of the inmate population in work-release programs. Horowitz found that most of the responding states had less than 10 percent of the population participating. *Id.* at 15. Similar survey results have been reported elsewhere. See, e.g., Richard M. Swanson, *Work Release: Toward an Understanding of the Law, Policy and Operation of Community-Based State Corrections* (Carbondale, Ill.: Center for the Study of Crime, Delinquency and Corrections, June 1973), Vol. II.

10. Savings are dependent on institutional wages. A 1974 survey of inmates in state institutions found that 29 percent received no wages for work assignments; 33 percent earned less than six cents per hour; and 25 percent received between six to twenty cents per hour. *Survey of Inmates of State Correctional Facilities 1974: Advance Report* (Washington, D.C.: Department of Justice, LEAA, 1976), Table 9, reported in Horowitz, *supra* note 5, at 13, n. 36.

Horowitz (*id.*, at iii, n. 11) reports the following estimates of average size of inmate savings:

Alaska	$10	Kentucky	$20
Arkansas	15	New Jersey	15
Georgia	75	New Mexico	15
Hawaii	40	New York	40
Iowa	50	Utah	100

11. *Id.*, at 21—23; and see Kenneth J. Lenihan, "The Financial Condition of Released Prisoners," 21 *Crime and Delinquency* 266, 278 (1975).

12. Horowitz, *supra* note 5, at 1–2.

13. Studt, *Surveillance and Service on Parole, supra* note 1, at 116–119.

14. Citizens' Inquiry, *supra* note 2, at 84–96.

15. David T. Stanley, *Prisoners Among Us: The Problem of Parole* (Washington, D.C.: The Brookings Institution, 1976), at 150.

Data collected in New York indicate that unemployment among employable New York State parolees is high. In 1975, the unemployment rate for those parolees was 19.7. State of New York, Department of Correctional Services, *Annual Statistics Report: 1975 Data* (Albany, N.Y.: Division of Program Planning, Evaluation and Research, n.d.), at 146, Table M–10.

16. See, e.g., Stanley, *supra* note 15, at 151–155; and Mitchell W. Dale, "Barriers to the Rehabilitation of Ex-Offenders," 22 *Crime and Delinquency* 322, 325–331 (1976); and see American Bar Association, Committee on the Legal Status of Prisoners, "Tentative Draft of Standards Relating to the Legal Status of Prisoners," 14 *American Criminal Law Review*, at 377, 615 (1977), for mention of progress in these areas; and Clearinghouse on Offender Employment Restriction, *Removing Offender Employment Restrictions* (Washington, D.C.: American Bar Association, March 1970).

17. See, e.g., Herbert S. Miller, *The Closed Door: The Effect of a Criminal Record on Employment with State and Local Public Agencies* (Washington, D.C.: Georgetown University Law Center, 1972).

18. Erickson *et al., supra* note 4, at 66–71: but see Marc Rensema, "Success and Failure Among Parolees as a Function of Perceived Stress and Coping Styles," (where he reports that the parolees in his study had problems "in abundance" but apparently little psychological stress), in Hans Toch, *Interventions for Inmate Survival*, Final Report submitted to LEAA, August 1976.

19. See, e.g., Studt, *Reentry of the Offender into the Community, supra* note 3; Irwin, *supra* note 4, ch. 5; American Bar Association, *supra* note 16, Commentary to § 9.6; A. Verne McArthur, *Coming Out Cold: Community Reentry from a State Reformatory* (Lexington, Mass.: D.C. Heath, 1974), ch. 6.

20. These programs are already in existence in some jurisdictions. For example, California has a furlough program for inmates who are within 90 days of release. A description of that program as implemented in one correctional facility found that inmates leave on furlough with a few fairly specific objectives (e.g., to obtain housing), and that the majority either accomplish or attempt to accomplish most of these objectives. See, Norman Holt, "Temporary Prison Release," in Carter, Glaser, and Wilkins, eds., *Correctional Institutions*, 2d ed. (New York: Lippincott, 1977).

21. See, e.g., Richard A. Tropp, "Suggested Policy Initiatives for Employment and Crime Problems," and Ronald Benjamin, "The Employment Problems of Ex-Offenders: A Suggested Approach," in Institute for Advanced Studies in Justice, *Crime and Employment Issues* (Washington, D.C.: Institute for Advanced Studies in Justice, American University Law School, 1978).

22. There is evidence that the service of locating sources of assistance might be useful, since ex-prisoners tend to be unaware of the available helping resources. A study of county jail releasees found both awareness and use of "the more prominent aftercare agencies" fairly low. See Peter C. Buffum, "The Phila-

delphia Aftercare Survey: A Summary Report," 56 *Prison Journal* 3, 12–15 (1976). Furthermore, Studt reports that community social service agencies are reluctant to accept parolees as clients. Studt, *Surveillance and Service on Parole, supra* note 1, at 129.

23. This role for parole agents was recommended by the National Commission on Criminal Justice Standards and Goals, *Corrections* (Washington, D.C.: Government Printing Office, 1973), at 410–11. And see R.J. Polisky, "A Model for Increasing the Use of Community Supportive Services in Probation and Parole," *Federal Probation*, December 1977, at 24.

24. John Stuart Mill, *On Liberty* (1859), chs. 1, 2 and 4, excerpted, e.g., in Feinberg and Gross, eds., *Philosophy of Law* (Encino, Cal.: Dickenson, 1975), at 123–134.

25. For citation in footnote: Gerald Dworkin, "Paternalism," in Wasserstrom, ed., *Morality and the Law* (Belmont, Cal.: Wadsworth, 1971), at 107–126.

26. See, e.g., American Friends Service Committee, *Struggle for Justice* (New York: Hill and Wang, 1971), at 98.

27. Norval Morris, *The Future of Imprisonment* (Chicago: University of Chicago Press, 1974), at 19.

CHAPTER 9: IMPLEMENTING THE REFORMS: WHICH DECISIONMAKERS? DUAL OR "REAL" TIME?

1. California Penal Code §§ 1170, 3000, 3040 and *passim*, as amended by Chapter 1139 of the 1976 session laws and subsequent amendments. For an analysis, see April K. Cassou and Brian Taugher, "Determinate Sentencing in California: The New Numbers Game," 9 *Pacific Law Journal* 5 (1978).

2. Indiana Penal Code §§ 35–50–1–1 through 35–50–6–6, which were mainly added by P.L. 148 of the 1976 session laws. Illinois Statutes, ch. 38, §§ 1003–3–1 through 1008–2–4, which were mainly added by P.A. 80–1099 of the 1977 session laws.

3. For example, a 1976 critique by Franklin Zimring of determinate sentencing proposals assumes that such standards would be written by the legislature. Franklin E. Zimring, "Making the Punishment Fit the Crime," *Hastings Center Report*, December 1976, at 13–17.

4. In *Doing Justice* it was suggested that such a nonlegislative standard-setter may be preferable. Andrew von Hirsch, *Doing Justice: The Choice of Punishments* (New York: Hill and Wang, 1976), at 102–104.

5. See American Bar Association, Project on Minimum Standards for Criminal Justice, *Standards Relating to Sentencing Alternatives and Procedures* (New York: American Bar Association, Official Draft, 1968), Commentary to Standard 2.1, at 56–61.

6. Association of the Bar of the City of New York, Joint Committee on New York Drug Law Evaluation, *The Nation's Toughest Drug Law: Evaluating the New York Experience* (New York: Association of the Bar of the City of New York, 1977).

7. See, e.g., Twentieth Century Fund, Task Force on Criminal Sentencing, *Fair and Certain Punishment*, (New York: McGraw-Hill, 1976), at 123.

8. See, Marvin E. Frankel, *Criminal Sentences* (New York: Hill and Wang, 1972), at 122; Kenneth Culp Davis, *Discretionary Justice* (Urbana, Ill.: University of Illinois Press, 1971), ch. 2.

9. Chapter 3 *supra*, text at notes 25 and 26.

10. Sometimes it is claimed that questions of desert are especially suited to legislative consideration. A 1975 parole study at Yale Law School thus asserts, "the legislature is the only political body with colorable claim to represent societal moral values relevant to the amount of punishment appropriate for certain classes of crime." The assumption made in this statement is that the standards for deserved punishment should mirror community mores. Is this assumption correct?

Certainly the criteria for the seriousness of crimes and the deserved severity of punishment would have to be distilled from the basic norms of conduct in this society. But the question remains: must those criteria reflect community attitudes *in detail?*

Not necessarily. The governing idea of desert, as we have explained it, is that a penalty is just only if its severity comports with the degree of harmfulness and culpability of the conduct. Even if surveys of popular opinion were to find, for example, that the crime of burglary was regarded as very serious, that would not settle whether it *should* be treated as such; one could still have legitimate questions about whether popular beliefs about the consequences of this crime were factually correct; or else one could have queries about the moral propriety of condemning so severely behavior that seems primarily to threaten property and privacy. Project, "Parole Release Decisionmaking and the Sentencing Process," 84 *Yale Law Journal* 810, 888–89 (1975), but compare Andrew von Hirsch, "Proportionality and Desert: A Reply to Bedau," 75 *Journal of Philosophy* 622 (1978).

11. A new LEAA-funded study, under the direction of Sheldon Messinger, Richard Sparks, and Andrew von Hirsch, will study the impact of the new California legislation on the amount and distribution of penalties in that state. Until the study is completed, conclusions cannot be more than tentative. Project on Strategies for Determinate Sentencing, University of California at Berkeley and Rutgers University at Newark, NILECJ Grant No. 78–NI–0082.

12. Indiana Penal Code, *supra* note 2.

13. For critiques of the high penalties and wide discretionary ranges in the Indiana statute, see Andrew von Hirsch, "The New Indiana Sentencing Code: Is It Determinate Sentencing?" Paper presented at the colloquium of the Indiana Lawyers Commission, September 20–23, 1978, Indianapolis, Indiana (unpublished); and Todd R. Clear, John D. Hewitt, and Robert M. Regoli, "Discretion and the Determinate Sentence: Its Distribution, Control and Effect on Time Served," 24 *Crime and Delinquency* 428 (1978).

14. California Session Laws of 1976, ch. 1139; as amended by California Session Laws of 1977, ch. 165; as further amended by Senate Bill No. 709, which became law during the 1978 legislative session. For discussion of the

problems created by such amendments, see Sheldon L. Messinger and Phillip E. Johnson, "California's Determinate Sentencing Statute: History and Issues" in National Institute of Law Enforcement and Criminal Justice, *Determinate Sentencing: Reform or Regression?* (Washington, D.C.: Government Printing Office, March 1978), at 13–58.

15. Frankel, *supra* note 8, ch. 9. For proposed and enacted legislation to create sentencing commissions, see notes 17, 18, and 19, *infra*.

16. See, e.g., the two U.S. Senate bills referred to in notes 17 and 19, *infra*.

17. S. 208, 95th Cong., 2nd Sess., the proposed "Federal Sentencing Standards Act of 1977," introduced by Senators Gary Hart and Jacob Javits on Jan. 12, 1978 [hereinafter referred to as "Hart-Javits bill"]. Richard Singer of Rutgers University Law School and one of the present authors, Andrew von Hirsch, assisted in the drafting of the bill. It is set forth in Appendix III.

18. Minnesota Session Laws of 1978, ch. 723; Pennsylvania Session Laws of 1978, ch. 319.

The Minnesota sentencing commission consists of three judges, a prosecutor, a defense lawyer, the corrections commissioner, and the chairperson of the parole board. The guidelines must prescribe (1) when a sentence of imprisonment is appropriate, and (2) the duration of any prison sentence. (The commission is also authorized to issue guidelines on non-incarcerative sentences.) While the guidelines are described as "advisory," sentencing judges are required to give reasons for any departures from the guidelines, and an appeal from sentence is established.

The Pennsylvania commission consists of four legislators (two appointed by the leader of each house of the legislature); four judges, appointed by the chief justice of the supreme court; and three gubernatorial appointments, one of whom must be a district attorney, one a defense attorney, and one a "professor of law or a criminologist." The commission's guidelines are required to stress the degree of gravity of the conduct; they must:

(1) Specify the range of sentences applicable to crimes of a given degree of gravity.

(2) Specify a range of sentences of increased severity for defendants previously convicted of a felony or felonies or convicted of a crime involving the use of a deadly weapon.

(3) Prescribe variations from the range of sentences applicable on account of aggravating or mitigating circumstances. [§1384]

The guidelines are to become effective 90 days after publication by the commission, unless rejected in their entirety by the legislature by concurrent resolution. Sentencing judges are required only to "consider" the guidelines, but must give specific reasons for sentences outside the guidelines. Appellate courts, moreover, have discretion to accept an appeal from sentence, and may vacate the sentence, if:

(1) The sentencing court purported to sentence within the sentencing guidelines but applied the guidelines erroneously:

(2) the sentencing court sentenced within the sentencing guidelines but the case involves circumstances where the application of the guidelines would be clearly unreasonable; or

(3) the sentencing court sentenced outside the sentencing guidelines and the sentence is unreasonable. [§ 1386(c)]

19. For citation in footnote: The Senate bill is S. 1437, 95th Cong., 2nd Sess., as amended and passed by that Chamber, Jan. 30, 1978. The House subcommittee's bill is H.R. 13959, 95th Cong., 2nd Sess., introduced by Hon. James Mann, chairman of the Criminal Justice Subcommittee of the House Judiciary Committee.

20. See, e.g., Pierce O'Donnell, Michael J. Churgin, and Dennis E. Curtis, *Toward a Just and Effective Sentencing System: Agenda for Legislative Reform* (New York: Praeger, 1977), ch. 9.

21. Hart-Javits bill, *supra* note 17, § 11.

22. See, Chapter 4 *supra*, note 49.

23. This problem of numerous decisionmakers, as it relates to the Federal system, is discussed at greater length in Peter B. Hoffman, "Reform in the Determination of Prison Terms: Equity, Determinacy, and the Parole Release Function," 7 *Hofstra Law Review* No. 1 (1979) (in press).

For a general discussion of the hazards of eliminating parole release, in the context of California, see Caleb Foote, "Deceptive Determinate Sentencing," in National Institute of Law Enforcement and Criminal Justice, *Determinate Sentencing: Reform or Regression? supra* note 14, at 133–141.

For citation in footnote: The Community Release Board's advisory review powers are set forth in California Penal Law § 1170(f), and discussed in Cassou and Taugher, *supra* note 1, at 70.

24. Hart-Javits bill, *supra* note 17, §§ 8, 13.

25. Maine Statutes, Title 17–A, § 1201; California Penal Code §§ 1170, 3000, 3040; Indiana Penal Code §§ 35–50–1–1 through 35–50–6–6; Illinois Statutes, Ch. 38, §§ 1003–3–1 through 1008–2–4.

26. For citation in footnote: The Indiana law, for example, allows a 50 percent reduction from sentence for good behavior in prison. Indiana Penal Code §§ 35–50–6–3 through 35–50–6–5. The California law also allows a large reduction for good behavior and program participation in prison, but with detailed "vesting" provisions that substantially limit the amount of time that can be taken away for any one infraction. California Penal Code §§ 2930 and 2931.

27. Minnesota Session Laws of 1978, ch. 723; Pennsylvania Session Laws of 1978, ch. 319.

28. For citation in footnote: Minnesota Session Laws of 1978, ch. 723, § 12.

29. For citation in footnote: S. 1437, *supra* note 19, §§ 2301, 994(b) (2); H.R. 13959, *supra* note 19, §§ 41305, 41306.

The Senate bill, unlike the Hart-Javits proposal, contains no unambiguous language that the commission adjust sentence durations downward as it shifts to "real time." The Senate bill does contain a provision in § 994(1) that the sentencing commission, in promulgating its guidelines, shall be guided by "the length of . . . terms actually served, unless the commission determines that such a length of term of imprisonment does not adequately reflect a basis for a sentencing range that is consistent with the purposes of sentencing described in subsection 101(b). . . . " As the latter subsection includes virtually all the purposes of punishment, however, the escape clause is a wide one. For a fuller critique of the Senate bill, see Testimony of Andrew von Hirsch, April 4, 1978, at Hearings of the Subcomm. on Criminal Justice of the Comm. on the Judiciary of the U.S. House of Representatives (record of hearings in press).

30. Oregon Revised Statutes (ORS) §§ 144.110—144.125, 144.775 through 144.790. The statute, in the form in which it was added by Chapter 372 of the state session laws of 1977, is reproduced in full in Appendix IV and is hereafter referred to as the "Oregon Parole Law."

This legislation was originally drafted by the state legislature's Interim Judiciary Committee, and substantially influenced by Ira Blalock, chairman of the state's parole board. Peter B. Hoffman of the U.S. Parole Commission, and one of the present authors, Andrew von Hirsch, also assisted in the drafting.

31. Vincent O'Leary and Kathleen Hanrahan, *Parole Systems in the United States* (Hackensack, N.J.: National Council on Crime and Delinquency, 1976), at 269—70.

32. Oregon Parole Law § 4(1), ORS § 144.110(1).

33. Oregon Parole Law § 4(2)(a), ORS § 144.110(2)(a).

34. Oregon Parole Law § 1, ORS § 144.175.

35. Oregon Parole Law § 2(1), ORS § 144.780(1).

36. Oregon Parole Law §§ 2(2) and (3), ORS §§ 144.780 (2) and (3).

37. The statutory language speaks of "[t]he protection of the public from further crimes by the defendant," which appears to refer to incapacitation, but might be interpreted to include rehabilitation as well (if rehabilitation is defined as we defined it in the beginning of Chapter 3).

38. Oregon Parole Reform Law §§ 5 and 6, ORS §§ 144.120 and 144.125. The provisions allowing the board to hold a prisoner beyond his initial release date for "serious" misconduct in the prison requires the board: (1) to define by rule what constitutes "serious" misconduct; and (2) to specify by rule the amount of any postponements for such misconduct. The provision regarding the prisoner's parole plan requires the board to adopt rules "specifying the elements of an adequate parole plan."

These provisions also contain a clause stating that the board "may choose not to set a parole date" where the offender's conduct was particularly violent, where it was preceded by two convictions for specified serious felonies, or where his record includes a diagnosis of severe emotional disturbance. It is not clear from the statutory language whether "not choosing to set a parole date" means: (1) deferring the parole decision until later; or (2) denying parole release altogether. The parole board's current rules take the second interpretation. Oregon Administrative Rules § 254—30—032(2).

39. The board's rules provide the following schedule for term-fixing hearings: for prisoners with sentences under 12 months, the hearing is to be conducted within 2 months of entry to the institution; those with sentences between

12 and 36 months are to be heard within 3 months; and those with sentences over 36 months are to be seen within 4 months of entry. Oregon Administrative Rules § 254–30–005.

Scheduling the decision in this fashion would not, of course, enable the time-fixer to learn any new relevant facts not knowable at time of sentence. The question is whether this delay—which should not be long enough to create a great deal of painful suspense—allows the decision to be made by an agency which, given present political and bureaucratic realities, would be better situated to formulate the standards and carry them out in individual cases. The proponents of the Oregon scheme would argue that for the reasons discussed in the text, the parole board is so situated.

40. For citation in footnote: for discussion of such good-time deductions and their problems, see Chapter 5 *supra*, text at notes 26–30.

41. The study is referred to in note 11, *supra*. The study will compare Oregon's experience with California's, where parole release has been eliminated.

42. See Testimony of Ira Blalock, April 17, 1978, at Hearings of the Subcomm. on Criminal Justice of the Comm. on the Judiciary of the U.S. House of Representatives (record of hearings in press).

43. The new rules were drafted in January, 1978, and adopted shortly thereafter. They are set forth in Chapter 254 of the Oregon Administrative Rules.

44. American Bar Association, Committee on the Legal Status of Prisoners, "Tentative Draft of Standards Relating to the Legal Standards of Prisoners," 14 *American Criminal Law Review* 377, 606–8 (1977), Standard 9.6.

The American Bar Association did not endorse any of the Committee's recommendations on release of prisoners, of which this was one, on grounds that the Committee's jurisdiction was limited to conditions *within* prisons.

45. In *Doing Justice, supra* note 4, at 103, it was noted that there might be other standard-setting bodies instead. The trial court might, either by consultation among its members or by establishing a special panel for the purpose, formulate standards for its sentencing decisions. Review of sentences might then permit the appellate court to affirm or modify those norms. Alternatively, the appellate court—were its rulemaking authority sufficiently broad—might promulgate standards, as it now prescribes rules of procedure in many jurisdictions.

46. H.B. 2424, Printer's No. 3117, General Assembly of Pennsylvania, 1978 Session § 303. Hearings on this proposal were held by the House Judiciary Committee on July 31 and August 1, 1978 in Harrisburg.

47. This suggestion was made, for example, in oral testimony by Andrew von Hirsch in the August 1 hearings on H.B. 2424, referred to in the previous note.

48. Oregon Administrative Rules § 254–70–042. For a description of these rules, see note 17 to Chapter 7, *supra*.

49. A.B.A. Committee on the Legal Status of Prisoners, *supra* note 44, at 606.

50. In practice, there are two types of parole discharge: the parolee may be formally released from supervision, or he may be discharged from "active" supervision, but retain the parolee status. It is the former, official discharge that we refer to here. O'Leary and Hanrahan, *supra* note 31, at 73–78.

51. California Penal Code § 3000(a),(b).

52. David Rothman, "Doing Time: Days, Months and Years in the Criminal Justice System," Pinterton Lecture delivered at the School of Criminal Justice, State University of New York at Albany, March 6, 1974 (unpublished); and David J. Rothman, "Doing Time," Op-Ed column in *New York Times*, September 9, 1977.

53. For a statement of these ideas in the specific context of the federal sentencing system, see Testimony of Andrew von Hirsch, *supra* note 29.

APPENDIX II: "PUNITIVE" SUPERVISION?

1. Andrew von Hirsch, *Doing Justice: The Choice of Punishments* (New York: Hill and Wang, 1976), at 119.

2. *Id.*, Introduction, at xxxv.

APPENDIX III: THE HART-JAVITS BILL

1. For example, the treatment of prior criminal offenses as an aggravating circumstance in Sec. 7(d) differs from how we would handle prior offenses—see Chapter 6 *supra*, note 39.

Index

About the Authors

Andrew von Hirsch is Associate Professor at the Graduate School of Criminal Justice, Rutgers University, Newark. During this project, both he and Ms. Hanrahan were also affiliated with the Center for Policy Research, Inc., in New York City. He is author of *Doing Justice: The Choice of Punishments*, the report of the Committee for the Study of Incarceration on the rationale for criminal sentencing, published in 1976. He is currently a co-director of a study of determinate penalty systems in California, Oregon and other states, funded by the U.S. Law Enforcement Assistance Administration. He is a graduate of Harvard College and Harvard Law School, and a member of the New York bar.

Kathleen J. Hanrahan is Research Associate at the Graduate School of Criminal Justice Research Center, Rutgers University, Newark. She is co-author of *Parole Systems in the United States*. She holds a master's degree from the Graduate School of Criminal Justice, State University of New York at Albany.